In Search of Consensus

In Search of Consensus

New Zealand's Electoral Act 1956 and its Constitutional Legacy

Elizabeth McLeay

Victoria University Press

TE WHARE WĀNANGA O TE ŪPOKO O TE IKA A MĀUI
VICTORIA
UNIVERSITY OF WELLINGTON

VICTORIA UNIVERSITY PRESS
Victoria University of Wellington
PO Box 600 Wellington
vup.victoria.ac.nz

First published 2018

ISBN 9781776561841

A catalogue record for this book is available from the National Library of New Zealand.

Printed by Ligare, Auckland

Contents

Preface

This book brings together several of my interests. I have always been fascinated by how political institutions work, especially their behavioural norms and formal rules. I have been engrossed in the relationship between those rules and the wider political and social world: their origins and the cultures that develop from them; the ways in which political actors invent rules and their subsequent evolution; and how rules can paralyse change. At the heart of this academic pursuit is the age-old agency–structure question of the relationship between humans and their environment, whether those humans are individual political leaders, their followers, or citizens. This relationship is at the heart of my own particular discipline, political science. An interest in rules connects intimately with my passion for democracy and social justice for all. Good institutions produce and protect good democracies; and good democracies foster societies that look after their people and are responsive to them.

My other intellectual involvement has been with the politics and government of parliamentary democracies, especially that of Aotearoa New Zealand. The study of New Zealand politics and government is a peculiar passion to nurture. On one hand it may seem a rather insular interest, speaking figuratively, of course. It may also seem like a lot of work to put in to understanding the culture of such a relatively unimportant state. I have a couple of responses to criticisms of this sort. The first is: if those living and working in New Zealand do not study its politics, who will? Overseas commentators take an interest in this polity, but the depth and the breadth of their research will inevitably be limited. My second response is that Aotearoa New Zealand is truly interesting in itself, with its bicultural history and more recent multicultural developments, its comparatively stable polity yet its startling periods of radical policy and constitutional change, and its historically high levels of political engagement. Aotearoa New Zealand can grab our attention. This is not a boring country. And other scholars and decision-makers can and do learn from us.

I am essentially a comparativist in that I learn from contrasting different and similar political systems. But we can learn from the past as well as from studies abroad, if we ask the right questions. Indeed, to delve back into New Zealand in the 1950s is to visit another country that is very different yet at the same time similar to how we are in the 21st century. It gives us cause to consider why so many aspects of that era have now disappeared – the very high rates of political participation, to take just one example – and why so many other characteristics remain the same. The faith that New Zealanders simultaneously hold in the virtues of popular sovereignty and the oft-noted belief in 'fair play' is an example of this country's cultural continuity. Furthermore, studying the 1950s has given me a reason to return to the writings of the excellent and innovative political scientists of that period and of the 1960s.

I have read many detective novels in my life. They make a great antidote to reading politics and history and being too much of a political junkie. However, some of the best stories in politics are themselves puzzles. One of my favourite scholars, Bernard Grofman, has edited a whole book of them.[1] He writes that there are three sorts of mysteries – 'whodunits', 'howdunits' and 'whydunits' – and political science problems can be one or all of these.[2] How and why the Electoral Act 1956, with its single entrenchment of some of its provisions, came to be invented is one of these political puzzles. This significant change to New Zealand's electoral law was made by Members of Parliament and their advisers. The construction of a device to make it very difficult for one side of the New Zealand House of Representatives to repeal or amend certain parts of our electoral system would influence its development thereafter and profoundly affect how we now think about the process of constitutional change. Yet few people know about the Act's significance, and there has been no full analysis of how and why it was introduced. This book attempts to solve the puzzle.

After many hours of research, and reading many more files in the Alexander Turnbull Library and National Archives than are recorded in my bibliography (p. 229), I still do not know exactly 'whodunit' – who persuaded those involved in drafting the Bill to try the experiment of singly entrenching some of its provisions. But I have narrowed the suspects down to a small group of men, mainly from the New Zealand National Party. Sir John Marshall was certainly the key protagonist. I most sincerely hope that someone who reads this book can tell us more about the making of the Electoral Act 1956. It might stimulate memories and the unearthing of files.

However, the constitutional and electoral problems of the 1950s, the political ideas and traditions that were then dominant, the principles that drove the architects of the Bill and the political compromises they made, became for me the most interesting aspects of the research and writing. These are the 'whydunit' questions. Especially challenging is the deeper puzzle that underlies this particular event: why do political leaders, so often derided as entirely self-interested and power-dominated, make self-denying decisions? Why do they constrain their own future actions and under what circumstances? It is important to understand this aspect of human behaviour and the circumstances that enable it, because when political leaders are not restrained by norms, values and formal constitutional rules, and when they cannot negotiate fruitfully with those who oppose them, democracy suffers. No democratic state can exist in a constant state of blissful consensus: policy advocacy, especially if it is founded on deeply held principles, will necessarily be adversarial and even perhaps strident. But the competition for power and resources must be controlled and shaped by constitutional rules and constitutional behaviour.

This is an interdisciplinary work, informed both by political science and constitutional law, which attempts to plug one of our many holes in New Zealand's political story. When I explain to friends that I am working on the Electoral Act 1956, too many respond with blank looks. Most people have no idea of the origins of one of our most significant constitutional traditions. I hope my book helps to remedy this.

Acknowledgements

I am immensely grateful to the New Zealand Centre for Public Law, Faculty of Law, Victoria University of Wellington, which has given me a lively intellectual environment since I retired from full-time teaching in the Political Science and International Relations Programme at VUW. I particularly wish to thank the past Dean of the Law School, Professor Tony Smith, and the present Dean, Professor Mark Hickford, for their warm hospitality. Their colleagues, too, have provided me with nothing but encouragement for my research, and at a seminar I presented on this topic I appreciated and learned from their comments. Special thanks go to Professor Claudia Geiringer for her support, encouragement and friendship. The book we wrote with Polly Higbee helped renew my interest in the New Zealand Parliament.[3] Emeritus Professor Sir Geoffrey Palmer has been a great supporter of this work and indeed encouraged me to turn what was supposed to be an article into a book. Whether he now thinks that this was a wise move is another issue. Professor Palmer also helpfully read chapters and commented on them. Dr Paul Harris, another of my wise experts, generously spent far too much of his time providing me with excellent feedback – his assistance was invaluable. Emeritus Professor Les Holborow not only had the misfortunate to live with the book but also commented on chapters, proofread them and patiently took part in many rewarding conversations about the work's structure, problems and ideas. Naturally the mistakes, omissions and misjudgements are mine alone.

I wish also to thank the librarians of the Turnbull Library, the National Library, National Archives, and the Wellington Public Library. They were invariably patient and helpful. And I thank Kathryn Patterson for sharing her expertise.

My heartfelt thanks, finally, go to Fergus Barrowman and Holly Hunter at Victoria University Press for being such encouraging and perceptive editors. The Press produces a very fine product. I am proud to be published by VUP.

This book is for my son, James Goldsmith.

1

The 'Remarkable' Electoral Act 1956

> Perhaps one of the most remarkable Bills that has been passed by Parliament for a good many years was the Electoral Bill, which was passed today. We were fairly evenly divided on that Bill. We met privately but officially, and reached conclusions which, I think, will improve our electoral laws. It is remarkable that we should have reached complete unanimity on the provisions of that Bill.
>
> *Sidney Holland, Prime Minister, 26 October 1956.*[1]

During the third term of the First National Government, a bill that would become one of Aotearoa New Zealand's most important constitutional documents was passed through its parliamentary stages. The Electoral Act 1956 would influence many of the constitutional changes that came after it, including the Constitution Act 1986 and the Electoral Act 1993, the Bill that put into law the mixed-member proportional (MMP) electoral system. From 1956 onwards, reforms to fundamental aspects of the electoral system would be decided either by a nationwide referendum or a super-majority of the House of Representatives, thereby moderating the influence of the party or parties in government over some of the most vital rules in a democracy. Furthermore, bills dealing with electoral issues would almost always be dealt with consensually in parliamentary select committees, although it would be a while before full and informed public consultation enhanced that process. The Electoral Act 1956 constructed the bones of the dialogue on how constitutional change should take place as well as stipulating how certain electoral reforms should be decided.[2]

The first achievement of the Act, and its original apparent purpose, was that it consolidated existing electoral law and remedied many – certainly not all – of its deficiencies. Although there had been a number of electoral bills over the previous few decades, they had been amendments to the Electoral Act 1927.

The second achievement was the decision to single out certain features of the electoral system that, it was believed, deserved to be placed above the level of ordinary statutes and protected against governing parties amending or repealing them through ordinary majority vote in the New Zealand House of Representatives. The protected features in Section 189 of the Electoral Act 1956 are: the triennial term of Parliament; the composition of the Representation Commission (which decides on electorate boundaries); the definition of the term 'European population', relating to the division of New Zealand into European electorates after each census; the allowance for the adjustment of the quota (that is, how much discrepancy is allowed between the population sizes of each electorate); the definition of 'adult', prescribing 21 years as the minimum age for persons qualified to be registered as electors or to vote; and the method of voting. (The term 'European' was much later changed to 'General' and refers to non-Maori.) Section 189 (2) states that 'No reserved provision shall be repealed or amended unless the proposal for the amendment or repeal—(a) Is passed by a majority of seventy-five per cent of all the members of the House of Representatives; or (b) Has been carried by a majority of the valid votes cast at a poll of the electors of the European and Maori electoral districts'. This meant that this part of the Electoral Act would have to be changed before any of the protected provisions could be amended or repealed.

The Act's third achievement was to invent a new parliamentary convention. The entrenching provision (Section 189 [2]) was not itself entrenched because at the time, as is explained more fully later, it was not believed that double entrenchment was possible in New Zealand's system of parliamentary government. This meant that, theoretically, any government commanding just a simple majority of the votes in the House could remove the entrenching clause and, thus enabled, could then amend or repeal the protected provisions. This has not happened: the entrenching provision has been respected. In his summary of the key features of the constitution, which forms a preface to the *Cabinet Manual*, Sir Kenneth Keith notes that certain electoral law changes may only be made using the prescribed procedures, that this requirement has been respected, and that 'It is also accepted, at the level of convention, that those voting requirements also apply to any proposal to amend that protective provision. Similarly, Standing Orders provide that an entrenched provision should be adopted by the House only by the vote which would be required for the amendment or repeal of the provision being entrenched'.[3]

The New Zealand constitution sprawls across a number of statutes, the common law, constitutional conventions and parliamentary standing orders. Conventions exist in every stable democratic state, whether or not they have codified constitutions. There are always gaps amongst the formal rules, gaps that are filled by the political actors developing their own behavioural norms. Conventions, however, play a particularly vital role when some of the most basic rules are unwritten.

The entrenching provision alone justifies research and

analysis, given that politicians seldom voluntarily enact self-denying ordinances such as this. When it comes to deciding and influencing their countries' constitutional arrangements, it is plausible to assume that politicians normally try to protect and enhance their careers. Personal and party enhancement of power is assumed to be more likely than their reduction. Indeed, that political actors aim to further their own self-interests is supported in the empirical literature on one particular constitutional issue: the fraught and contested area of changing electoral rules. Although politicians frequently make strategic errors that lead to perverse electoral rule outcomes – New Zealand politicians promising a referendum on electoral reform in the early 1990s, for example – the main goal of political actors when confronting constitutional issues is to pursue personal and party electoral success, either through preserving the status quo or altering the rules of the political game to suit their own purposes. So the politicians' actions in confining their future freedom to change aspects of the electoral law in the 1956 legislation need to be explained. But it seems as though they left themselves a loophole in that, fascinatingly, the clause that set out the conditions for repeal or amendment was not itself entrenched.

Early in New Zealand's history the idea of parliamentary sovereignty became received wisdom in New Zealand's version of the Westminster system. At the time of the 1956 Act's conception and birth it was believed that Parliament could not bind the actions of future parliaments: thus the protecting provision had moral rather than constitutional authority. So why do it in the first place? Just why single entrenchment was selected as a means of restraining Parliament's actions is one of the puzzles tackled in this book. Was it a quasi-self-denying ordinance or something more heroic? Who was responsible for this novel constitutional rule (a difficult, perhaps impossible, question to answer so many years after the event)? Whatever the motives behind it, the effectiveness of the single entrenchment has been undeniable and would almost certainly have surprised its architects.

One might have expected that a statute demanding higher than usual decisional thresholds for particular constitutional changes (requiring either a parliamentary super-majority or approval in a referendum), would be discussed and debated by those whom it would most affect (the voters) before being passed into law. Nevertheless, the elements of the Bill outlined above were not put before the people at the previous general election in 1954; and although the select committee that considered the Bill called for public submissions, voters were given only a matter of days to respond. Furthermore, the Bill's content was not placed before the people for approval via a referendum. There was some discussion about a possible plebiscite, but it never happened. Instead the Bill was rushed through the formal parliamentary process under urgency, albeit being passed through its three stages with the unanimous support of the House of Representatives. Effectively, the Act handed over some major constitutional decisions to the people without seeking their prior consent. It is just as well that those decisions furthered constitutional democracy rather than retarded it.

The Electoral Act 1956 was the first constitutionally significant response to the implications of abolishing the Legislative Council in 1950. New Zealand's appointed upper house had become a refuge for party loyalists and, since the beginnings of party government at the end of the 19th century, had played an inadequate role in legislative scrutiny.[4] Despite the severe shortcomings of the upper house, the ideal of bicameralism remained important in the eyes of many, even after the Legislative Council was no more, as the story told here will show. If the New Zealand Parliament were to remain unicameral, what could constrain single party governments from doing anything they liked? In particular, what could stop such governments manipulating the electoral rules in their own interests, thereby placing oppositions at a substantial disadvantage? The Electoral Act 1956 was an attempt to stop such game-playing and thus was an important development in the evolution of New Zealand's House of Representatives.

Note that the decision-makers during the 1950s had no ideal model of a unicameral Parliament to guide them. Keith Jackson points out that New Zealand's adoption of unicameralism 'was widely regarded as a radical development without significant precedent in the English-speaking world'.[5] Bicameral parliaments predominated in democratic polities. They still dominate our models of ideal legislative architecture. We instinctively understand that a second institution provides a 'veto point' to powers exercised in another chamber, an institutional blockage to legislative power exercised unwisely. The idea that there should be 'checks and balances' on legislative power fits with bicameralism more easily than unicameralism. Instead, in the Electoral Act 1956 'veto players' – in this case opposition politicians or voters – were given the role of stopping or approving changes to key components of the electoral law.[6]

However, the New Zealand architects of the Electoral Act 1956 were dealing not only with the implications of having become a unicameral Parliament but also with an overall constitutional design that put parliamentary supremacy at the heart of political power and oversight by the courts on its perimeter. This prevailing doctrine of parliamentary sovereignty, when combined with an electoral system that tended to produce single-party majority governments, was a formula for untrammelled political power that rested solidly in the hands of the governing political party. Answering to the public's vote at the triennial general elections was the only formal accountability mechanism. A wary press and watchful, constitutionally informed public servants were the only other constraints against the abuse of power, but these were persuasive influences rather than formal bulwarks against the actions of overweening governments. The Electoral Act 1956 was a step towards moderating the power of governments to change aspects of the electoral law without seeking the approval of others. This alone makes it an important constitutional document.

As will already be apparent, I have a broad understanding of what constitutes the 'constitutional'. A state's constitution includes all formal and informal rules (including conventions) that allocate, regulate, and adjudicate upon the exercise of power within a given polity. Thus, whether a constitution is codified or uncodified, it consists of rules about the state and its powers, individual rights, and how the constitution can be changed.[7] The Electoral Act 1956 is certainly a constitutional document in terms of its substance – the rules that dictate how MPs are to be elected and define the limitation to their terms in power – and the specified processes to be followed whenever those rules are to be changed.

Theoretically, of course, after the 1956 Act one party could win three-quarters (or more) of all the seats in the House of Representatives, thereby having the necessary number of votes to amend or repeal any of the protected provisions. As it happened, there was no such opportunity for this to occur under the simple majority, single-member district electoral system that remained in place until the first election under MMP in 1996. This would have been a true test of the moral strength of Section 189. However, even though the First-Past-the-Post rules (FPP) advantaged the two major political parties by making it very difficult for smaller parties to win parliamentary seats and rewarded the winning party by allocating it more seats that its nationwide vote warranted, the highest percentage of seats any governing party managed to win during that 40-year period was when the National Party won 69% of all the parliamentary seats (67 out of 97) in 1990, with 48% of the nationwide vote.

Under proportional representation it is even less likely that one party will win an overwhelming majority; it tends to produce multi-party parliaments by bringing in small parties. Indeed, between 1996 and 2017, no single party won more than half the seats: coalitions and support-party agreements were required by every major party in government. And because the two major parties, Labour and National, continued to dominate voters' loyalties, coalitions tended to be one major party supported by one or more very small parties. Under MMP, a formal or informal coalition of parties who favour amendment or repeal of any of the protected provisions could be formed to repeal the entrenching provision that was repeated in the Electoral Act 1993 – if, together, they can provide the numbers required to dominate the House. But both reaching the three-quarters super-majority and also creating a legislative coalition willing to challenge what is now an accepted part of the constitution is unlikely. Alternatively, a grand coalition of the two major parties could be formed and decide to amend the protected provisions. Any such moves, however, might now be challenged in the courts, given the increased judicial activism of the decades since the mid-1980s.

Why and how the Electoral Act 1956 was passed and in what ways it influenced constitutional development during the following six decades is a worthy and interesting tale to tell. How did a bill that had begun life with relatively modest, if nonetheless important, consolidating goals metamorphose into a statute that had enduring importance not only for future electoral law but also for New Zealand's overall constitutional development? What was the story behind single entrenchment? There was no precise precedent for this in New Zealand constitutional history.

The other untold story is how and why single entrenchment was selected to protect some provisions and not others. Most notably and unfairly, the four Māori seats are not protected in the Electoral Act 1956. Even under the Electoral Act 1993 they can be amended or even abolished by simple majority vote in the House of Representatives.

Furthermore, legislatures are generally regarded as particularly 'sticky' institutions, organisations that are captured by their past histories and rules. I address this generalisation with reference to the Electoral Act 1956 in Chapter 8 (pp. 180–185) when I discuss the circumstances in which radical change tends to occur and the role played by unintended consequences. More generally, what does the story of the Electoral Act 1956 tell us about the circumstances in which important constitutional changes occur? This is a particularly salient question to ask in an era when there have been two government-led initiatives that have sought public views on the future of the Aotearoa New Zealand constitution,[8] conferences involving academics and community and political leaders,[9] and a book published in 2016 – six decades after the Electoral Act – advocating a written constitution with protections modelled on that earlier legislation.[10] Māori have been particularly active proposing new constitutional arrangements that reflect their status as first settlers and equal partner to the Crown under the Treaty of Waitangi 1840.[11]

This case study of electoral rule change also raises the thorny issue of whether the debates around the 1956 legislation and since indicate whether or not New Zealanders discuss constitutional issues within a context of a coherent body of political ideas. I say that this is a 'thorny issue' because it has often been asserted that New Zealand has a paucity of original constitutional ideas. We borrow from abroad, amending where appropriate, it is claimed. We don't talk about the big ideas. We are essentially pragmatic: we look for small-scale, feasible solutions that plug into our existing arrangements as seamlessly as possible. Our political culture, it is often said, is one that favours doing things incrementally, bit by bit, a pattern that follows naturally from pragmatic attitudes. Is it the case that, as Mark Hickford has argued when discussing the Constitution Act 1852, 'What may be referred to less than illuminatingly as "pragmatism" may conceal or divert attention from a range of intellectual and political genres and changes in them through time'?[12] I tackle these issues briefly in the last part of this book.

Writing About the 1950s

The National Party's first term in government is a fascinating example of how a new administration conserves policies inherited from its predecessor, even those it had opposed, while implementing much of its election manifesto. As the story of the Electoral Act 1956 shows, National's period in office also illustrates how pulling down one part of New Zealand's constitutional structure, the Legislative Council, led to further architectural alterations. But there has been no full analysis of the 1949 to 1957 period, unlike, for example, the attention paid by historians and political scientists to Labour's first and fourth terms in government (1935–1949 and 1984–1990).[13] Furthermore, New Zealand's post-war constitutional history has been largely untold, at least until Labour's fourth term, when that government became active on Māori rights and other constitutional issues.

Historians have also identified the 1950s as a period of social change. Philippa Mein Smith, for example, discusses the 'unsettling of settler society';[14] and Michael King's chapter on the period between 1946 and the 1960s is entitled 'Cracks in the Plinth'. King focuses on social developments, such as the post-war burgeoning birthrate, the reassertion of domesticity, suburbanisation, consumerism, the impact of the intellectual refugees, university development and the arts, and the Mazengarb Report (which made recommendations to control youth sexual behaviour). King also covers major political events such as the 1949 general election, the debate over conscription in the late 1940s, the abolition of the Legislative Council, and the 1951 waterfront dispute.[15] The 'unsettled' state of the constitution tends to drop from attention once the upper house has made its exit. In his classic *A History of New Zealand*, first published in 1959, Keith Sinclair finishes his narrative in 1956 with neither a mention of the Electoral Act of that year nor of the ferment within the National Party over constitutional issues after the abolition of the Legislative Council. Robert Chapman analyses the political events and policy developments between 1935 and 1975, but he, like others, mainly disregards constitutional developments.[16]

The Electoral Act 1956 also tends to be ignored in biographies and autobiographies of important politicians and public servants of that era. The exception is a two-volume memoir by John Marshall, one of the Act's architects, which includes much interesting material about the first National Government and devotes a couple of pages to the Act.[17] Keith Sinclair's biography of Walter Nash, Leader of the Opposition in 1956, pays little or no attention to constitutional developments of the period, including the abolition of the upper house and the Electoral Act 1956. A key political actor of the period was of course the National Party leader and prime minister, Sidney Holland (usually called Sid), but as of yet he has not had a chronicler, although he has appeared in brief chapters, and he did not write his memoirs.[18] There are two biographies and a collection of essays about Keith

Holyoake, however his years as prime minister, rather than his years as deputy, naturally overshadow the 1950s, and nowhere is the Electoral Act discussed.[19] Clifton Webb's daughter wrote a book about her father, but, despite his interest in constitutional issues, she chooses to focus primarily on other aspects of his life.[20] Unfortunately, scarcely any other key actors of the time either wrote autobiographies or inspired biographers. One of the most perceptive and distinguished public servants of that era, Dr John Robson, who occupied the positions of Assistant and then Deputy Secretary of Justice, published an autobiography which – although he was a scholar of constitutional and administrative law – mainly deals with criminal justice policies.[21]

Thus there is little written on the 1950s that could help the writing of this present research. The only political events that have been fully researched are the abolition of New Zealand's upper house, the Legislative Council (which has much to do with the story told in this book); and the waterfront dispute in 1951. For most historians, New Zealand post-war political history does not really get going again in an interesting way until the 1960s and 1970s. Those decades saw New Zealand's controversial involvement in the Vietnam War, the quickening of Māori political protest and the revival of debate on the Treaty of Waitangi, the emergence of the campaign for nuclear disarmament (CND), the development of concerns about human rights, the feminist movement, and the flourishing of the environmental movement.[22] On many of these issues, though, the seeds that fermented over the following decades began in the 1950s: the beginning of the CND movement, for example, and New Zealand's protesting of South Africa's treatment of Māori and their own Indigenous peoples when it came to participating in rugby. The 50s are a rather more interesting decade than is usually acknowledged.

Experts on public and constitutional law have of course acknowledged the importance of the 1956 legislation and its successor, the Electoral Act 1993,[23] and yet, in the otherwise helpful report of the 2005 Constitutional Arrangements Committee, the Electoral Act is not included in the list of New Zealand's significant constitutional milestones.[24] In its report, the Royal Commission on the Electoral System in 1986 includes an excellent discussion of entrenchment, recommending double entrenchment.[25] The most complete description of the evolution of the 1956 Act is in the Royal Commission's invaluable history of New Zealand's electoral law.[26] Also, Neill Atkinson, whose history of the vote in New Zealand is also invaluable, succinctly tells the Act's tale;[27] and James Christmas analyses its significance in the context of the history of electoral law since 1927.[28] Much earlier, Kenneth Scott, who was closer to the actual event, discusses the Act in his book on the New Zealand Constitution.[29] This book builds on, and expands, the stories related in those earlier works.[30]

2

The New Zealand Constitution in the 1950s

> Because, in our unitary state, the duly elected Parliament of the day is the repository of supreme power, no Parliament can bind its duly elected successor.
>
> *John Marshall, 1983*[1]

Before analysing the puzzles presented by the Electoral Act 1956, we must first consider the constitutional context and political culture of the 1950s, which helps to disentangle the story of how such an innovative new convention came to be established.

The Constitution and the Political System

After the signing of the Treaty of Waitangi in 1840, the imposition by Westminster of New Zealand's Constitution Act in 1852 and the beginnings of responsible government in 1854, Aotearoa New Zealand underwent far-reaching constitutional changes. Although some parts of the Constitution Act 1852 required approval from the UK Parliament for repeal or amendment, most of those provisions were removed with scant fanfare and little debate, thus facilitating continual constitutional evolution. During the

1950s the constitution was largely uncodified. The courts had no role in the judicial review of legislation.

The doctrine of parliamentary supremacy reigned supreme during the 1950s, and would not be seriously challenged until the 1980s. In other words, the prevailing belief was that no Parliament could bind its successor and that Parliament was the supreme decision-making authority. This credo would be significant in the framing of the Electoral Act 1956.

It is important to remember that for most of the 20th century the Treaty of Waitangi did not play a significant role in debates about the New Zealand constitution and was not regarded as part of it. The significance of the Treaty was remembered and understood by Māori, but not by members of the political elite – except for Māori MPs – and certainly not by non-Māori voters. The finding by Chief Justice Prendergast in 1877 had a long and pernicious impact. He had ruled that 'as an instrument for transferring sovereignty, the Treaty was "a simple nullity", and that Māori claims to customary land, based on the Treaty, could not prevail against the Crown'.[2] For the Treaty to have effect it would have to be explicitly included in statutes.[3] The debates from the 1980s onwards regarding whether or not the Treaty might be incorporated into New Zealand law, and the constitutional implications of regarding the Treaty as a form of higher law, took the country into a new era of debate about the rights of Māori under the Treaty and the state's obligations to respect its provisions. If the Treaty had been regarded as a living document in the 1950s, discussions over the Electoral Act 1956 might have taken a different shape.

Despite the haphazard nature of New Zealand's constitutional development and the scattered sources of the constitution itself, by the 21st century it was one of the longest-lived in the world. In comparative terms, it was already old during the 1950s. Such endurance is not the normal condition for states, even democratic polities.[4] By the 1950s, the New Zealand constitution, although evolved and still evolving, had survived the stresses of colonisation with its severely adverse impact on Māori, the New Zealand land wars, several major economic depressions, the pressures towards authoritarian government during two world wars, and the constant risk of dictatorial executive power enabled by the combination of the winner-take-all electoral system and cabinet government strengthened by strong party discipline in Parliament. Control from the centre had been enabled early in the country's history: the provinces were abolished in 1875, making New Zealand into the unitary state that it is today. A US political scientist observed in 1948 that because New Zealand democracy had had to adapt to the new environment, it was 'not just a slavish imitation of the British model'.[5]

Formal constitutional sovereignty would be achieved with New Zealand's 1947 ratification of the Statute of Westminster 1931, an event that would enable the appointed upper house, the Legislative Council, to vote for its own abolition in 1950 – this would become pivotal in the story of the Electoral Act 1956.

An important element of the country's colonial origins continued into the 1950s and beyond: New Zealand's Head of State was the British monarch, with a Governor-General acting on his or her behalf in New Zealand. During the 1950s, New Zealand still had non-New Zealander representatives from the imperial power acting as Governors-General. Even the appointment of the Governor-General was in the hands of the British until Peter Fraser, at that time a Labour prime minister, nominated Sir Bernard Freyberg, who then held office between 1946 and 1952. Lord Norrie succeeded Freyberg; and Viscount Cobham became Governor-General in 1957. By then the appointment was entirely in the hands of the New Zealand government, with formal approval coming from London. Sir Arthur Porritt (1967–1972) was the first New Zealand-born Governor-General, although he was a British resident. His successor, Sir Denis Blundell, was the first Governor-General who was both a New Zealander by birth and also resident at the time of his appointment in 1972. Since that time, only New Zealanders have occupied the position.[6]

Government Formation and Cabinet

In the style of Westminster government, political power in New Zealand was and is fused: the political executive (cabinet) is drawn from the legislature (indeed, must be so drawn) and is responsible to it for its actions and its continued existence in office.[7] If the government loses the confidence of Parliament by losing a vote of confidence, then it must resign. In New Zealand, National Party prime ministers have selected their cabinets, as happens in both the British Conservative and Labour parties, while New Zealand Labour caucuses have elected theirs, although there have been periods when Labour prime ministers made the choice. There was and is no constitutional limit to the number of ministers who can be appointed, but all ministers must be parliamentarians. Before the Legislative Council was abolished, one or two ministers were selected from that body. Sidney Holland's cabinets comprised fifteen to sixteen ministers.

Unlike Westminster, where power transition takes place immediately when a governing party loses a general election, the Wellington power exchange has been a slower process. Writing before the adoption of proportional representation in 1993, Keith Jackson explains that 'following a clear defeat in a general election, the outgoing government has, in effect, some twelve to fourteen days to hold post-mortem cabinet and caucus meetings, clear out offices, finalise minor decisions, and depart'.[8] A major reason for this delay is that the special votes have to be checked so that the final count can be done and the writs returned. As Jackson writes,

> The New Zealand practice which has attained the status of a constitutional convention (and has been followed since the first government to be overturned at a general election fell in 1887) appears to be unique and avoids both the undignified haste of British practice and most of the problems of a 'lame-duck' administration associated with the United States.[9]

Power transition is similar to that in the United Kingdom, however, in that a new prime minister does not have to be formally endorsed by a majority of the legislature.

Under FPP in New Zealand, between 1935 and 1993, there was no doubt which party held the majority of seats after an election, could command a majority in the House, and would form the government. This could of course change mid-term if a prime minister lost the confidence of the House. The absence of constitutional requirements for formal parliamentary approval of a new prime minister is a contributory factor in the formation of minority governments, a feature that would become evident after MMP.

The New Zealand Cabinet has historically been a collective institution. Although some cabinets more than others have been dominated by their prime ministers, generally they have been far more collegial than in similar jurisdictions. This might be a consequence of the comparatively small sizes of the ministry and indeed of the legislature itself: everyone knows everyone else. And when prime ministers hold their leadership positions at the behest of their party colleagues, personal allegiances have to be fostered, and it is advisable for prime ministers to carry their ministerial – and caucus

– colleagues along with them when making important policy decisions.[10] During the 1950s ministers and the prime minister had small personal staffs. We can hypothesise – and I do not know of any research on this topic – that the smaller the number of ministerial staffers, the more ministers have to coordinate with their cabinet colleagues as well as their senior public servants in order to achieve policy change. Cabinet at that time was infamous for dealing with the smallest of policy and administrative decisions.

Prime ministers, especially in the National Party, had and have the power of patronage, making them the most powerful figures in their administrations, at least until their powers wane and plausible challengers emerge.[11] Sidney Holland, National's prime minister between 1949 and 1957, took advantage of the credit he accrued by winning a general election to change aspects of the cabinet system as well as to abolish the upper house. Holland inherited some degree of reorganisation because in 1948 Peter Fraser had decided 'to admit to the Cabinet Room a Secretary whose primary task was to establish a systematic record of proceedings'.[12] After 'an experimental period and the 1949 General Election', Holland directed that a cabinet manual be put together.[13] Also, as John Martin relates, Holland took the advice of his cabinet secretary, Foss Shanahan, to establish a cabinet secretariat. Under Holland's prime ministership, the whole process of cabinet was regulated and made more orderly.[14] A Cabinet Economic Committee was established, supported by an officials' committee.[15]

Parliament and the Electoral System

New Zealand has had a triennial parliamentary term since the abolition of the provincial system of government. There were, however, three occasions during the 20th century when the term was extended: during World War I; during the 1930s depression years; and during World War II. Memories of these postponed elections, including some resentment and unease about the delays, would be formative during the making of the Electoral Act 1956. Prime ministers can call early elections, provided they can assure the Governor-General that they can still command a majority in the House of Representatives. Sidney Holland availed himself of this power in 1951.

During the 1950s, the 80-member New Zealand House of Representatives was elected through the FPP electoral system, which used simple plurality electoral rules in single-member constituencies. This system would not be changed until the referendum in 1993 approved the introduction of MMP. Elections under FPP were decided in the marginal seats, mostly situated in the mixed income-level city seats and the secondary centres. The Labour strongholds were in the poorer city seats, and National held sway in the richer suburbs and in rural New Zealand.[16]

From the 1946 election until 1966, the House of Representatives comprised entirely Labour and National MPs. Minor parties faced a dual problem: two-party hegemony through voter loyalty, and the FPP electoral system that made it very difficult for minor party candidates to be elected unless they could consolidate substantial voting support in particular electorates. This latter strategy would not work successfully until 1966, when the New Zealand Social Credit Party would win one seat. Parliamentary politics during the period of the Electoral Act 1956 were based on two competing parties, each with its distinctive voting support. Despite the emergence of Social Credit in the 1950s, the two decades after the ending of World War II were the heyday of two-party politics, at least in so far as parliamentary politics were concerned.

A particularly important feature of New Zealand's adaptation of its Westminster heritage and, indeed, its FPP electoral system, was the insertion of the Māori seats into Parliament in 1867, originally intended as a temporary measure. The country was divided into four Māori electorates comprising Māori voters, each seat electing a Māori MP. Thus, in this early and almost accidental constitutional fumbling, the new colony began its painful journey into biculturalism and a somewhat more representative Parliament.

The Māori seats were created essentially to protect the settlers' political interests and to further their ambition for Māori land whilst at the same time paying lip service to minority rights and responding to pressure from the British government for fair recognition of Māori rights. Nevertheless, there were settlers and MPs who argued that Māori ought to be able to vote and be represented in Parliament.[17] A Bill resolving (among other things) that Māori have 'fair representation in both Houses' had only narrowly failed to pass.[18] At that stage, the franchise was property-based and, in order to vote, male citizens (who were 21 years old or older) had to own or lease land of a particular value. But there were very few Māori who had individual title to their land because they owned land communally (a feature of Māori society that non-Māori were doing their utmost to change through the courts). Further, many realised it was desirous that Māori cooperate with government: in 1860 war had broken out at Waitara between Māori and the settlers over the unfair seizure of Māori land; and a King movement had developed with the main goal of withholding land from sale.[19] Thus, self-interest alone dictated that the settler government and Parliament incorporate Māori into the electoral system, although some MPs who favoured the seats did so on the grounds of democratic fairness. Like most constitutional arrangements, the solution of creating four seats specifically for Māori was a compromise between competing interests and goals. The seats also built on precedent, for special seats had been formed for the non-property owning gold miners.

The 1867 Act gave all Māori males over the age of 21 years the franchise regardless of property, unlike non-Māori men. (It would be another 12 years before males in that age group were enfranchised.) But Māori were grossly underrepresented in Parliament. Neill Atkinson reports that in 1867 'between 40,000 and 50,000 Māori were (temporarily) allocated four seats, while some 220,000 Europeans had 72'.[20] In 1872 the Māori seats were continued for another five years, and four years later their lives were extended indefinitely. These separate constituencies were an example of how 'long-term institutional consequences may be the byproducts of actions taken for short-term political reasons'.[21] The underrepresentation of Māori electors in the Māori seats would continue until the Electoral Act 1993, when the number of seats was linked with the number of Māori who chose to enrol on the Māori voting register. As we shall see in Chapter 4 (see 87–93), there were further undemocratic features of the Māori seats. These seats play an important part in the story told in this book.

As far as parliamentary processes were concerned, the *Standing Orders of the New Zealand House of Representatives* were modelled on *Erskine May*, the House of Commons rule book. New Zealand's Parliament was thus the product of borrowed rules adapted for new purposes. (Indeed, much later, New Zealand's *Standing Orders* were rewritten in anticipation of the new parliamentary environment that was likely after the advent of MMP, after the Standing Orders Committee examined how multi-party parliaments managed to organise themselves.) During the 1950s, Parliament had a committee system but not all bills were referred to committees for scrutiny.[22] That would not come until 1979, when all but financial bills would normally be referred to committees.

The press was almost never permitted access to committee hearings.[23] The government dominated the House, both in terms of the time devoted to the ruling party's business rather than that of private members and, also, in terms of controlling voting outcomes. Urgency, whereby bills could be propelled through the House rapidly through skipping one or more of the usual legislative stages, and thus escaping adequate parliamentary and public scrutiny, was prevalent during the 1950s (and beyond).[24]

Strong party discipline and cohesion was a feature of the House. Party caucuses met regularly when the House was sitting and caucus committees were influential in shaping party policy. Armed with compliant MPs, governments could get their policies through the House. The small size of the House (80 MPs during the period under discussion) and the high proportion of the governing caucus who were ministers made it easy for those in the political executive to dominate their parliamentary caucuses. On the other side of the Treasury benches sat the Opposition, ready to criticise, oppose and propose alternative policies. With its system of spokespeople (the term 'shadow cabinet' was not used in New Zealand), the Opposition, as in Westminster, was the government-in-waiting. The legitimacy of opposition was reinforced by the formal position of Leader of the Opposition, occupied by the leader of that party.[25]

The Westminster Tradition

Despite the evolution of New Zealand's constitution between 1852 and the mid-20th century, it could still be classified as a Westminster type of parliamentary system. According to Arend Lijphart's typology, parliamentary systems divide into two main groups: the Westminster (or majoritarian) and the consensual models. Majoritarian characteristics are 'logically based on the principle of concentrating as much power as possible in the hands of the majority'. Consensual characteristics, Lijphart continues, 'are based on the principle of sharing, dispersing, and limiting power in a variety of ways'.[26] The nature of the relationship amongst governing political actors is at the heart of Lijphart's categorisation of the institutional features of different forms of democracy.

In its 'pure' form, the Westminster system, which Lijphart amended as he elaborated his model, has the following characteristics:

(a) concentration of executive power in one party and bare-majority cabinets;
(b) cabinet dominance;
(c) a two-party (or one-dimensional) party system;
(d) majoritarian, disproportional electoral systems;
(e) interest group pluralism;
(f) unitary and centralised government;
(g) concentration of legislative power in a unicameral legislature;
(h) constitutional flexibility;
(i) an absence of judicial review; and
(j) a central bank controlled by the executive.[27]

Writing in 1999 (before the advent of MMP), Lijphart used New Zealand under FPP as the exemplar of a Westminster system:

> With only two exceptions – the parliamentary seats reserved for the Māori minority and the earlier shift to central bank autonomy – democracy in New Zealand was, until 1996, more clearly majoritarian and hence, a better example of the Westminster model than British democracy.[28]

Of course the shift to central bank independence came in New Zealand several decades after the 1950s, so at that time the four Māori seats were the only 'consensual' ingredients of the New Zealand constitution, according to Lijphart's model.

Other authors, attempting to avoid categorisation, are more interested in understanding 'Westminster' as a tradition, a cluster of beliefs about the constitutional framework, the structure and conventions of the core executive, and the party system and electoral process. According to the literature on the subject, the Westminster constitutional tradition includes the following aspects: 'a centralized unitary state'; the absence of separation of powers and hence an absence of judicial review of the constitution; bicameralism; 'doctrines of parliamentary sovereignty and "responsible government"'; and an 'unwritten constitution with flexible constitutional conventions'.[29] Clearly, New Zealand until the abolition of the upper house fits into this set of intersecting practices and traditions. And as we shall see, the idea of 'Westminster' will influence the shape of the Electoral Act 1956.

The Westminster inheritance has had a further effect upon New Zealand politics, one that follows from having an unwritten constitution. The constitution before the passage of the Electoral Act 1956 did not include designated processes for changing its rules. As the UK Parliament's power over New Zealand's diminished, governments in Aotearoa accrued increasing flexibility to make changes, compliant parliamentary majorities making this an easy process. There were no institutional constraints that might act to protect minority rights. Neither were there constitutionally prescribed uses of supermajorities or referendums to slow down or prevent change. For most of the 20th century the upper house, a possible constraint against change, was the creature of the government. After it disappeared in 1950 even this cardboard cutout veto point had gone. With the exception of some turbulent years during the 19th century, the political executive easily dominated the legislature, thus allowing wide scope for elected representatives to alter the constitution. The achievement of the Electoral Act 1956 was to provide minority party political players with veto powers over certain aspects of the electoral system.[30] More than this, however, it accelerated the development of institutional norms that would in the future act as significant informal constraints on legislating constitutional change. As important as this change was, the pathways to change the New Zealand constitution in aspects beyond the electoral law remain obscure.

Documents and conventions establish the road-map and rules in constitutional democracies. The ways in which political actors then behave in those spaces, however, evolve according to a looser set of norms and values than conventions prescribe. I now turn to unpicking these other contextual features of the New Zealand polity in the 1950s.

Governments and Behavioural Norms

As various scholars have observed, in the 1950s the two major political parties shared key political values. As well as a generally held belief in the value of consultation beyond the public sector, as explained later, they recognised 'a strong public commitment to the principles of fairness and equality and a belief in grassroots democracy', as evidenced by strong party membership and high electoral turnout.[31] Richard Mulgan argues that the political culture before 1984 was distinguished by three 'tendencies' in political attitudes.[32] The state should be 'active', looking after its people; it should be 'fair', stressing egalitarianism and fairness; and it should be 'accessible'.[33] That governments should respond to voters' expressed needs was a behavioural norm which had developed decades earlier. It can be assumed that this norm was a product of the developmental, settler state that set up expectations about the active state. The dominant influence of Keynesian economics reinforced this tendency. The state 'had an active interventionist role to play in managing the economy to maintain full employment and stimulate economic growth'.[34]

Accessibility was valued: MPs, including ministers, were expected to be readily available to their constituents, and ministers were expected to be available to members of the public, including pressure groups.[35] As a scholar who surveyed MPs in 1981 writes, he gained

> an overwhelming impression of close constituency work, of MPs with small districts who live in them, return home often, and do an astonishing amount of constituency and casework themselves. The strong party system, if anything, reinforces this tendency by removing national policy and parliamentary votes from the responsibility – and influence – of the individual MP.[36]

Thus, along with the two-party, cohesive and disciplined parliamentary system and the strong political executive that was characteristic of Westminster systems, there was a highly participatory political culture, at least in so far as conventional involvement was concerned: voting, joining political parties, and being involved in pressure groups. I explore these behavioural tendencies further in the next chapter. The links between governed and governors were strong, leading to expectations about how the state should respond to citizens' wishes and needs. Again, this point should not be exaggerated, for the tradition that governments should be responsive to voters' expressed views was not always complied with: governments followed policies according to their own preferences for much of the time; and governments listened most closely to those groups who were closest to their own ideological views. It is important to note that, without opinion polling and focus groups, feedback came through contact between MPs and constituents, then was directed to caucus discussions, newspaper editorials and letters to the newspaper. This meant that voters' views were mostly mediated either via partisan players or through editorial opinion.

Closely connected with the value of governmental responsiveness to needs and views was the notion that political parties should put forward full election manifestos in front of voters and these construed promises that should be kept if elected to office. The doctrine of the 'electoral mandate' held strong in the post-war period. This included the belief that governments had the duty to carry out their manifesto promises; that, concomitantly, failing to do this would be a dereliction of that duty; and that any such failure would court voter disapproval.[37] To call the idea of mandate a constitutional convention would be to inflate its significance and exaggerate the extent to which it was actually complied with, but it was certainly part of the system of political norms and values of the 1950s. As K. J. Scott writes, 'That pledges should in normal circumstances be regarded as binding is recognized by politicians and public. A party that dishonours too many of its pledges is likely to be punished by the electors. There is in fact a neat correspondence between propriety and expediency.'[38]

Richard Mulgan makes the point that the doctrine of mandate also played a useful role in uniting government caucuses behind the prime minister and the party policy programme.[39] This meant that the doctrine could be used to justify decisions that might otherwise have been challenged from within the party. Note the following quotation from Sidney Holland, faced with doubts within National concerning his plan to get rid of the upper house after abolition had been included in the Party's manifesto for both the 1946 and 1949 elections: 'The Government has a clear mandate from the people, and it would be an intolerable situation for any Government to find itself in a position where the non-elected members of the legislature were in a position to block the passage of legislation which the people had, by their votes, authorised.' Holland went on to say that he had hoped the councillors would have indicated their willingness to pass legislation but this had not happened, and so appointments would be made to the Council 'to ensure the passage of its legislative programme'.[40]

A measure of the seriousness with which this era of politicians regarded the mandate is shown by the Holland government's determination to implement the promises made in their 1949 election-winning policy. Four years later, the government was privately checking off the policies against what had been achieved (or not).[41]

Discussion of the mandate doctrine takes us to the last characteristic of the political culture that I wish to highlight here: there was broad agreement over the main rules of the political system, albeit with some significant partisan differences that will be discussed in Chapter 4 (p. 66).

The Political Parties and the Constitution

Labour and National took it for granted that the essential ingredients of the Westminster system, as it had developed in Aotearoa New Zealand, were appropriate for their country.

By the 1950s, both political parties agreed that FPP was the best electoral system for New Zealand. Proportional representation had been Labour Party policy from the time of its 1919 general election platform but had been dropped in 1934, just a year before Labour won office.[42] Bruce

Brown reports that 'proportional representation became the cause of much uneasiness during the early thirties' and the party executive reported on its workings in other countries in 1931.[43] The report stated that majorities and minorities were awarded their appropriate shares of seats, and the party conference continued to support proportional representation. However, 'scenting the prospects of victory, Labour saw no reason why its potential majorities should be cut down to a more strictly proportionate size. In 1934, after several years of wavering, a remit to delete proportional representation from the platform was carried by a large majority.'[44]

This means that by the 1950s the parties were united in their acceptance of the basic tenets of majoritarianism: the party that won the most seats also won the right to implement its policies. Janet McLean, following Bruce Ackerman, calls this 'monist'.[45] No negotiation with the loser or losers was necessary or indeed desirable. The idea of mandate reinforced this belief system. Furthermore, majoritarianism had its normative foundation in a particular interpretation of representative democracy: while MPs were elected to represent their constituencies, the winning party was elected to govern. This was New Zealand's version of popular sovereignty. An appointed house, as is shown later, had little legitimacy to draw upon for its continued life; and the courts were expected to keep away from policy issues and policymaking.

Despite the bipartisanship over the basic FPP rules, however, there were significant differences between the two parties concerning how, in practice, electorates were defined and people were counted – working rules that could influence election results. These differences would become a source of tension, and were fundamental to the development of the Electoral Bill in 1956. The two parties also had different attitudes towards the four Māori seats: voting support plus philosophical differences on Māori rights meant that Labour accepted their existence while National largely wanted them to be abolished.[46]

Both parties believed in representative democracy as expressed in the composition and powers of the House of Representatives, a belief that trumped ideas about upper houses with constraining powers. Power should be in the hands of those representatives elected by the people. It had long been Labour policy to abolish the ineffective, appointed Legislative Council, but it suited its purposes meanwhile to retain it as a safe place for retired politicians, whereas Sidney Holland passionately wanted its abolition. This was not the universal view of his colleagues, as explained later.

No politician, and hardly anyone else in the political and intellectual elite, believed that the constitution needed thorough overhauling: belief in the utility of gradual reform, where necessary, was near universal.[47] This led to a particular mode of constitutional reform process that will be discussed in the last chapter. At present it is sufficient to note that, when constitutional problems arose, there was normally the political will to deal with them, although this spirit of enterprise seldom included improving minority rights. Too often this readiness to legislate led to overreaction and undemocratic legislation, as was the case with the Police Offences Amendment Act 1951, passed at the time of a major industrial dispute and which targeted 'seditious material' and restricted the rights of protest, 'a devastating weapon in a democracy'.[48] The year 1951 was thus a busy one for constitutional legislation that had a repressive impact, as the Official Secrets Act was also passed. This required all government information to be secret, binding public servants to confidentiality, a situation that existed until the passage of the Official Information Act 1982.

At times circumstances led politicians to clarify rules in a piecemeal and bipartisan manner. In National's first term, the Civil List 1950 was passed, pertaining to the payment of the Governor-General, ministers and MPs, and, for the first time, an additional payment for the Leader of the Opposition. Section 6 of the Civil List Act 1950 provided that ministers must be MPs. Previously this had been practice rather than law.[49] In 1951, MPs' remuneration was included in the adjudication of the Commission on Parliamentary Salaries and Allowances (along with ministers, parliamentary under-secretaries, the Speaker of the House, and the Chairman of Committees).[50] This helped remove MPs' salaries from accusations of feathering members' own nests.

In 1954 Sid Holland was forced to deal with the problem of ministerial conflict of interests. His Minister of Industries and Commerce, Dean Eyre, decided to go overseas to pursue his personal business interests as an importer – a clear example of a conflict of interest between private gain and public office. This led to the clarification of rules around ministerial interests, largely drafted by another minister, John Marshall.[51] The committee appointed to examine the new rules met during 1956 and reported back to the House on 25 October of that year. Thus New Zealand's rules around the behaviour of ministers was being debated at the same time as the Electoral Bill 1956.[52] Another issue relating to New Zealand's constitutional structure that surfaced at this time was pressure for a permanent Court of Appeal. According to a draft speech of Marshall's, the pressure from the legal profession for such a court went back to 1907.[53] Just fifty years later, a permanent Court of Appeal was established.

Thus, as well as complying with New Zealand's political traditions, the First National Government had a busy eight years when it came to issues around the constitution, even excluding major policy changes such as the abolition of the upper house and the passing of the Electoral Act 1956. The new government was a reforming government when it came to public law issues.

The Political Culture and Constitutional Change

I have argued in this chapter that the New Zealand political culture during the 1950s had a number of distinctive features. Government was supposed to be approachable, accessible and responsive. Despite its gender-bias, with the political and economic elite almost completely male-dominated, and despite the institutional and societal discrimination against Māori, the polity demonstrated the prevalence of political values that emphasised government's responsiveness to people's needs and demands. The small parliament meant that MPs knew each other, their capacities, their faults and their views. Contact between cabinet and the rest of the caucus was close, and wise prime ministers used proximity and intimacy to keep in touch with backbench views. This was one way of testing how well government was doing, as Holland and his successors appreciated.

There were elements of consensual decision-making in how governments behaved, and these practices also linked closely with the prevalent ideas of responsive government and fulfilling election promises. Despite the differences between the two major political parties on aspects of the operation of the electoral system, there was a high degree of acceptance of the legitimacy of the basic constitutional rules and beliefs. The constitutional and political structure of the 1950s would consolidate the culture of dominant single-party government and two-party competition that had existed since 1935 and would continue until the advent of the MMP in 1993. At the same time, however, critics of the power of unconstrained executive dominance would emerge from both sides of the political spectrum.

In the next chapter I explore the wider political context of the 1950s to set the broader scene in which the Electoral

Act 1956 was conceived and born. Constitutional change does not occur in a political vacuum: institutions, political traditions and political actors matter a great deal.

3

Politics and Government in the 1950s

When the National Party entered government for the first time, World War II had ended merely four years earlier. New Zealand was still reconstituting a society that had lost more than 11,500 of its citizens, the highest casualty rate per head of population in the Commonwealth. 'In all, 194,000 men and 10,000 women had served in the country's armed forces, 140,000 of them abroad.'[1] Those who were overseas had to pick up their usual lives again at home, re-forge their relationships with family, whānau and friends, and yet continue to cope with the exigencies of rationing petrol and foods. The task of peace-time reconstruction was well underway. By 1949, for many New Zealanders it was time for a change.

The First Labour Government had been in power since it won the general election in 1935, led by Michael Joseph Savage. Labour had increased its majority in 1938.[2] But unlike the situation in 1935, when it had faced several parties at that general election, this time it was fighting the National Party, a coalition of anti-socialist forces formed in 1936 and led by Adam Hamilton.[3] Savage died in 1940, to be succeeded by Peter Fraser. At the postponed 1943 general election, Labour won 45 seats (56.3% of the seats in the 80-member House) against National's 34 (42.4%), with one Independent also elected. In terms of the percentages of the nationwide valid vote won, however, the distance between the two parties had narrowed: 47.6% against 42.8%. The National Party was gaining support. For the moment, anyway, Labour held the loyalty of voters, and when Labour faced the voters again in 1946 it won its fourth consecutive general election. Although Labour gained 42 seats (51.3% of the votes), National had continued to improve its performance, being rewarded with 38 seats (48.4% of the valid vote).

By 1949, New Zealanders were tired of wartime controls and rationing, only gradually lifted and removed, and chose a new set of faces with different ideas about the role of government and a new leader, Sidney Holland. National, with 46 seats, garnered 51.9% of the valid vote, against Labour's 34 seats and 47.2%.

National in Government: The People

When Sidney Holland's party won the 1949 general election it had had 13 years to build a parliamentary team and establish its credentials as a government-in-waiting. Holland deserved credit for binding the disparate elements of three former parties together: Reform, United and the Democrats, each with different electoral bases (country versus town) and political ideas (conservatism versus liberalism).[4] Their common goal was to defeat Labour. Lessons had been learned from the three-party politics of the 1920s and the unity of purpose displayed by their opponent.

Holland himself had been in Parliament since 1935, when he won Christchurch North. Five years later he succeeded the uninspiring Adam Hamilton as party leader. Keith Holyoake, a possible rival for the position, had been defeated in the 1938 general election but would be re-elected in 1943. From 1947 onwards, Holyoake was Holland's deputy, representing the rural wing of the party. Evidently Holland consulted each caucus member on who should take this position, and 'reluctantly Holland was forced to accept Holyoake over his personal favourite [Bill] Sullivan'.[5]

The National Party contingent in the 80-seat Parliament had grown steadily: 25 MPs in 1938; 34 in 1943; 38 in 1946; and 46 in 1949. The gradual accretion of seats meant that, when it at last won office, National had years of parliamentary experience behind it, if not experience in governing. The number of new National MPs entering Parliament peaked in 1943 when there were 15 newcomers, eight of whom became ministers during National's first term.[6]

With a team of 46 when he won political office in 1949, Holland had some flexibility of choice of ministers for his 16-person cabinet. There were eight brand new MPs, regarded as ineligible for immediate promotion, leaving 38 caucus members with at least three years' parliamentary experience.[7] Holland had observed his MPs thoroughly during the Opposition years. He held regular caucus meetings and created specialised caucus committees covering a range of areas. This gave his MPs valuable experience as well as provided an opportunity for the leader to test their capacity. According to a National MP who knew Holland well, he 'looked for bright young men' to supplement the stalwarts, those who had been in Parliament during the opposition years. Evidently Holland had a 'kind of inner circle', involving Keith Holyoake, William Goosman, Clifton Webb, Fred Doidge and Thomas Macdonald (who went into cabinet after the 1954 election). Bill Sullivan was 'a very close confidant'.[8] However, the historian of the National Party, Barry Gustafson, holds the view that Holyoake never had a close relationship with Holland and, indeed, during the 1954–57 term the two 'were reluctant even to talk with one another'.[9]

According to Austin Mitchell, regular caucus meetings and consultation with the parliamentary team continued after the election victory in 1949.[10] Caucus, however, was mostly informed of policy change and legislation after cabinet had already made its decision. 'The caucus was inadequately informed about the highly controversial Police Offences Amendment Act of 1951 on the grounds that this measure was too delicate and urgent for consideration by the entire caucus', and instead a 'few selected backbenchers' were involved in the cabinet subcommittee that considered this bill.[11]

For the times, Holland's ministers were well-educated, unlike their leader. Just four ministers had been through primary education only, ten had university degrees and three had experienced other forms of tertiary education. Of the 25 ministers who served in the First National Government, eight had been farming, six had been in business, and seven had been lawyers. (There was also an accountant, a schoolteacher, a housewife and a journalist.)[12]

Holland himself retained the Finance portfolio between 1949 and 1954, which 'probably showed a lack of confidence in anyone else to do the job'.[13] Holland had no background in finance. Keith Holyoake held two portfolios, Agriculture and Marketing. These were substantial jobs. His ministerial papers, although voluminous, provide little evidence of an interest in constitutional affairs. Who, then, would play leading roles on electoral and constitutional matters? These players were: Thomas Clifton Webb, Attorney-General, Minister of Justice, and Minister in charge of the Electoral Department; Ronald Algie, Minister of Education; and John Marshall, Minister Assistant to the Prime Minister.[14] They were all lawyers. Algie had been a professor of law at the University of Auckland. In 1937 he had formed the Auckland Provincial Freedom League, which supported National from 1938.[15] From all reports, Algie was a notable parliamentary debater.[16] Clifton Webb, John Marshall writes, was 'one of the most influential members of the Holland Cabinet. He had an uncommon amount of common sense, a clarity of mind, and a facility for simple expression.'[17] The journalist Keith Eunson, who knew Holland, refers to Algie, Webb, Marshall and Jack Watts as the 'intellectual elite'.[18] In the 1949 team, Watts, another lawyer, became Minister of Health and also Minister of Social Security.

Holland appointed Matthew Oram, also a lawyer, who had a strong interest in constitutional affairs, to be Speaker of the House after the 1949 general election and he retained this position for the whole of National's first term. Oram had been 'tipped to become minister of education. However, his poor relationship with Prime Minister Sidney Holland, his right-wing views and his somewhat difficult personality may have counted against him.'[19] The position of Minister of Māori Affairs, along with the Lands and Forests portfolio, went to Ernest Corbett; there were no Māori in the National caucus. At least Corbett had had contact with Māori throughout his life, having been brought up in a rural area (Taranaki) and attended a predominantly Māori primary school. He would be responsible for the Maori Affairs Act 1953 (on land disaggregation) and the Maori Reserved Land Act 1955. Corbett was friends with Whina Cooper, the then president of the Māori Women's Welfare League, and, as minister, 'spent much of his time visiting maraes [sic] in the remotest corners of New Zealand'.[20]

Holland's first ministry included a member of the Legislative Council, William Polson, who was a minister without portfolio. His cooperation would be essential for Holland to succeed in his mission of abolishing the Council. The only National woman MP, Hilda Ross, was Minister for the Welfare of Women and Children (without a department).

After the 1951 snap election Marshall was elevated to the position of Minister of Health, and there were other portfolio reshuffles. Webb became High Commissioner to London and did not contest the 1954 election. Between 1954 and 1957

Holland gave himself the position of Minister of Police, Algie and Corbett remained in their main portfolio positions, Watts was allocated Finance, and Marshall, crucially, was now Attorney-General, Minister of Justice, and Minister in charge of the Electoral Department. Ralph Hanan, another lawyer with an interest in constitutional issues, was in 1954 elevated to become Minister of Health and Minister of Immigration.

And what kind of person and leader was Holland? He had politics in his background: his father had been a Reform Party MP, and Sidney succeeded him as MP for Christchurch North (later Fendalton). The National leader had a reputation as being 'ebullient, domineering, belligerent'.[21] Barry Gustafson calls Holland 'a determined, vigorous, naturally aggressive speaker with an exceptional memory'.[22] Austin Mitchell writes:

> The jaunty, ebullient Holland quickly emerged as the most effective opposition leader in New Zealand's history. A self-confident and determined fighter, he was absolutely convinced that his own party, whatever its policy, was right, if only the other side was wrong. A flair for the New Zealand idiom, a few over-simplified ideas, and an inexhaustible energy concealed a real intellectual vacuum. [23]

Marshall provides a somewhat more flattering pen portrait of his leader:

> He was a man of action, a vigorous, buoyant, positive personality. Because he was a practical man of action, not given to contemplation, he did his leading out in front, but he also had a remarkable capacity for reconciliation, an ability to bring differing points of view and conflicting personalities together. This was shown in a willingness to discuss, to inform and to consult. It produced that quality of team leadership which brought a response of loyalty and confidence.[24]

He also writes that Holland's 'political philosophy could be written on the back of an envelope, and sometimes was'.[25] Moreover, 'He had little appreciation of constitutional theory, and presided over the abolition of the Legislative Council with gay abandon'.[26] Marshall writes as a confirmed bicamerist. Keith Eunson acknowledges Holland's shortcomings but also shrewdly observes that while Holland 'could not compete with many of his Cabinet colleagues intellectually or academically, he nonetheless ran a tight ship and his reign was notable for the lack of schisms or coup attempts, perhaps because he had the good sense to delegate and to let his ministers get on with their tasks'.[27]

Holland's leadership style emerged in interviews conducted during the early 1970s with some of his former colleagues. One of them commented that when the House adjourned at 10.30pm Holland used to get three or four backbenchers up to his room to talk about their problems and get their comments.[28] This was a useful way of keeping in touch with backbench views on the government performance and provides insight into Holland's leadership style. But it was also a way of remaining the dominant leader he was, at least until his health deteriorated from late 1956 onwards. A few months before the 1957 general election, Holland's colleagues persuaded him to stand down in favour of Keith Holyoake.[29]

Holland had regular meetings with senior National Party officials, especially Alex McKenzie, Party President. Holland looked for feedback on the performance of his government, as is shown in later chapters. Behind the scenes sat Martin Nestor, National's Research Director, who was responsible for writing speeches and gathering policy material.

The Holland Government was supported by able public servants, including those closely involved with policy development generally and constitutional matters: the Permanent Head of the Prime Minister's Department, the distinguished Alister McIntosh; officials from the Department of Justice headed by N. C. Butcher; and the parliamentary draftsman, H. D. G. Adams.

On the opposite side of the House sat Labour's front bench, led first by Peter Fraser and then by Walter Nash. The rump of the Labour team was a dispirited group of just thirty MPs after its resounding 1949 defeat and the divisiveness of the referendum on conscription held at the time of that general election. Then there was Fraser's death to deal with, the difficulties of dealing with the 1951 waterfront dispute and contesting the 1951 election, all of which took its toll on the party and on Nash, as Keith Sinclair shows.[30] Although Nash won the leadership election unanimously in January 1951, in early 1954 he had to face down a leadership challenge led by Rex Mason ('who detested Nash'), Bill Anderton and the future Labour leader, Arnold Nordmeyer.[31]

The 1954 general election brought into Parliament ten new Labour MPs, a much-needed intake of energy and talent. The front bench during that period included Nash's deputy, Clarence (Jerry) Skinner, a former Minister of Rehabilitation and Lands. The MPs who would take an active part in debates on the Electoral Bill 1956, some of whom would also sit on its special select committee, were: the former ministers Fred Hackett, Mason, Nordmeyer and Eruera Tirikatene; John Mathison, who had won a 1947 by-election; and Phil Holloway, Walter Hudson and Frank Kitts, new MPs elected in 1954.

National in Government: Policies and Elections

> If you want to condense our policy, you can say that we are against them and we stand for private ownership . . . If we could define a long-range policy, I would say that it is the

> private ownership of the means of production, distribution and exchange.[32]
>
> *Sidney Holland, July 1948*

Like all new governments, National was determined to make some radical changes. The party wished to displace what they saw as a socialist regime by lifting the controls over the economy and reducing welfare. In the end it left much alone, including Labour's social security scheme and compulsory unionism. Institutions take a while to reform, let alone abolish; and Keynesian economics ruled.

Soon after the 1949 victory, the government was faced with discontent among trade unionists, particularly those who worked on the wharves. This was not new: Labour had also dealt with industrial unrest, and had been much criticised by National for how it had managed the trade unions and the strikes. Then 1951 saw the ugliness of the waterfront dispute, when the country was bitterly divided and many of the usual civil liberties were suppressed, as were the watersiders. Holland, deciding to capitalise on his victory against the strikers, called an early general election. This he won with an increase in parliamentary seats, now holding 50 compared with Labour's 30, and a resounding 54% of the valid vote. Labour did badly; and according to Robert Chapman, the percentage of people who did not vote went up almost 5%.[33]

After National's second electoral success, it went into its third general election in 1954 with some confidence. Earlier that year, however, a new challenger to National had appeared in the form of the Social Credit Party, previously an interest group intent on reforming the monetary system. In a letter to Keith Holyoake, Holland reported that the 1954 campaign was going well, that he was not worried about Walter Nash (who had included a family allowance in Labour's election policy), and that National had a practice of not mentioning Social Credit during campaigning. He thought that the new Party 'would harm Labour more than they will injure us. All the fellows seem to be doing well and there is every ground for quiet optimism and confidence'.[34] Social Credit managed to gain a surprising 11% of the nationwide vote, although it gained no seats in Parliament. National remained in office with 45 seats, compared with Labour's 35 (a reduction of the government's majority from 20 to 10), having won 44.3% of the valid vote, slightly more votes than gained by Labour (44.1%). According to Chapman, National was helped by Social Credit and 'a skewed redistribution of electorates accentuated by the inclusion of the total population in boundary assessment and by the doubled allowable difference in electorate populations' due to the passing of the Electoral Amendment Act 1950, both issues that will become part of the story of the Electoral Act 1956, as described in Chapter Four.[35]

National's first governing term came to an end in 1957 when, now led by Keith Holyoake, it was narrowly defeated. National won 39 compared with Labour's 41 seats. In 1960 National was returned to the government benches, and there the party remained until 1972.

During its first term in government, National moderated some of its policies. All governments in liberal democratic states are lobbied by pressure groups expecting to be listened to by government. In both the First Labour Government and its National successor, governmental accessibility and tolerance of group opinion, earlier noted as a feature of the political culture, meant that many policy decisions of the adversarial, all-powerful governments that reigned under FPP were less radical than they might have been. Furthermore, during the Holland years a whole range of formal consultative committees and inquiries were established, many of which impacted on government policy.[36] In the 1950s this was 'consultation' rather than 'stakeholder engagement', the moniker of the 1980s and beyond. These elaborate consultations, informal and formal, brought a degree of consensus to the policy process in terms of how decisions were made and also of the policy compromises that resulted.

Thus despite National's election rhetoric, some policy directions established under the previous government were allowed to continue, including retaining the welfare state and Labour's health reforms. It is far easier to leave voters with what they have gained than to remove those benefits. National also continued with a considerable degree of state intervention over the economy. After showing that the number of state servants that had gone up as a consequence of Labour's new state functions and the tasks of fighting war did not go down in peacetime, John Martin pithily notes that 'National's enterprise rhetoric was not matched by a bonfire of controls after Mr Holland became Prime Minister in 1949'. For example, Holland retained price controls, despite his manifesto promise to the contrary.[37] Austin Mitchell notes that Sidney Holland 'instinctively grasped the fact that Labour had changed the pattern and that political clocks would not go backwards. Any party anxious to win power had to accept what had been done, particularly in the welfare sphere.'[38]

Indeed, the political culture of the 1950s (and into the 1960s) exhibited a high level of political consensus across the political elite. This informal bipartisan agreement covered 'harmonious industrial relations based on a commitment to full employment, private enterprise (especially small-scale private ownership), an agrarian economy heavily reliant on trade with Britain, and foreign and defence policies which centred on the old Western alliance structure'.[39]

This last point is important. The 1950s was a period of rapid development in New Zealand's relationship with the rest of the world: during the post-war period New Zealand took part in the debates around the formation of the United Nations; New Zealanders were included in the occupying forces of Japan until 1952; the Colombo Plan was established in 1950; and in the same year New Zealand troops became involved in the Korean War; New Zealand signed the ANZUS Treaty in 1951; in 1956 New Zealand was elected to the United Nations Security Council and joined SEATO; in 1956, there was the Malayan Emergency; in 1957 bomb testing in the Pacific began, and this was controversial in New Zealand. There was plenty to occupy the new government, but the general bipartisanship over these issues made the task somewhat easier.

Yet it would not do to exaggerate the extent of consensus during the 1950s. Although National had campaigned against Labour's socialistic state – one of National's pamphlets, for example, is headed 'Russianising New Zealand' – and then left much of that state intact, the two parties differed on a number of issues.[40] National, after all, had to respond to the expectations of its supporters and mostly behave in accordance with its election policies. For example, there were strong differences between the two major political parties on such issues as housing policy (National adopted a policy of selling state houses), taxation and the death penalty. Labour had abolished the death penalty (except for treason) in 1941, having commuted all since 1935. National reinstated the death penalty in 1950.[41]

Writing in the mid-1960s, Austin Mitchell characterises the National Party as not 'conservative' in the sense of returning the country to what it was like before the First Labour Government, 'but conservative in that the only substantial field in which it has taken an innovating role is in the government and constitutional area. Here it is motivated both by its concern for the individual and his rights and its feelings about efficiency in Government'. Mitchell lists (among other actions) the abolition of the Legislative Council (1951), the reorganisation of cabinet (1949–51), the creation of the Ombudsman (1962), the consideration of a Bill of Rights (early 1960s), and the establishment of the Royal Commission on the State Services (1962). Interestingly, like so many other commentators, Mitchell does not mention the Electoral Act 1956.[42] Yet anxieties regarding the general absence of formal constraints over powerful political executives (including the ease with which the electoral laws could be changed) and of protection over human rights can be traced back to the debates about state, society, government and the people that were simmering away during National's first term in government.

The National Government was itself a coalition of interests and ideas: urban and rural, conservative and liberal. It was led by a man with huge determination and energy, albeit with few original ideas of his own. Holland was fortunate to have some capable ministers to carry out National Party policies.

I now turn to the broader political context of the Electoral Act 1956. New Zealand in the 1950s was a highly participatory society: politicians did not make decisions in a hermetically sealed central political system.

The People: Parties and Participation

Although the major parties mobilised their supporters at election time, they could expect that, by far, the majority of those qualified to vote would do so. When expressed as a percentage of enrolled voters, turnout was very high between 1949 and 1960, although compared with the figures for those *eligible* to vote, the turnout is less impressive.[43] Nevertheless, in contrast to recent elections in New Zealand, turnout was remarkably healthy in the 1950s. In the three general elections that National won during its first term, turnout was 93.5% of registered voters in 1949, 89.1% in 1951, and 91.4% in 1954. In 1957, turnout was 92.9%.[44]

The explanations for this highly participatory political culture are certainly various and probably include factors such as the high number of party activists who would have mobilised others to vote, the social expectation that it was everyone's duty to vote, the habit of voting passed down and across New Zealand's small communities, and perhaps the absence of opinion polls – for turnout tends to increase when the competition between the major parties is perceived to be a tight one. In the 1950s, voters could not reliably tell whether an election would be a close contest or a foregone conclusion (although it is interesting that turnout went down in 1951 when most people supported the National Government's actions against the watersiders).

Except for the four Labour MPs representing the Māori seats, the parliaments of the 1950s were Pākehā in composition and culture. After Sir Āpirana Ngata was defeated in 1943, no Māori candidate won a general electorate seat until Ben Couch and Rex Austin were elected in 1975, representing National. Māori were confined to the four Māori seats. Until 1974, Māori who were 'half-caste' or more had to enrol in the Māori seats while those who were less than 'half-caste' had to enrol in the general seats. Neill Atkinson writes, 'In line with the Maori Affairs Amendment Act 1974, the electoral definition of "Maori" was altered from one based solely on race, with its references to "pure descent" and "half-castes", to one of cultural self-identification . . .'[45] At the five-yearly censuses Māori could choose whether to enrol and vote in a Māori or European electorate. This issue is explored further in Chapter 7 (p. 168).

The parliaments were male-dominated. Women were very active in the National Party, but their support was not recognised at its top levels. During the National Party's first term in government, there was merely one MP who was a woman, Dame Hilda Ross (MP for Hamilton between 1945 and 1959). There were only three Labour women MPs: Mabel Howard (1943–69); Iriana Ratana (1949–69); and Ethel McMillan (1953–75).[46] Indeed, between 1935 and 1975 just 14 MPs were female (4.5% of all members), eight representing Labour and six National.[47] The 1950s were notable for its gendered society, with women back in the domestic sphere after working in factories, the armed forces, the public service and on farms during World War II. Men dominated the memberships and the mores of all the powerful institutions, including Parliament, cabinet and senior positions in the public service. Aotearoa New Zealand during the 1950s was a highly participatory society, but the phenomenon was characterised by its social and ethnic biases.

During the 1950s both major parties were 'mass' parties rather than the Parliament-centred, cadre parties that they would become in later years. Labour, the older political party, had led the way by building up its membership in the long years between 1906 and 1935. National, the inheritor of three caucus-based parties that worked closely with local notables, generally copied the Labour organisational model.[48] However, National instituted a divisional (regional) structure, unlike Labour (until 1971); and candidate selection was more widely participatory, as explained below. Furthermore, the bases of party membership differed. Labour membership could be through belonging to an affiliated trade union or becoming a branch member, while prospective National members joined as individuals.

Party membership during the 1950s was huge compared with later decades. Evidently in 1947–48 there were 201,765 Labour Party members;[49] although by 1960, according to Robert Milne, there were about 180,000 with an estimated

80% of those being affiliated members.[50] As with National, membership levels fluctuated, going up in election years and then down again. National had worked hard to build up a mass membership.[51] Writing in the mid-1950s, Robert Kelson noted that the total financial membership of the National Party was 'in the vicinity of the 200,000 mark, that is, something like 40% of the voting strength of the Party'.[52] Indeed, 'nearly half of those who vote for the party at elections are also members of the party.'[53] (In 1952 New Zealand had a total population of just under two million.[54]) From the time National was formed it had focused on having a large membership. According to Milne, there was 'regular collection of the minimum annual membership fee of 2s. 6d.'. Writing in the early 1960s, he reports that National Party membership had 'fluctuated from 250,000 in an election year to 143,000 in an "off year"'.[55] Both Kelson and Milne note that whole families were signed up, some without their knowledge.[56] Despite this, the National Party, along with Labour, could be labelled a 'mass' membership political party.[57]

The National Party historically has selected its candidates through involving its members at the electorate level, albeit after some winkling down at the divisional level. The process could involve many party members voting to choose their candidates in electorates with large memberships, since the more members an electorate had on the books, the more representatives were eligible to be involved in selecting the candidate. As Milne notes, 'the requirement that an electorate organization must normally have 2,000 members in order to be allowed to choose its own candidate stimulated the drive to obtain more members'.[58] One might add that there was also the incentive for anti-Labour New Zealanders to join a party that was having its first exciting period in government and to attempt to influence that government. Expectations were high. In comparison, Labour candidates were selected by a panel of six or seven members and included national representatives who could dominate the choice over the locals, themselves selected by the party branches. There was a vote of members present at the selection meeting, but this was advisory only, and did not always sway the committee.

Membership of the two major parties involved a sizeable proportion of the New Zealand population in the political process. If we take Milne's estimate of 1,300 National Party branches by the early 1960s, and make the assumption that branches overall had an average of ten active members, then some 13,000 people were participating in National Party politics (excluding paid Party workers and MPs).

The fundamental organisational unit in both parties was (and is) the branch. Branches in both parties sent representatives to electorate committees, to the divisional conferences and committees in the case of National, and in both parties to the annual conferences. These gatherings elected officers, considered remits, and made any changes to their parties' constitutions. The most influential National Party body during Sidney Holland's time was the executive committee of the Dominion Council, which met more frequently than did the Council itself.[59] Also influential was the policy committee, constituted by equal numbers of MPs and non-parliamentary party members and chaired by the party leader.[60] The policy committee was 'an agency for synthesising attitudes of the top leadership in the two branches of the party. Formal votes are never taken, and it is left to the Leader to sense the consensus of the meeting.'[61] The leader's policy views were undoubtedly paramount, an important point to remember when it came to constitutional change during the 1950s.[62] As we shall see, Holland had a close working relationship with the party president, Sir Alex McKenzie, who held that position from 1951 until 1962.[63] The task of a party president, whatever the party, is to look two ways at once: to the organisation outside Parliament, its campaigning, its memberships, and the selection of parliamentary candidates; and to the parliamentary party, especially communicating with the party leader.

Political participation was not confined to joining political parties. Post-war Aotearoa New Zealand possessed a plethora of actively lobbying groups, social and economic. The country was extensively unionised, with most trade unions in their umbrella organisation, the Federation of Labour (formed in 1944), affiliated to the Labour Party. Milne's estimate was that affiliate members made up about 80% of the Labour Party's membership.[64] A Joint Council of Labour linked the party with the unions.[65] Many other pressure groups existed. The organisation that was most closely tied to National was Federated Farmers, formed in 1944, an umbrella organisation of various farmer interests. At its peak in the early 1950s, Federated Farmers had about 49,000 financial members.[66] There were also women's groups such as the National Council of Women, the Women's Division of Federated Farmers and the Maori Women's Welfare League (formed in 1951). Robert Milne's explanation for the many groups pursuing economic goals is worth quoting in full:

> Perhaps there are two reasons why such economic groups are especially prominent in Australia and New Zealand. For one thing, because of the prevailing materialistic atmosphere, cultural and intellectual groups play a less important role than in, say, Britain. Secondly, the prominent role of the State in economic life, and consequent concern with the economic benefits or losses from arbitration, import selection, tariffs, marketing schemes for farm products, price control, public works schemes, and so on, is a powerful incentive to activity on the part of economic groups. In some spheres, such as arbitration and marketing, groups may be strengthened by

> government activity and so may become 'implicated' in the governmental process. Indeed, groups have actually been *created* by state intervention; the National Milk Scheme (1943) quickly resulted in the formation of the Town Milk Producers' Federation and the Milk Vendors' Association.[67]

Hence an active civil society comprising many organised groups, including those with business interests, was a notable characteristic of the 1950s.

Electoral Law and the Limitations of Consensus

As I have indicated above, despite their policy disagreements, during the 1950s there were pronounced consensual tendencies concerning the operation of the state and its relationship with society, both in terms of employing consultative policy processes and pursuing shared policy goals. I have also stressed that there were important differences. Although the two parties agreed with the bases of the constitutional system they had inherited, including the Westminster tradition with its parliamentary supremacy and the FPP electoral system, they disagreed profoundly over certain aspects of the electoral law. These differences, combined with general discontent with the workings of the Electoral Act 1927 and internal National Party debates over unicameralism and its consequences, would be the catalysts for the Electoral Act 1956. As we shall see, it would be the product of backroom deals, internal National Party disagreements, and bargaining between the National Party Government and the Labour Party Opposition in an attempt to resolve their historic grievances.

Before addressing the passage of the Electoral Bill, I discuss the electoral issues on which there was little or no bipartisan consensus and which helped shape the Electoral Act 1956.

4

The Unsettled Electoral Issues

During the 1940s and 1950s, despite bipartisan consensus over the basic rules and practices of the constitution, the two major parties strongly disagreed on important aspects of the electoral system. These were the criteria to be used when determining electorate boundaries and the composition of the Representation Commission, which was responsible for carrying out the task of defining those boundaries. Within the National Party there was also a difference of opinion: whether or not New Zealand should revive bicameralism after the Legislative Council had been abolished. It is these differences – the partisan disputes between Labour and the National Party and the internal disagreements within the latter Party – that propelled the revisers of the Electoral Act 1956 to include Section 189 with its selected entrenched provisions. Less divisive, but also unsettled, was the legislation defining the length of the parliamentary term. There was considerable anxiety on both sides of the House about the ease with which a governing party could extend its rule by legislating to delay a forthcoming general election.

The story of the passage of the Act through the House of Representatives and the analysis of Section 189 will be the foci of later chapters, but they cannot be understood without first discussing the decisions and debates of the preceding years. Moreover, non-decisions can be as important as decisions when it comes to constitutional design and amendment. The non-entrenchment of the Māori seats in 1956 was a significant omission that would have long-lasting consequences. In the last part of this chapter I outline the historical treatment of the four Māori seats to provide the background for further discussion of what happened in 1956.

Defining Electorate Boundaries: Arguments about Fairness and Equality

The bases on which constituency boundaries are drawn matter a great deal for final electoral results, particularly in single-member district, simple plurality electoral systems. How should electoral populations be counted when the electorates are decided upon? By the number of qualified voters or by total population? The latter formula was at that time more likely to favour parties that depended heavily on rural support because those areas tended to have more children per family. Furthermore, how does one balance heavy support for one party in an electorate against marginal support in another? Corralling party supporters into particular electorates can lead, especially in FPP systems, to many 'wasted' votes in those areas and, concomitantly, work against a party's representation that is proportionate to its nationwide party support. And how can boundaries be defined in such a way as to make each constituency roughly the same size in terms of their electoral populations whilst still respecting communities of interest such as towns and neighbourhoods? And who should make these crucial decisions? These issues were the subjects of partisan disagreement and they reached a crescendo in the post-war period.

To understand the quarrel between Labour and National over these particular issues, we need to return briefly to the politics of the 19th century, when politicians made some crucial decisions. In 1879, George Grey, premier from 1877–79, introduced a Representation Bill that, as well as increasing the number of general seats to a total of 91, proposed creating an independent board tasked with redrawing the boundaries after each census. Previously the boundaries had been decided upon by members of the House of Representatives. The basis for dividing up the country into electorates was to be total population; and the Bill proposed then adding 25% to the electoral populations of country districts when deciding upon the boundaries of their seats.[1] This was known as the 'country quota'. The Bill's electoral reforms were unsuccessful.[2] Two years later, under the next premier, John Hall, the government introduced another, very similar bill. This time it passed.[3]

In 1887, the independent Representation Commission was created. The invention of an organisation independent from politicians, tasked with the responsibility of drawing electoral boundaries, was a democratic milestone for New Zealand. There were two officials on the Commission, the Surveyor-General and the Property Tax Commissioner, and three 'unofficial' persons who were to be neither members of the public service nor MPs. These 'unofficial' members were nominated by the House of Representatives. In 1896 the Representation Commission was split into two, with one Commission for each of the North and South Islands. Now there were three official members and two unofficial members on each body. According to Alan McRobie, the appointment of the non-official members was not controversial until the development of intense two-party politics during the 1930s and Labour's Electoral Amendment Act 1945, which I discuss below.[4] As the Royal Commission on the Electoral System states, the first Commission embodied four important principles: independence (from parliamentary interference); membership (balanced between neutral public servants and members nominated by Parliament); representation (apart from the country quota, a limit was set on drawing up unequal electorates); and revision (regular reviews).[5]

A 'country quota' was also included in the Representation Act 1887. After a brief period at 19% (1887–89), the country quota settled at 28% (Representation Act 1889). It was a measure 'with the design of curtailing the representation of the four largest cities'.[6] The country quota added 28% to the populations of electorates that had no cities, boroughs or town districts of more than 2000 people. This meant that, as Lipson writes, 'a New Zealander's vote counted for one, if he lived in a city, and for one and twentyeight hundredths, if he lived on a farm'.[7] It is not surprising that this formula was the subject of debate. According to Lipson, there was only one argument on each side that had merit: National's argument that 'the economic importance of the rural minority warranted an electoral adjustment in their favour';[8] and Labour's retort that it was 'unfair that a farmer's vote should count for more than a city dweller's' and that the country quota meant 'the basic democratic principle of equality at the voting booth was violated'.[9] Lipson writes that, 'The animosity aroused during debate over the "country quota" signaled the emergence of a new political division in post-provincial New Zealand: town versus country.'[10]

From its formation in 1916, the Labour Party had opposed the country quota on principle, regarding it as undemocratic because it weighted different electors' votes differently. Plainly, however, self-interest also provided a powerful incentive to oppose the country quota, given that Labour's voting strength was mainly in the urban areas. Despite its opposition, for various reasons including the onset of war at the end of the 1930s, Labour left the country quota alone for most of its first term in government.[11] Until 1943, Labour attracted significant numbers of rural voters, meaning that the effects of the formula on the party's results during that period were minimal.[12] When Labour's rural support dissipated, however, government acted to rid itself of the country quota. In 1945, it put an Electoral Amendment Bill through the House, using urgency to hasten its passing, abolishing the quota in time for the general election scheduled the following year. Delegations from the rural sectors lobbied Labour ministers to retain the quota, but in vain.[13] Federated Farmers fulminated on the Bill's iniquities, even creating a fighting fund to oppose the Bill,[14] and *The Evening Post* scolded, editorialising that the government aimed 'to change the rules in the middle of the game in the hope of benefitting itself and playing the Opposition at a disadvantage, and it is doing so without any authority whatever from the people'.[15] John E. Martin reports that, when the Bill was passed through the House, 'Labour members sang "The Red Flag". When National responded with "God Save the King", Labour broke into "God Defend New Zealand".'[16]

Labour's 1945 legislation not only abolished the country quota but also changed the Representation Commission by abolishing the two separate bodies and creating one Commission for the whole country. Its membership now comprised three official members (the Surveyor-General and the Commissioners of Crown Land for South Auckland and Canterbury) and four non-official members, all nominated by the government of the day.[17] The new composition was strongly criticised by the National opposition.

Closely connected with the country quota formula and the composition of the Representation Commission was the vexed question of how to count people when determining electoral boundaries. Should total population be the basis for calculation? Or should the electoral population be based on adults alone, that is, the age-eligible members of the population? Note, however, at this stage we are talking about the 'European' (now 'non-Maori') population only:

the Representation Commission at that stage did not decide upon the boundaries of the Māori seats (see below). Labour's 1945 Act required the electoral quota to be calculated using adult population rather than total (European) population, as it had been since 1887. This further reduced country representation, as explained above.[18] Neill Atkinson observes that, 'In anticipation of a close contest in 1946, the [Labour] government had no desire to maintain a system that gave disproportionate voting power to increasingly hostile rural electors.'[19]

The 1945 legislation stirred the pot in another way: the permitted allowance for the adjustment of the quota was yet another contested ingredient of the business of drawing up electorate boundaries. The electoral tolerance allowed for some numerical variation in electorate population in order to allow communities of interest, topological features and communication links to be acknowledged while also treating the weight of each person's vote as equally as possible. Boundary-drawing has been a particularly difficult issue in a long, skinny, jagged country such as New Zealand. In 1935 the Surveyor-General, a member of the Representation Commission, proposed that the extent of electoral tolerance when drawing up electorate boundaries should be changed. It was felt that the existing margins by which the population quota could be exceeded or reduced in any one electoral district (1250, or 250 in urban areas) should be altered to 10% and 5% respectively. This would allow for more weight to be given to geography and community of interest.[20] These criticisms were repeated two years later.[21]

With its voting strength in the rural areas, National favoured wider tolerances while Labour preferred narrower ones. And Labour was in government, so it provided that a 'uniform tolerance relative to the quota of 500 for all electorates' was included in the Electoral Amendment Act

1945.[22] Such a low tolerance fitted with Labour's belief that each voter's choice should be as equal to everyone else's as possible, as well as reflecting its dependence on urban voters. As noted above, the lower tolerance was contrary to the advice of the Representation Commission. Farmers and the National Party were outraged. As James Christmas points out, both sides, Labour and National, were demarcated by clear self-interest. Christmas also notes that the National Opposition criticised the Bill on the grounds that the Labour Government had no democratic mandate for the measure since it had not appeared in its election manifesto.[23]

The National Opposition argued against the 1945 Bill on the grounds of abuse of process because it was pushed through by the use of urgency. Arguments about the legitimacy of change processes concerning electoral law matters had emerged on the political agenda.[24]

Insofar as electoral boundaries were concerned, adversarial politics, with its seesawing between polar policy alternatives, moved into a new phase after National won office in the 1949 general election and had revenge over its opponents. As promised in its 1946 and 1949 election manifestos,[25] the Electoral Amendment Act 1950 reversed the earlier legislation so that the electoral quota would be calculated on the basis of total 'European', not adult, population figures, thus favouring many of its core supporters, the rural voters. Also, the tolerance was increased to 7.5%. Yet the new government did not change the composition of the Representation Commission, thereby retaining the possibility of influencing the nomination of the unofficial members. National replaced the four nominees with its own supporters. Despite appearances, however, according to McRobie 'there is no evidence that the unofficial members used their majority to force a particular result in either 1946 or 1952'.[26] Nevertheless, perceptions of bias dominated the rhetoric on both sides of the political divide.

The 1950 legislation did not go so far as reinstating the country quota, but debate over it continued after its 1945 abolition. In 1956 the issue bubbled up again as an enduring cause of resentment, as shown in the next chapter.

As can be seen, adversarial politics over the determination of electoral boundaries and the composition of the Representation Commission had been lively issues for decades. The differences between Labour and National were partly based on philosophical differences. Labour stressed the importance of the equality of the vote, with each elector's vote weighing as closely as possible to every other elector's vote. National, on the other hand, was more interested in the end result – representing all communities of interest, insofar as that is possible. Tucked into the normative concerns were partisan interests. National's strength was in the rural areas and the richer city electorates, while Labour's was in the poorer urban parts of the country.

So far I have discussed the electoral issues that divided the two parties and have highlighted intensely adversarial differences that would influence the Electoral Bill of 1956. I turn now to the anxieties and differences that had developed within the National Party.

Bicameralism, Unicameralism and the National Party

Abolition of New Zealand's appointed and ineffectual Legislative Council had been Labour Party policy since its 1919 general election manifesto.[27] Once in office, though, it benefited from being able to appoint party loyalists to the upper house for renewable seven-year terms. Moreover there was no ceiling on its total membership. Thus there was no immediate incentive for Labour to get rid of the Council: everything was in favour of leaving it alone. The opposition

National Party, in particular its leader Sidney Holland, had a different viewpoint, viewing the Legislative Council – stacked with Labourites – as an obstacle to implementing National policies once the Party won office. Abolition was promised in the 1946 National Party manifesto and repeated in 1949.

In 1947, Holland put forward a private member's bill to abolish the Council. As Keith Jackson records, this bill, even though unsuccessful, 'triggered the constitutional steps necessary if abolition was to be undertaken seriously'.[28] Although New Zealand had long behaved as if it were a sovereign state, constitutionally it still had a degree of dependence on Westminster.[29] In particular, Parliament could not abolish the upper house without referring the matter to the UK Parliament: the Constitution Act 1852 stated that New Zealand's General Assembly consisted of a Governor, a Legislative Council and a House of Representatives, and this section could only be amended or repealed by the UK Parliament.

In 1931 the UK Parliament had passed the Statute of Westminster Act 1931, the necessary initial step in releasing New Zealand and other former colonies from constitutional dependency. Despite recognising the constitutional limitations inherent in continued non-ratification, particularly in the area of foreign affairs, New Zealand had not got around to ratifying this agreement.[30] In 1944, via the Governor-General's speech at the opening of Parliament, the Labour Government announced its intention to ratify the Statute of Westminster.[31] Nothing happened for a couple of years. Then, as Harshan Kumarasingham notes, the prime minister, Peter Fraser, introduced an amendment to Holland's 1947 private member's bill during its second reading to the effect that, before any change was made to the constitution, New Zealand would ratify the Statute of Westminster.[32] The Labour Government then formally set in train the adoption of Sections 2–6 of the 1931 British Statute of Westminster to make New Zealand legally sovereign 'and able on its own national authority to exercise the constitutional power to abolish the Legislative Council – if desired'.[33] The Statute of Westminster Adoption Act and the New Zealand Constitution Amendment (Request and Consent) Act were passed in 1947. Both statutes were necessary if New Zealand was to change its Parliament, because bicameralism had been included under Section 32 of the New Zealand Constitution Amendment Act 1857 (UK), and Section 8 of that same Act had prohibited New Zealand from repealing certain provisions of the Constitution Act 1852.[34]

Under pressure from the National Opposition, Prime Minister Peter Fraser agreed to the establishment of a Joint Constitutional Reform Committee (with members from both chambers) to investigate the future of the Legislative Council. In 1948, the Committee called for submissions. Letters were sent to New Zealand and overseas experts and practitioners requesting their views. Many proposals were received, and these included descriptions and assessments of how other bicameral systems worked.[35] Perhaps predictably, the Committee failed to agree on a replacement upper house.[36] As Holland commented, 'It was difficult to expect the Legislative Council members of the joint Committee to be very enthusiastic about the abolition of the Council.'[37] However, he did not give up at this point, putting forward a further private member's bill on abolition in 1949, although this was allowed to lapse.

As well, we should refer to National's full constitutional policy put before electors in 1949, recalling that in those days the Party took its pledges particularly seriously.

> (a) The Legislative Council as present constituted has failed in its purpose as a revising Chamber and should be abolished.

> As the Government, the National Party will examine the possible alternatives to provide for some form of safeguard against hasty, unwise or ill-considered legislation.
>
> (b) Introduce the British White Paper System [discussion documents circulated before legislation was introduced to Parliament].
>
> (c) The Electoral Act will be amended to give effect to the unanimous recommendations of the 1938 and the 1946 Representation Commissions and to provide that the total population be the standard for determining the boundaries of each electorate.
>
> (d) Right of Inheritance to be strictly preserved.
>
> (e) The possibilities of introducing a written constitution for New Zealand will be examined and, if possible, adopted.[38]

Once National gained office after the 1949 general election, Holland set out to fulfil his Party's election promise and his own personal ambition by abolishing New Zealand's upper house. There were normative as well as practical issues at stake. One of those issues had arisen during the debate in the House, when the *Report of the Constitutional Reform Committee* was tabled. What was the legitimate role of the House of Representatives in changing the shape of Parliament, even after ratification of the Statute of Westminster? There was a rancorous exchange on whether or not such a decision should be made by plebiscite rather than by the House of Representatives. According to Keith Jackson, two National Party lawyers, Clifton Webb and Ronald Algie, advocated holding a referendum to decide on the future of the Legislative Council, and Holland himself flirted with this strategy.[39] Fraser, the Leader of the Opposition at this time, rejected any such suggestion. This meant, as Jackson points out, that Holland actually benefitted, because since the Opposition had rejected the idea of consulting the people through a referendum, the prime minister could now work out how to abolish the upper house by other means.[40] With the help of his newly appointed Legislative Council suicide squad – thanks to the absence of a constitutional limit on how many upper house members there could be – Holland did just this, arguing that his government had a mandate to get rid of the Council.

The abolition bill passed through both the House of Representatives and the Legislative Council. The National Party bicamerists had held their noses and voted along party lines, appeased by the prime minister's promise to consider the establishment of a new and better upper house. Furthermore, as Clifton Webb pointed out during the Second Reading of the Legislative Council Abolition Bill, National's party platform included the statement that 'we would explore the possibility of a written constitution'.[41] Holland endeavoured to placate his dissidents by moving to establish a second constitutional reform committee to look again at bicameral solutions. Labour acted against its own party policy on the Legislative Council by voting against the abolition Bill. According to one commentator, 'Labour's consciences were salved by claiming that they could not vote the old Council out because the Government planned to put a new and monstrous one in its place.'[42]

With the abolition of the Legislative Council, New Zealand's constitution had been radically changed through a simple majority vote in Parliament. The legality of this move was not in question but its legitimacy was worrying to some. Should a referendum have been employed? This was not a novel way of settling policy issues in New Zealand, as shown in Chapter 6 (p. 136), although referendums had never been employed on constitutional matters. The process of constitutional change became an issue that bubbled away within the National Party, just under the surface of the official constitutional agenda. It is not surprising that, for some National Party members, the manner in which the Parliament had gone about abolishing its upper house – without consulting or seeking approval from voters, despite the issue being heralded by election promises – sat uncomfortably with them. The death of the Legislative Council through the combined action of its suicide squad and MPs led to wide-ranging questions about the appropriate processes to be used for changing the constitution. And because many National Party MPs and supporters regarded abolition as the pathway towards creating a new and better upper house –rather than the beginning of de jure as well as de facto unicameralism – constitutional change and constitutional propriety were in the parliamentary air. As Keith Jackson writes, 'the key to the situation within the National Party lay in the fact that abolition did not necessarily imply unicameralism'.[43]

Senior members of the National Party outside Parliament had been discussing the problem of inadequate constitutional constraints. For example, one writer advocated 'finding some brake which would curb the damage a subsequent Government might be able to do, and safeguard the fundamental rights of the people'. Given that 'sovereign power rests with the people', surely a constitution could be drawn up, approved by the people in a referendum and 'if the constitution included a clause to provide that subsequent alterations to the constitution could only be made by a referendum of the people, then surely such action would be binding on Parliament'.[44] Clifton Webb responded to this proposal with some vehemence:

> I received your letter of the 1st instant, and am pleased that you have written me as it gives an opportunity to correct a misapprehension under which many people like yourself are labouring.

> The important point to bear in mind is that the only body that can make laws is Parliament; laws cannot be made by the people themselves, but only by the Members whom the people choose for the purpose.
>
> It is for this reason that one Parliament cannot fetter a successor, and I go further and say it would be wrong if one Parliament could fetter its successor. It would be a two-edged sword and it does not require much stretch of the imagination to picture what our friends on the opposite side might do, and indeed might have done, if your view of the power of Parliament were correct. [45]

The possibility of a written constitution surfaced during the 1950 debates on the abolition of the upper house. Leading National Party politicians expressed their views on whether or not a written constitution could be protected by, for example, entrenchment of the relevant clauses in a constitutional statute. Clifton Webb argued that even if an Act required a referendum to amend it, a subsequent Parliament could repeal that provision.[46] Ron Algie concurred, saying that 'if one Parliament cannot bind its successor, it is no use writing a Constitution now, because this Parliament having written it, hands over to another which can repeal it at once'.[47] Jack Watts cited Dicey and opined, 'There is nothing one Government can do to bind its successor.'[48] Holland said, 'We could extend this Parliament – its life – for ten years. You cannot stop us. No one can stop us if we make up our minds. It is important we should have these things cleared up. We could extend our life if we wanted to, but we will not.'[49] Bob Semple intervened from the other side of the House, commenting that Labour could also do this. Holland agreed; and Nash pointed out that public opinion would be against it.[50] Parliament had been extended in the past, as related below.

In mid-1950 there were newspaper reports that a written constitution was being considered by the Attorney-General and Minister of Justice, Clifton Webb.[51] Thus, while the abolition of the Legislative Council was underway, evidently there developed a lively debate on constitutional issues behind the scenes. A memorandum from the Law Draftsman, H. D. G. Adams, to Webb entitled 'New Zealand Constitution Act' referred to a recent conversation on these matters and suggested that a new act might replace the 1852 legislation before the scheduled royal visit. Adams pointed out that many parts were obsolete and inconsistent since New Zealand's adoption of the Statute of Westminster. He suggested what a written constitution might include, but he did not touch upon issues of how such a statute might be protected from simple-majority parliamentary amendment.[52] Professor Robert McGechan (Victoria University College) and Clifton Webb exchanged letters on that very question, however, focusing particularly on the sovereignty of Parliament. McGechan argued that Parliament could indeed set out a procedure that required a referendum be held to amend or repeal a particular law, with such a law not coming into effect unless approved by that referendum. Webb disagreed.[53] In July 1950 Webb wrote a memorandum that proposed a reformed Statutes Revision Commission 'as a check against the risk of hasty or ill-considered measures being pushed into law'. He suggested that it could be a powerful cross-party bills' revision committee that included a few officials and would hear submissions, could revise bills after the Second Reading, and could delay the progress of bills if a majority on the Committee opposed a measure.[54]

Thus, although there was public and private skepticism within National on the efficacy of a written constitution in a system characterised by parliamentary supremacy, there were enough constitutional worriers in the Party and amongst the public to keep the issue alive. Furthermore, given the liveliness of the opposition within his own team, Holland was saddled with having to work out how to pacify the vocal, pesky bicamerist elements of his party. Indeed, constitutional issues would continue to bubble away for most of his prime ministership, only diminishing with the passing of the Electoral Act 1956. In the meantime, Holland had to deliver on the second part of his election promise concerning the abolition of the upper house, that is, how to design and establish its replacement. Fulfilling this commitment might also put the issues of second houses and written constitutions safely away in the cupboard for some time.

Very quickly, in September 1950, a second constitutional reform committee was established. Labour decided to boycott it. In a letter to Holland Peter Fraser wrote that

> as the Government decided to abolish the Legislative Council as part of the work of the first session of Parliament after it assumed office, without any prior consultation with the Opposition in regard to any possible substitute or new form of revisionary body, they are of the opinion that the question is solely and entirely the responsibility of the Government.[55]

The Opposition decided that the new situation needed 'an adequate trial'.[56] National's committee membership would prove to be significant, however, for its deliberations, and the submissions to the Committee would influence the content of the Electoral Act 1956, as is discussed more fully in the next two chapters. Sir Ronald Algie took the chair after the first, T. O. Bishop, died. The other members were: Eric Halstead, Ralph Hanan, Thomas Hayman, John Marshall, Duncan Rae and William (Blair) Tennent. There was also a mirror Legislative Council committee: the two would sit together and, after the latter's abolition, its committee members would sit with the MPs. Algie's role was pivotal and, according to his biographer, the final report 'was largely a product of Algie's learning, drafting skills and political wisdom'.[57]

In 1952 the Committee unanimously recommended the creation of an appointed 32-seat Senate.[58] The senators would be nominated by the Government and Opposition in proportion to their numbers in the House of Representatives. They would serve for three years, delay legislation passed in the House for up to two years, negotiate and initiate legislation, and reject money bills. As academics at that time commented, 'It is true that the members of the Committee came almost exclusively from the National Party, but the divisions of opinion within that party on this issue are known to be so wide that substantial agreement must be regarded as a triumph.'[59] However, as another contemporary commentator wrote, 'It would seem, then, that in recommending the establishment of a Senate the Parliamentary Committee sought to please those who had stressed the urgent need for a second Chamber; then, to please the Prime Minister and the Opposition, it divested the Senate of any effective powers against the political executive.'[60] Despite the unanimity of the Committee on its recommendations, the report would go no further than being tabled in the House, at least in so far as the establishment of a Senate was concerned. John Marshall, himself a unicamerist writes:

> The report and recommendations were received without enthusiasm by our colleagues and were rejected out of hand by the Opposition. I was given the dubious privilege of presenting the report to the next Dominion Conference of the party. In the debate which followed, the party was almost equally divided. When put to the vote, the recommendation to set up a Senate was lost by four votes.[61]

Thus, although 'a large element' of the National Party favoured the proposed new upper house, the leadership 'was not interested in any restrictions on its own power, once it was in office'.[62] Barry Gustafson tells an illuminating story about Holland's attitude to the report on the proposed Senate. When he was asked by a journalist what he would do with it, Holland responded, 'I'm going to take it home, I'm going to bore a hole through the top left hand corner, and I'm going to put a piece of string in it and take it up and hang it in the outhouse.'[63]

It seemed that the upper house cause was now lost, but the Committee's deliberations were to bear other fruit because it interested itself in more than the structure and powers of a new Senate. The Committee was also concerned with constitutional reform processes and constraints, in particular, how any new upper house might be protected from subsequent amendment to its constitution or, more radically, be protected from being abolished.[64] This was in contrast to the previous committee that had reported in 1948, just a few years before. Neither the earlier report nor the submitters to that earlier Committee had proposed how radical constitutional reconstruction might be carried out and, moreover, subsequently protected from future abolition and amendment. The political and institutional contexts had changed. Plainly, the recent experience of seeing just how easily the New Zealand Parliament could divest a part of itself once the Statute of Westminster had been ratified, had been an instructive lesson in the dangers of unprotected constitutional elements.

While the substance of the recommendations – the composition and powers of a new Senate – was contained in the main body of the report, constitutional reform processes and protections were addressed in two appendices. It would be the arguments contained in these that would be significant influences on Section 189 of the Electoral Act 1956, as I later explain.

Despite the rejection by their party of the report's recommendations to establish a new upper house, National Party bicamerists in and out of Parliament kept the issue on their party's agenda. In late 1953, the National Party Executive Committee considered two remits advocating new second chambers (as well as remits on other electoral issues, including a couple wanting increased electorate tolerances).[65] There were two remits on the issue at the 1954 annual conference.[66] In July 1955, according to *The Dominion*, despite Holland's 'uncompromising opposition to the Old Legislative Council, and indeed to the committee's recommendations at the time it reported', the party's annual conference 'passed a resolution requesting the Government to reconsider the Constitutional Reform Committee's report with a view to the establishment of a revised second Chamber'.[67] As can be seen, there was considerable discontent within the National Party with the lack of constraints on powerful governments. The party's own actions, by abolishing the upper house rather than reforming it, exacerbated concerns that were already present within the party before it was elected.

I now turn to the disquiet felt by many MPs concerning the ease with which governments and parliaments could extend their terms of office.

Extending the Parliamentary Term

The maximum parliamentary term had been fixed at three years since 1879. The three-year cycle was, however, interrupted at the time of World War I. There was a general election in 1914, but the next one was postponed until 1918 and then again until 1919. The Electoral Act 1927 stated:

> (2) Every such House of Representatives shall, unless the General Assembly is sooner dissolved, continue for a period of three years, computed from the day fixed for the return of the writs issued for choosing such House, and no longer.

Despite this provision, there were no obstacles in the way of governments extending their tenures by amending the Act using their parliamentary majorities, although they risked courting public disapproval and Opposition criticism.

During the depression of the late 1920s and 1930s, the Parliament elected in 1931 was controversially extended by the United–Reform Coalition Government for one further year (to 1935). Its legislative authority for this action was an amendment to the Finance Act 1932 (Section 35). The extension was unsuccessfully opposed by the Labour Opposition. The Government then went further and in the Electoral Amendment Act 1934 2 (1) amended the principal Act, changing the parliamentary term from three to four years. Not only had the Government not sought an electoral mandate for this move but also it drove through the amendment under urgency: the Labour Opposition and the Independent MPs bitterly opposed it. The 1935 general election, however, brought the Labour Party to power for the first time and, although under the new law that Parliament had been elected for four years, restored the triennial term in the Electoral Amendment Act 1937. The next general election was held in 1938.

During World War II, the tables were turned and the Labour Government postponed the 1941 general election, initially for one year and then for a further year, in successive Prolongation of Parliament bills. (The previous election had been in 1938.) The problem of whether or not the 1941 general election should take place in a period of war was mixed with the controversial issue of whether or not, given the circumstances, New Zealand should be governed by a coalition government, an arrangement that was opposed by Labour and the Federation of Labour. In July 1940 a War Cabinet had been formed as a compromise. Adam Hamilton, the then National leader, and the former leader of the Reform Party, Gordon Coates, represented the Opposition in the War Cabinet. As Keith Sinclair relates, Sidney Holland, who replaced Adam Hamilton as National Party leader in November 1940, declined the invitation to join the War Cabinet on the grounds of National's disapproval of Labour's policies.[68] In June 1942 a War Administration was created that included Holland, but this arrangement lasted only four months. National resigned from that body because the party did not approve of the Labour Government's treatment of a miners' strike. The War Cabinet lasted to the end of the war.

Even within Labour, whether or not the scheduled 1941 general election should take place, despite the ongoing war, was a fraught topic. 'Caucus was unanimous in wanting an election', while Nash 'could not see how an election could be avoided if there were to be no coalition. The situation was thus very confused.'[69] The prime minister, Peter Fraser, overseas at the time, favoured a coalition government: 'It would unify the nation: the responsibility for difficult and unpopular tasks would be shared.'[70] There was dissent within the party and discontent over Fraser's leadership.

When the Bill to extend the parliamentary term was introduced into Parliament, Holland said that until he had received a letter from Fraser he had been unaware of the Government's intention to defer the election and said that 'I thought an election was on'.[71] Although Holland would not participate in anything other than a full coalition, he did agree to the elections being put off for one year. In return for this cooperation, Fraser committed himself to refrain from introducing partisan legislation.[72] Fraser stated in the House that there had been much 'soul searching' within Labour but that he had been approached by MPs from both parties asking him to postpone the election.[73] The Bill was passed.

Just over a year later Parliament was extended for a further year in the Prolongation of Parliament Act 1942. Speaking for the Opposition, Holland said that there was general approval of postponement but that the situation must be reviewed every year.[74] Three parliamentarians voted against the Bill.

Although wartime prolongation had bipartisan support, the actions of the wartime and depression governments gave rise to unease among many New Zealanders, including MPs. As was shown above, during the debate on the abolition of the Legislative Council the power to extend the life of a parliament was one of the issues that MPs felt was problematical, no matter that abolition had really changed nothing in this respect. As E. A. Olssen observed in 1952, 'Yet the act of abolition did give renewed emphasis to the manner in which political power has come to be concentrated in the executive.'[75] Fixing the maximum term of Parliament was another issue that needed resolution.

I now turn to a further unsettled part of the constitution: the four Māori seats that had been established during the previous century.

Māori Representation and Attitudes Towards the Māori Seats

When it comes to the Māori seats we find that philosophical differences about what construes just and fair representation were intertwined with pragmatic interests founded on different voting supports, as was the case with the criteria that dictated the drawing up of electorate boundaries.

From 1943 onwards, Labour dominated all four Māori seats, thanks to the alliance with the Rātana Church and also Māori voters' attraction to the party that brought Māori citizens, then and now amongst the poorer members of society, under the umbrella of the social security state. Once in office, Labour made some effort to democratise the seats, in contrast with its liberal and conservative predecessors.

Non-Māori voters had been granted the secret ballot in 1870, but Māori seat voters were not included in this important democratic reform. The secret ballot was strongly advocated by Māori MPs such as Eruera Tirikatene (MP for Southern Maori 1932–67), who was also concerned that dual- and triple-voting was occurring.[76] Labour included the secret ballot for Māori in an Electoral Amendment Bill in 1937.[77] As John Wilson observes, the immediate effect was to increase Māori seat voter turnout in the 1938 general election.[78] In 1949 Māori seat voters were for the first time given voting rights in two nationwide referendums on off-course betting and compulsory military training.[79]

Labour took much longer, however, to create Māori electoral rolls. This had been promised for the 1938 general election. Between 1910 and 1948, Māori electors voting in the Māori seats voted by declaration. The United Party had proposed the creation of electoral rolls for the Māori seats in 1928 but no action had been taken.[80] The creation of Māori electoral rolls had been Labour Party policy since 1925. Finally, in 1948 the Electoral Amendment Act created rolls for the four Māori electorates, centralising them in the Chief Electoral Office. (After then, Māori could vote by declaration only after the rolls had closed.) It seems that officials were at least partly to blame for the very long delay in implementing this change: 'The Electoral Office had continued to exaggerate the difficulties of compiling a roll until Fraser decided to use the welfare officers of the Maori Affairs Department to flush out Māori enrolments in time for the general election.'[81]

One of the problems was to determine eligibility. From the

time of the creation of the Māori seats, eligibility to vote in those four electorates had not been determined by identifying as Māori but by proportion of Māori- or non-Māori 'blood'. The advent of a Māori roll brought up the ambiguity of the status of those New Zealanders who were half-Māori and half-Pākehā. Hence the Electoral Amendment Act 1948, as well as creating the electoral rolls, clarified the position of 'half-castes'. According to Labour's Walter Nash, the Act gave them 'the option of being registered either as Maori or European in the various Maori or European electoral districts . . . Previously they could register as Europeans only, and vote as such. If they were not registered, they automatically had the right to vote as Maoris.'[82] This might have clarified issues of eligibility but it certainly created problems for those who identified as Māori but who were now restricted as to their electoral roll. It would not be until 1975 that further legislation permitted those who identified as Māori to choose either the Māori or the General roll, thus avoiding the troubling issue of defining ethnicity through blood percentages.

Interestingly, however, 'The manner in which the [1948] Bill was dealt with was, perhaps, as important as its contents. While the 1945 Electoral Amendment Bill had been debated with considerable bitterness, parts of this Bill were clearly the result of agreement before it was introduced into Parliament.'[83] It seemed that negotiation between the Government and the Opposition resulted in agreement that the Chief Electoral Office would deal with the Māori roll.[84]

The Labour Government had been willing to cure a couple of the problems of the unfair electoral functioning of the four Māori seats. Undoubtedly the credit should go to Labour's Māori MPs: the presence of a political minority in a parliamentary party matters a great deal, even when that presence is a small one. But, as has been shown, Labour's responsiveness to Māori representation had its limits.

The Māori MPs wanted the Māori seats to increase to six, reflecting the population increase, but this was ignored.[85] In 1946, for example, the average population of the non-Māori seats was 21,799 while in the Māori seats it was 25,391.[86] Furthermore, as Keith Sorrenson points out, during the 1946–47 period Peter Fraser was 'unwilling to hand over the portfolio of Native Affairs to one of the Maori members'. Tirikatene was given a minor portfolio.[87] During Fraser's time as minister, though, and due to his ministerial Secretary, MR (Mick) Jones, 'Native' was replaced by 'Maori' in all official documents. [88]

Once created, the Māori rolls were not reliable. Sorrenson notes that, despite concern at their state, the Minister of Maori Affairs during the first National Government, E. B. Corbett, rejected the suggestion that Māori welfare officers be used to recruit Māori voters, seemingly because he feared that they would recruit for the Labour Party.[89] Nevertheless, despite – or perhaps because of – National's suspicion of the seats, once in power it was instrumental in legislating in 1950 and 1951 to have the Māori seat elections occur on the same day as the elections in the General seats.

There was another anomaly which neither Labour nor National cleared up. Under the Maori Representation Act 1867 the Māori electorate boundaries were declared by proclamation of the Governor (later the Governor-General). The Electoral Act 1927 did not specify the criteria that were to be heeded in drawing up the boundaries. In effect the government made the decisions. In 1954, the National Government made well overdue electoral boundary changes, although the inequality between constituency populations remained much greater than amongst the European seats. Regular fair and equitable boundary determination would have to wait very much longer. Indeed, Māori seat electoral boundaries were not defined by the Representation

Commission until Labour legislated on this matter in 1975. And it would be not until 1981 that Māori electorate boundaries would be reviewed every five years, almost one hundred years (1887) after the non-Māori seats were granted this regular assessment.

Voter registration had been made compulsory for general electorate voters in 1924. As we shall see, Māori-seat voter compulsory registration would be included in the Electoral Act 1956.

When it came to justifying the very existence of the Māori electorates, the two parties differed. Labour was prepared to argue for group rights to political representation, via the vehicle of the seats. National, in contrast, was less happy with the whole concept of 'special' representation.[90] For example, although the National Opposition supported the Electoral Amendment Act 1937, evidently a number of its members saw it 'as a prelude to the abolition of the Maori seats'.[91] To take another example of National Party attitudes to the seats, during the 1956 Address in Reply parliamentary debate, one of its MPs said, 'Now that the Maori people have attained equality of status and equality of privilege with the European population should not the privilege of separate representation given to the Maori people be withdrawn?'[92] The notion that the Māori seats constitute some sort of privileged position in the New Zealand electoral system is still present in some quarters during the 21st century.

As Richard Hill observes, for the first time since 'the third quarter of the nineteenth century, New Zealand had a government with no Maori support in Parliament'.[93] Why then did National not abolish the seats, in its reforming zeal during its first term in government, especially given that it was not winning those electorates? It could have achieved this change by a simple-majority parliamentary vote. Sorrenson writes that, 'National, unwilling to eliminate the Maori voice from Parliament, continued to hope that it would win back at least one of the Maori seats. In the meantime, it was content to tinker with the existing system.'[94] Sorrenson also reports that Ernest Corbett, the Minister of Maori Affairs, wanted to get rid of the seats and unsuccessfully wrote to Marshall in 1957 favouring giving Māori the option of enrolling in the general electorate if they wished. Then, if the numbers on the Māori electoral rolls fell below a certain minimum, then the Māori seats could be abolished.[95] While the seats existed, and while Māori voted predominantly Labour, the 'Maori problem' was not National's to worry about. As we will see in the coming chapters, it would be far easier simply to leave the seats unprotected by entrenchment, thus leaving National's future options flexible.

It should be noted that Māori MPs themselves were generally treated with disrespect by the mass media during the 1950s, and this was related to the prevailing belief that the reason for the existence of the seats – to ensure that the Māori voice and interests were expressed in representative politics – was illegitimate. One researcher examined 91 articles on Māori affairs published in newspapers between 1949 and 1951. He found that 'forty-one of these were devoted to politics, all but one being unfavourable to the Maori political position and expressing disfavour ranging in degree from near neutrality to bitter hostility'.[96] The newspapers recognised, however, that the mechanics of the Māori seats needed to be improved. The author reports that the National Party views of Maori politics expressed in its publication *Freedom* were vitriolic.[97]

Neither party ever denied the right of Māori citizens to participate as individuals in the polity, and to that extent there was consensus about basic democratic rights. But with neither Labour nor National selecting Māori candidates for winnable General seats, it was unlikely that Māori themselves would have wanted the Māori seats to disappear, despite their manifold problems and disadvantages. The recognition of group rights in a democratic policy is always problematical. But these rights are inherently difficult to justify in a majoritarian political culture where the primary instrument for the exercise of political rights is the ballot – essentially an exercise of individual choice. The Māori seats, which represented a culture as well as the individual and collective interests of Māori citizens, were part of the unsettled elements of the New Zealand constitution. In the following chapters we will again see the ambiguity and weakness of the Māori seats within the New Zealand constitution when it comes to the making of the Electoral Act 1956. Their democratic deficiencies would be only very slowly resolved over the next decades. The absence of widespread public and elite legitimacy for the Māori electorates would be an issue that would continue to haunt the Māori electorates, delaying reforms to democratise them and weakening the voices of Māori in Parliament when it came to electoral and constitutional reform, at least until the advent of MMP.

Towards Reform

By the mid-1950s adversarial party politics had noisily played out over several electoral and constitutional issues: the weighting of votes, especially concerning rural and urban voters; the extent to which electorate sizes might vary in order to respect communities of interest; and the composition of the Representation Commission. Given the recent history of seesaw politics over these electoral issues, each side of politics could rightly fear the actions of their opponents when the other side regained political power. There was also the quieter issue that gnawed away: the ease with which the triennial term of Parliament could be, and had been, extended.

Furthermore, discontent over the electoral law and the

constitution surfaced when some MPs thought about the implications of becoming a unicameral Parliament. This was particularly intriguing given the 20th century Legislative Council was hardly an instrument of constraint when it came to vetoing or amending constitutional or any other type of legislation. National Party MPs who were concerned about the future of the constitution in the aftermath of the abolition of the Legislative Council would be involved in the search for solutions to ameliorate their worries during the passage of the Electoral Act 1956.

5

The Making of the Electoral Act 1956

> An Act to consolidate and amend the enactments relating to the election of members of the House of Representatives.
>
> *Preamble, Electoral Act 1956.*

Although by the 1950s the two dominant political parties accepted the basic design of the electoral system, namely the FPP voting rule, those involved in New Zealand's general elections were identifying problematic elements of the voting and vote-counting processes. The critics included electoral and departmental officials as well as members of political parties. A consolidated, reformed statute was needed: the Electoral Act 1927 needed to be thoroughly revised. As we have seen, however, National MPs such as John Marshall and Ronald Algie were concerned with wider constitutional issues, searching for solutions to remedy the absence of constraints on Parliament and the executive. Such potential solutions included constructing a written constitution or even resurrecting an upper house.

The two sets of pressures – to reform the voting process on the one hand and to reform aspects of Parliament and the constitution on the other – would converge and produce the Electoral Act 1956. But there was a third electoral irritant that would also influence the Bill, as shown in the previous chapter. Certain aspects of the electoral system were the subject of adversarial party politics. The resulting legislation would not satisfy those yearning for radical reform but would provide some compensatory constraints on the exercise of untrammelled power, albeit concerning a narrow range of issues. This chapter shows how the three political trajectories – statute consolidation and reform; the search for effective constraints on majority power; and the unsettled issues around electoral law – affected the shaping of the Electoral Bill 1956. Here I piece together the story of the making of the Bill, leaving the detailed analyses of the entrenchment clause and the protected (and unprotected) provisions of the Electoral Act to the next chapters.

Consolidating New Zealand's Messy Electoral Legislation

We must return to the 1940s to understand the origins of the consolidating electoral Bill. There had been ongoing concern about voter eligibility and vote-counting processes. Voting irregularities in the Raglan electorate in 1946 had led to a magisterial recount involving issues such as the residential qualifications of voters and the registration of 'half-castes'.[1] The court, after hearing an election petition, 'disallowed 15 [votes] because each of these electors had "too much" Maori blood to be entitled to enrol and vote in that electorate district'.[2] (Only 'half-castes' could choose to enrol either in a European or Māori seat at that time.) The Raglan decision also related to the rules to be followed when casting special votes. Some of these anomalies had been dealt with in Labour's Electoral Amendment Act 1948. This legislation, as earlier related, also allowed for the compilation of electoral rolls for the four Māori seats. Much more, however, was needed to fix the faults and omissions of the 1927 legislation.

The Electoral Office, responsible for administering elections, had been under the remit of the Department of Internal Affairs from 1943 but was returned to the Department of Justice in 1950. Events then accelerated. During the next year the Justice Secretary 'invited all Deputy Returning Officers to offer their recommendations as to how the electoral system could be improved'.[3] In November 1952 the Chief Electoral Officer conveyed these recommendations to the Secretary.[4] A departmental committee was established to discuss these issues. In his 1953 *Annual Report*, the Secretary [of Justice] pointed out that, 'The subjects under consideration by this committee do not touch the basic principles of voting. The review is being made purely to improve the conduct of elections'.[5] In 1954, the committee attempted to remedy some of the worst defects of voting and counting procedures by producing a new set of electoral regulations.[6]

In 1952, the annual conference of the National Party called for the electoral law to be rewritten.[7] Three years later, the Deputy Chief Officer, responding in part to urges for reform by the Wellington Central branch of the National Party, wrote that 'There has been much popular demand for a consolidation Act from political, licensing and other sources and also within the Department. The many amendments make the present Act difficult to follow, and much of the law is obsolete.' Hence, 'We hope to have a consolidating measure before Parliament in 1956, incorporating various improvements arising from suggestions received following the last two General Elections and also from a close examination of the present Act'.[8] Not only did the National Party and electoral officials communicate with each other on the problems of the Electoral Act 1927 and its subsequent amendments, but John Marshall also wrote to the Leader of the Opposition, Walter Nash, asking for his suggestions on improving the Act.[9] As the Department of Justice subsequently reported, the Bill's aims were to:

> give greater recognition than hitherto to the principles that no qualified person should be deprived of the opportunity to register and vote, that no vote should be invalid because of an official mistake, that voters should be free on polling day from all influence and propaganda, and that where an election is disputed, the Courts should look to substance and not to technicalities.[10]

Hence it is clear that the Electoral Act 1956 began life as a consolidating bill aimed to clarify the law and clear up its anomalies. Its primary goals were to clean up electoral operations, especially concerning residency requirements, registering to vote, casting votes at the ballot box and vote counting. But, as we shall see, the Electoral Bill would increase in scope as it took shape, reflecting wider electoral agendas including past contested issues around voting fairness and equality and, also, the debates within the National Party around the constitutional consequences of the abolition of the Legislative Council.

John Marshall, as the Minister in charge of the Electoral Office and also Minister of Justice, initiated the Bill's public and parliamentary process in a February 1956 press statement announcing 'a complete revision of procedural and legal matters' in a new, consolidating electoral act.[11] At the beginning of the 1956 parliamentary year, in his speech from the throne the Governor-General simply pronounced that there would be 'a consolidation and revision of the electoral law'.[12]

Revisiting Old Grievances

Despite the unadventurous description of the forthcoming electoral Bill, its imminence gave political actors the opportunity to return to the contested issues that were at the heart of the differences between the two political parties.

More radical electoral reform was back on the political agenda.

MPs raised various electoral issues in the traditionally wide-ranging Address in Reply debate that followed the Governor-General's speech. The dominant topics, however, were not the problematic voting and vote-counting processes, which were nominally the focus of the electoral law revision, but the two interconnecting, highly contested issues that had engrossed the two major political parties during the 1940s: who counts when electorate boundaries are drawn; and who makes those decisions by being appointed to the Representation Commission. There could be a strong element of bipartisan consensus over the issue cluster involving voter eligibility and counting, but strong partisanship marked the second of these issue clusters, the rules around boundary-drawing.

Familiar battles were re-fought in the parliamentary arena with the protagonists even referring back to the country quota, although this time the debate was on how it had been first imposed and then later removed. Frank Kitts (Labour), commenting on criticisms that the Labour Government should have had a referendum on the abolition of the country quota, said that it had been 'introduced without the consent of the people, it was amended without the consent of the people, and I submit that in abolishing the country quota the Labour Government was fifteen years overdue in carrying out the intent of the original legislation.' Abolition had restored 'the status quo . . . to give every vote an equal value'.[13] Arthur Kinsella put National's case: the quota had been introduced because 'in the young state of New Zealand distances were so great in country districts that it was absolutely impossible for a country Member to cover the whole of his electorate if it was arranged on the same population basis as a city electorate'.[14] Other MPs made similar points. During this debate the

Opposition also accused National of gerrymandering: National had appointed the four non-officials to the Representation Commission.

Meanwhile, the results of the 1954 general election were worrying the National team. Not only had the Party lost seats but Social Credit had appeared to split the vote more than had been anticipated, although its presence had actually harmed Labour more than National (as pointed out earlier). Social Credit was a threat that had to be combated. A report by the party General Secretary pointed out that National could not govern if it lost four-to-five seats in the 1957 general election. Moreover, boundary changes were anticipated. Anxieties were expressed concerning the disappointing numbers attending National Party branch meetings; and members' criticisms of the performance of the Government had been expressed in a questionnaire sent out to the wider party. One of the points made by the General Secretary was that an electoral act would be introduced during the current session and copies would be sent to directors and electorates.[15]

Constitutional Agitation in the National Party

The pressure from within the National Party, urging its Government to embark on further constitutional reforms, continued unabated. In particular the idea of a new upper house was still alive. At the end of April 1956, Holland wrote to the president of the National Party, Alex McKenzie, regarding the Constitutional Reform Committee (usually referred to in the Holland papers as the 'Algie' Committee).[16] Holland reported that Speaker of the House Matthew Oram and Major Neil Rattray had recommended creating a mixed upper house, partly elected and partly nominated, and with a fixed number of members, a proposal that had been discussed the previous year. Without an upper house to block electoral law changes, it was feared, Labour might change the electoral boundaries or impose some sort of 'town quota'. In his letter Holland wrote:

> There appears to be the same fears in both the Labour Party and National Party but for different reasons. The Labour Party fear that we will enact legislation to prevent them from doing as they wish if they win a general election. One of the chief intentions of a 'fixed number' Upper House is to do precisely that thing.
>
> We of the National Party fear that a Labour Government might alter the electoral laws to make it virtually impossible to win a general election in the future – once Labour regains power. Therefore we ought to have an Upper House to prevent that from happening.[17]

The Representation Commission, Holland went on to suggest, should include no nominated non-official members. The Party should confer with Labour and ask them to agree to drop the nominated members from the Commission and also retain the present basis for fixing electoral boundaries (total population). Also discussed with Labour would be the qualifications for membership of Parliament and the triennial parliamentary term. Holland continued: 'Finally, I think the conference between the Organisation side and the Political side should now be arranged. My nominees are Messrs Holyoake, Algie, Sullivan, Marshall and myself.'[18] The correspondence between Oram and Holland indicates that the prime minister's pledge during the Second Reading of the Legislative Council Abolition Bill that there would no replacement of the upper house put paid to the revival of any upper house. This refers to a heated exchange between the Government and the Opposition in 1950. Labour, referring to National's 1949 Manifesto commitments on the constitution, feared that after the Council was abolished National would create a new one, one that could obstruct a Labour Government by having a fixed number of members (removing the possibility of appointing government loyalists) with fixed terms to serve. Labour had sought Holland's assurance that this would not happen.[19] Holland, appearing to want the support of Labour for abolition, especially as it was Labour Party policy, eventually declared that so far no alternative upper house had been found but, given the views of 'friends', National would continue the search. However, Holland had promised that alternative would not be brought forward under that Parliament and any alternative would have to be put before the people.[20] Plainly, Holland was using his assurance to the Opposition party as an argument to bolster his own unicameral preference when dealing with dissidents – his 'friends' – within his own party. Holland was searching for other solutions to the problem of party advantage gained from electoral law manipulation; this was his priority, not creating a senate.

Nevertheless, during 1956 the pressure to restore the upper house continued. At the beginning of May, Oram wrote to Holland about the 'Algie Report', advocating that the Government take its proposal for a Senate to voters at the next general election. Oram set out his own recommendations.[21] Shortly after receiving this letter, Holland wrote to McKenzie commenting that Oram and Rattray 'continue to busy themselves over the Upper House'.[22] Holland met with them and was told that 'there is much more support than I realise. I had a talk in Caucus and all agree with my views.'[23] National's Dominion and National Executive Councils were asked to circulate the Oram paper: because Oram was Speaker he should not participate in party policy matters, so would not himself distribute the paper. There was pressure to include a policy on an upper house in the party's manifesto for the next election but, Holland wrote somewhat hypocritically, 'This is a constitutional matter and I'm not so sure that an election policy is the proper place for it.' He goes on to say that 'If it wasn't that we are committed to a referendum on "hanging" I might try with the idea of a vote at the time of next election.'[24]

On 16 May there was a meeting in the prime minister's office that included Algie, Marshall, McKenzie and two officials. The purpose was to consider the Report of the Constitutional Reform Committee, the Memorandum by Sir Matthew Oram, and a letter and enclosures from Holland to McKenzie.[25] It was resolved to send the above letters to the Divisions and debate the question further at the forthcoming annual conference. An 'Electoral Amendment Bill' would provide that: (a) the 'Boundaries Commission' members would all be officials; (b) that it would 'establish the method of voting'; (c) 'establish life of Parliament'; and (c) 'include a clause in the Bill that changes in (a), (b) or (c) above can only be made after a majority of voters, at a referendum, have approved the proposed changes'. A 'Note' was added: 'It was appreciated that any Government could alter such a law without first having a referendum but it was felt that the voters would object strongly to any Party which ignored a right given to electors by statute.'[26] An important step was made within the top ranks of the National Party towards protecting parts of the constitution from majority government interference. A special caucus committee would be established to consider how this could be done.[27]

In early August 1956 it was reported that there were branches of the National Party that wanted an upper house restored.[28] All this discussion was going on during a parliamentary term in which, for the first time, there had been no constitutional or electoral policies outlined in National's previous election manifesto.[29] However, the political discourse was now focusing more on constitutional process – how to effect and thwart change – than on the creation of a new institution such as an upper house.

Holland now had to act firmly and stamp his authority on constitutional initiatives coming from within his own party. The opportunity came at the National Party conference in August 1956 (when, for the first time for either of the two main parties, the media were permitted to follow conference proceedings). In a major speech, widely reported, Holland argued that without a second chamber, Parliament could extend its life to five or more years, alter the electorate boundaries, and change the electoral quota system, the adult franchise and the boundary tolerances. The present law was unsound because the design of the Representation Commission 'gives a right to the party of the day to have members on the boundary commission and it can exclude the Opposition. It acts in favour of the party which is in power.'[30] There should be no party appointees on the Representation Commission and it should include between five and seven officials. Further, Holland said, 'I do not think Parliament should be allowed to tinker with these laws without the consent of the People.' There should be a referendum before enactment or repeal, although this would be difficult.[31]

Holland expressed the view that the government would make proposals, through laws approved by Parliament, and then those laws would be submitted to referendum:

> The essence of the proposals which the Government will shortly make to Parliament is that the sovereign rights of the people shall be further safeguarded and strengthened and that these new safeguards shall bear the direct imprint of the people's approval . . . That is why the principle of a referendum has been included in the proposals. . . . The objective is that we

> shall have on the statute books legislation relating to electoral procedure which shall have had the plainest endorsement of the nation. A Government is not bound by the actions of its predecessors, but I would think that any future Government which wished to amend the electoral laws would consider it desirable to submit its proposals to the opinion of the nation.[32]

The prime minister appeared to be taking back control of the constitutional agenda by promising to turn over some decisions to the people. By this time, Holland had become increasingly ill and was facing criticism from within the party over his leadership. One newspaper assured its readers, however, that rumours of a split within the party had been dispelled by Holland's conference performance, including his 'firm lead on the question of re-establishing a second chamber – strongly urged by, shall we say, the intelligentsia of the party – which swung the conference to agree to leave the establishment of an Upper House in abeyance while other measures were considered to safe-guard any abuse of unicameral Government'.[33] Another newspaper opinion was that National was still 'searching around for some suitable alternative to single-chamber government'.[34]

In response to Holland's public speculations, Walter Nash observed that it would be worthwhile ensuring that a 'completely judicial and independent' boundaries commission was established. As well, 'a referendum for the purposes of handing over the responsibilities of Government and Parliament does not appear a wise way of governing, although the principle of the referendum is excellent'.[35] Inside the House, Labour MPs again criticised the total population formula and accused National of interfering with boundary-fixing.[36] Walter Hudson complained that, although his party got more votes (not actually the case, although the two parties were very close to one another), National won 45 MPs in the 1954 general election compared with Labour's 35.[37] Referring to the prime minister's conference speech, Labour stressed the primacy of parliamentary supremacy, with one MP stating that 'when we come to an examination of these proposals we will demonstrate that you cannot tie the hands of future legislators' and (referring to a newspaper editorial), 'for the Prime Minister to abolish the Upper House without a referendum, and then to pass a Bill to say that no one in future can do what he has done is surely colossal conceit on his part. As was said at the conference, such a Bill could be upset within forty-eight hours . . .'[38]

Towards the end of August 1956, *The New Zealand Herald* was predicting the imminent introduction of the Electoral Bill. It was expected to include the provisions suggested by the prime minister at the party conference and to 'include the provision for referring any changes to a referendum'.[39]

The Electoral Bill Takes Shape

Already, however, Cabinet had been considering a number of the issues covered in the forthcoming Electoral Bill. Various clauses had been dribbling through the legislative system. In May, for example, Cabinet had directed that the Bill provide for general re-enrolment of electors after the act was passed and 'at regular intervals thereafter', referring to a cabinet paper it had received.[40] The next month it directed that the compulsory re-enrolment provisions be also applied to Māori.[41] In early September Cabinet approved 'the adoption of the measures necessary to base the right to vote at Parliamentary elections in New Zealand on the qualifications of permanent residence in New Zealand'.[42] And at the next week's meeting Cabinet decided that a revised form of the ballot paper would be taken to Caucus for consideration.[43]

On Monday 8 October at 9am, 'Electoral Bill – L.D.O. 59/2' was considered by the Cabinet Committee on Legislation, chaired by John Marshall. Also present were S. W. Smith (Minister of Internal Affairs and Forests) and Ralph Hanan (Health and Immigration). As is usual with cabinet committees, officials were present: N. C. Butcher, J. Cameron and I. Irwin from the Justice Department, and 'Mr Adams', a law draftsman. Officials were requested to redraft the definition of electoral expenses in Clause 2 of the Interpretation. Further consideration of the Bill was deferred to the next meeting.[44] The Bill, at this stage, included Section 12, Duration of the House of Representatives, and Section 15, relating to the Representation Commission. However, this draft stated that the official members of the Representation Commission were to be the Surveyor-General, the Commissioner of Crown Lands for the South Auckland Land District, and the Commissioner of Crown Lands for the Canterbury Land District. And, 'The remaining four members shall be such persons, not being public servants or members of the General Assembly, as the House of Representatives from time to time nominates as unofficial members of the Commission.' The Surveyor-General was designated Commission Chair. Total population was to be the basis for dividing the electorates, with references to the 'European population' in Section 16 (on dividing the European population after each census), and Section 17, the allowance for adjustment of the quota. At this stage this was not to exceed 7.5%. In other words the final version of these sections of the Bill had not been included. Sections 38 and 39, the qualifications of electors, are present in the Bill but would undergo some changes. Section 106, on the method of voting, was in the Bill and would remain exactly as first drafted and appear in the Act itself. The entrenchment clause (Section 189 of the Act) is absent. [45]

The Committee met again on Tuesday 9 October, meeting three times that day for a total of five hours. This time Algie was also present for most the time, and an additional law draftsman, Mr Todd, was present. A. C. Shailes from the Cabinet Office was also present. The Committee considered the Electoral LDO 59/2 in further detail. The minutes list a number of significant changes to the Bill, including several definitions and the qualifications of electors, and many alterations to wording. They make no changes to the Bill relating to the substance of the clauses that would be entrenched in the Act. [46] On 11 October Cabinet agreed to place the whole Bill before Caucus – along with the Rabbits Amendment Bill.[47] The Electoral Bill was in frisky company.

We cannot tell whether there had been consultation with the Opposition during the pre-Introduction drafting of the Bill. However, the prime minister's diary includes a meeting on the evening of Tuesday 2 October between Holland, Marshall (who, as Minister of Justice, sponsored the Electoral Bill) and, for the Opposition, Nash, Mason and Nordmeyer – the Leader of the Labour Party and two of his most senior MPs.[48] There were, however, other bills going through the House at the same time.

The Bill is Introduced and Amended

It was now very late in the 1956 parliamentary session. On Friday 12 October, John Marshall, as Minister in charge of the Electoral Department, announced in Parliament that the Government was introducing a consolidated electoral Bill.[49] The Bill included reforms that were 'designed to prevent attempts to influence or interfere with voters'.[50] Changes were made to enrolment procedures, including the requirement to reregister after each census, and the residential qualifications were rewritten.

Unsurprisingly, the Bill as introduced was substantially the same as the Bill scrutinised by the Cabinet Committee on Legislation. There was still no Section 189, with its provisions that would transform the Bill from a consolidating statute to a seminal document. In the House, Marshall noted that the provisions for the Representation Commission were the same as in the present legislation but that these might be subsequently amended.[51] *The Dominion*, citing Holland's speech at the National Party Conference, quotes Marshall saying that 'the Representation Commission question was the subject of discussions now and if satisfactory agreement was reached then the new provisions could be introduced by the special select committee to which the Bill would be referred, or later'.[52] *The New Zealand Herald* editorialised that the Bill was 'incomplete in its present form'.[53]

Marshall recommended that the Bill be sent to a select committee, perhaps a special committee 'if that is acceptable'.[54] Holland suggested that the committee comprise six MPs representing the Government plus four from the Opposition: 'That is the usual committee distribution of Members.'[55] No details of the Bill were available at the stage of Introduction, but copies, Marshall said, would be available when the House rose.[56] The Bill then passed its first reading.[57]

A measure of the haste in which the Bill would now proceed is supplied by letters from the Secretary of Justice (N. C. Butcher) sent on Monday 15 October to the Registrars of Electors and their Deputies, along with copies of the Electoral Bill as introduced into Parliament. The Secretary asks for their comments and writes that he realised how little time there was for them to study the provisions and to respond, given that the session would end at the end of the following week and the Bill had to be dealt with before that. 'Unfortunately because of the need to meet the Parliamentary deadline we were unable to release drafts of the Bill at an earlier stage to officers outside Wellington, as we had hoped to.' The Secretary wanted responses by the beginning of the following week at the latest.[58]

On Tuesday 16 October, the select committee was appointed by motion of the House.[59] It comprised Bertie Cooksley (National, Wairarapa), Fred Hackett (Labour, Grey Lynn,) Ralph Hanan (National, Invercargill), Cyril Harker (National, Hawkes Bay), Phil Holloway (Labour, Heretaunga), Hallyburton Johnstone (National, Raglan), John Mathison (Labour, Avon), Clarence Skinner (Labour, Buller), Sidney Smith (National, Hobson), and John Marshall (National, Karori). The committee included two ministers: Hanan, Minister for Health and Immigration; and Marshall, Attorney-General, Minister of Justice and Minister in charge of the Electoral Department. All four Labour representatives were senior MPs – each would be elected to cabinet after Labour won the general election the following year. Note also that there was a cross-section of rural and urban MPs and the select committee included three MPs from the South Island, although no mention of committee representativeness was made in the House. Nash did not select a Māori MP to serve on the Committee, and there were no Māori MPs at all in the National caucus. Thus no committee member directly represented Māori views. The Minister of Maori Affairs, Ernest Corbett, was not a member of the Committee, although the Leader of the Opposition had been Minister of Maori Affairs during the last years of the First Labour Government. At the time, there were only four women MPs in Parliament (with the only National female MP, Dame Hilda Ross, serving in Cabinet) and none was appointed to serve on the Committee. The Bill was referred to the ad hoc Electoral Bill Committee the following day.

Apparently, at the same time as the select committee was meeting, informal cross-party meetings were discussing the

Representation Commission and other issues.[60] The *New Zealand Herald* reported that, 'During the past few weeks an informal committee of Government and Opposition members has been studying the question [of amendments]. They are expected to tidy up final details of the legislation tomorrow.'[61] It was reported that referendums would be used to approve major constitutional changes, and that the Bill would increase the size of the House in order to stabilise South Island representation at 26 MPs.[62] No mention was made of the composition of this group. The prime minister's diary, however, reports a particularly busy time for Holland. Apart from the normal (and extra) cabinet meetings, there was also a rash of extra caucus meetings. The National caucus usually met on Thursdays, but apart from those regular weekly meetings, between Thursday 4 October and Thursday 25 October (the day of the last meeting of the Electoral Bill Committee) there were five further occasions when Holland met with his caucus. Again, the topic of those meetings is not stated. However, on Tuesday 23 October there was a cross-party meeting, with those attending being Holland, Holyoake, Marshall, Nash, Nordmeyer and Mason, 're boundaries'. We can assume that, at the very least, these senior politicians discussed the provisions relating to the Representation Commission and any agreements were passed on to the Electoral Law Committee. The meeting with the senior Labour politicians was immediately followed by one with 'Algie and Marshall, followed by Executive' (presumably the National Party executive) and, after that, a caucus meeting.[63]

The Electoral Bill Committee itself met four times, with the first a brief meeting on Wednesday 17 October to elect a chair (Harker) and discuss future meetings.[64] The next day, 'the Committee considered the question of evidence on the Bill. It was agreed that interested political parties be invited to submit evidence on the Bill. The Clerk was instructed to notify the Social Credit League, the Communist Party and, if possible a Liberal Organisation.'[65] The first two of these parties had stood candidates in 1954.[66] It can be assumed that the Labour and National parties, being part of the process, did not need to be asked. Indeed, there are many references in the files to National Party submissions on the Bill (although no evidence that there were proposals on entrenchment). The Committee agreed to all the clauses on which there was no amendment and held over to later meetings the clauses 'on which it was possible evidence would be brought, also those Clauses showing amendment in the original provisions'.[67] The many clauses that were held over included the sections on the composition of the Representation Commission and the allowance for the adjustment of the quota, the meaning of 'ordinarily resident in New Zealand', the details of the qualifications of electors, and Section 189. However, this last section does not appear in the file copy that presumably went to the Committee (Electoral Bill No. 89–1). It can be assumed, therefore, that the draftsman, presumably on instruction from the minister, presented this addition to the Committee at either this or its previous meeting.

A press statement issued by Marshall for the morning newspapers on 19 October said that so far only procedural clauses had been dealt with but no doubt there would be 'some organizations who would wish to make representations to the Committee' and 'they should get in touch with the Committee Clerk'.[68]

On Tuesday 23 October the Committee considered Clauses 2, 25, 30 (re-committed) and 37, and it was resolved that the clauses as amended were agreed to. None of these related to the reserved provisions of the final Act. The next day the Committee heard evidence from A. P. O'Shea, representing the Federated Farmers of New Zealand, and R.

Nunes, representing the New Zealand Communist Party, who presented verbal evidence only. O'Shea's submission consisted mainly of a response to Labour's accusations of bias by the Representation Commission, on which he had been an unofficial member.[69] The witnesses were questioned. The Committee then agreed to a number of further clauses.

At the Committee's last meeting on the Thursday, the Bill, as amended, was agreed to.[70] Although the report on the Bill was formally submitted to the House in accordance with standing orders, no details of the select committee's recommendations, let alone any justification of them, were included in the published report, but the Bill as reported back by the Committee shows which parts were struck out, which were reworded, and the new clauses that were inserted.[71]

Several provisions remained substantially the same as in the earlier bill drafts, namely the triennial parliamentary term (Section 12), the sections on the qualifications of the voters, Section 99, on who may vote, and Section 106, on the method of voting. As far as the reserved provisions are concerned, the Bill now included the major changes to the Representation Commission that were to appear in the final Act (Section 15). The official members would be the Surveyor-General, the Government Statistician, the Chief Electoral Officer, and the Director-General of the Post and Telegraph Department (Section 15a). There would be two unofficial members (Section 15b), not being public servants or MPs, one nominated to represent the Government and the other the Opposition. The Commission Chair (not a public servant or MP) would be 'appointed by the Governor-General by Order of Council on the nomination of the official and unofficial members of the Commission, or a majority of them' (Section 15c). The electoral tolerance was reduced from 7.5 to 5% (Section 17) and the basis on which the electorates would be divided was total (European) population.[72] Plainly some significant negotiations had taken place between Labour and National, and compromises had been made.

The addition of Section 189, which would significantly influence New Zealand's future manner of changing its constitutional arrangements, was also added in the very last stages of Select Committee consideration. Section 189(2) stated that:

> No reserved provision shall be repealed or amended unless the proposal for the amendment or repeal – (a) Is passed by a majority of seventy-five per cent of all the members of the House of Representatives; or (b) Has been carried by a majority of the valid votes cast at a poll of electors of the European and Maori electoral districts.

The reserved provisions related to: the three-year duration of the House of Representatives (Section 12); the composition of the Representation Commission (Section 15); the definition of the term 'European population' in Section 2(1), the number of European electorates and the criteria for determining their boundaries after each population census (Section 16); the 5% allowance for the adjustment of the population quota for European electorates (Section 17); the definition of the term 'adult' (Sections 2(1) and 99(e)) setting the minimum voting age of 21; and the secret ballot and the method of marking the ballot paper (Section 106).

The Electoral Bill Is Passed and the House Congratulates Itself

Because the parliamentary year was nearly at its end, the Government was in a hurry to get the legislation passed through the House. On 25 October, urgency was sought for the Electoral Bill, along with the Electricity and Gas

Co-Ordinating Bill, the Bay of Islands Harbour Board Empowering Bill and the North Shore Drainage Bill.[73] Urgency was uncontested by the Opposition.

When Marshall moved that the Bill be committed on 26 October, he was now saying:

> I do not think it is an exaggeration to say that this Bill represents a major advance in the progress of democratic government in New Zealand. I think it will be said by legislators of the future, by students of political science, and by others interested in good government, that this Bill is a genuine, and I believe successful, attempt to place the structure of the law above and beyond the influence of Government and party.[74]

The Bill went to the Committee of the Whole on the same day. With the unanimous consent of the [Select] Committee the amendments made by the Electoral Bill Committee were read into and deemed part of the Bill.[75] Minor changes in wording were agreed to in the Committee of the Whole (and these are recorded): there were no votes called for.[76] The Bill was reported back with amendments and it was read a third time.[77] The Electoral Bill 1956 then received the Royal Assent, also on 26 October.

A Consolidating and Innovative Act

The progress of the Electoral Bill through the House had been extraordinarily fast. There was scant time given to the Bill by the select committee and, moreover, it was passed using urgency. Geoffrey Palmer, discussing the rapidity of the legislative process in New Zealand, notes that in 1956 123 bills were passed in 67 sitting days. There were also 224 regulations made.[78] The number of sitting days in 1956 was particularly low for a non-election year, but in 1956 the parliamentary year ended early because Parliament would be the site of the Colombo Plan Conference as soon as Parliament adjourned for the summer. By comparison, in other non-election years during the same period and under the same government, Parliament met on 92 sitting days in 1950 (National's first year of office), 70 days in 1952, 77 in 1953, and 81 in 1955.[79] Poor parliamentary time-tabling, the desire to get things in order before the next general election in a year's time, and the compulsion to get a controversial measure through the House with as little public attention as possible are all possible reasons for a major constitutional statute being hurried through the House of Representatives in such indecent and undemocratic haste.

The Electoral Act 1956 significantly reformed the voting process.[80] Many anomalies were cleaned up; and some important changes made, as intended by the original revision of the Electoral Act 1927. The changes included the new residency requirements, the compulsory enrolment for Māori, and the compulsory re-registration of all voters after boundary changes. These reforms fitted tidily with New Zealand's habit of making incremental changes to its constitution. As the Department Report said in its subsequent summing up of the Act, however, the Act also protected particular aspects of the electoral system and these were 'perhaps the most interesting' changes in the new Electoral Act.[81] The Act 'records the unanimous agreement of both parties represented in Parliament that certain provisions in our system of government have a particular character and should not be altered at the whim of a bare majority'.[82]

Thanks to the confluence of three reform tendencies – tidying up existing legislation, resolving historical party differences on electoral matters, and settling some constitutional concerns consequential on the abolition of the Legislative Council – the Electoral Act 1956 marked a seminal change in New Zealand's constitutional history. But despite the public and private discussions on what construes due process, including considering taking the key electoral decisions to the people for them to decide, voters were given almost no opportunity to voice their views on the substance of the legislation.

The choice of electoral aspects that were included as reserved provisions or else omitted altogether appeared to be eccentric, although the entrenchment provision demonstrated a significant degree of ingenuity and innovation. In the next two chapters I attempt to explain how Parliament arrived at the single entrenchment device, with its particular choice of approval devices, to protect the selected provisions; why those provisions were included in Section 189; and what happened to them subsequently.

6

Entrenchment

'What we are doing has a moral sanction rather than a legal one'

John Marshall, Minister of Justice, 26 October 1956[1]

The need to revise the inadequate Electoral Act 1927 had put the contested electoral issues on the official agenda. But once the Holland Government had decided to resolve them in the new Bill, it then had to work out its primary goals and its policy strategy. Using its parliamentary majority, National could have legislated for its first preferences: a Representation Commission comprising officials only; the use of total population as the basis for defining electorate boundaries; and a wide population variance among electorates. Implementing these first preference options would have carried a high level of political risk. If National were to lose power in the forthcoming general election, then Labour might introduce new electoral legislation that reflected its own party preferences. The 1960 general election might then be an even harder election for National to win. This was a risk even if National were to do nothing at all about the contested electoral issues.

As we have seen, the National Party chose an alternative strategy: to negotiate with the Labour Opposition to find solutions which both parties could tolerate but which would involve compromise. Resolving these issues through discussion, even if this meant giving way on one or more first preferences, became the preferred strategy for National to follow, especially if somehow a way could be found to fix any agreements in a manner that overrode adversarial rule-fiddling by successive governments. Rule stability through an agreed entrenchment clause was thought a more desirable outcome than getting one's own way in the short term but not guaranteeing it after the next general election.

In the final stages of the debate on the Electoral Act 1956, the Minister of Justice, Jack Marshall, said that the entrenchment provision was unusual, 'but I feel I should make it perfectly clear that the effect of these reserved sections is not in their legal force to bind future Parliaments but in their moral force as representing the unanimous view of Parliament'. He was 'very happy to be in the position to say that Parliament is unanimous on these points, and I do want to express the appreciation of the Government for the co-operation that has been received in bringing about this position. It represents what we all agree is a fair and reasonable and impartial method of protecting the electoral system.' Marshall continued, asserting its effectiveness depended on the people. The rules 'will only really be entrenched if they become universally accepted as rules which commend themselves to the sense of fairness of the people as a whole. Only then can they be regarded as a permanent part of our democratic way of life'.[2] Speaking for the Labour Opposition, Walter Nash supported the Bill in general, saying, 'The objective on both sides was the same. We wanted to find a way by which everyone qualified to vote would have the right to vote without interference. We wanted to ensure that democratic principles should prevail in the determination of who should write the laws.'[3]

Two main areas of concern with Section 189 were expressed by the MPs in 1956. First, what was the legal status and force of a referendum to amend the Electoral Act? A Labour MP asked whether a government had 'a legal requirement to follow a referendum decision?'[4] In response to this and other points, National's Duncan Rae agreed that a government could indeed override a referendum. At this point Ron Algie added that this would not happen 'without telling the citizen that it was taking away one of his rights'. Rae came back with the highly sanguine comment that it was most unusual for a government to override rights.[5]

The MPs' second concern regarded the capacity of the entrenching clause to bind future Parliaments. Nash doubted that future Parliaments could be bound by single entrenchment, although he said he supported the 'so-called reserved provisions'.[6] Phil Holloway (Labour) asked whether the reserving clause was not 'a farce – can it be enforced?'[7] Ralph Hanan then entered the debate, stating that 'history has shown that the only possible way to satisfactorily make a major change in the electoral laws is where you have an element of agreement between the political parties'.[8] It was true that the legislature cannot bind future parliaments, but there is 'a strong moral obligation on any future Government not to alter the "rules of the game" unless with a 75 per cent vote in the House of Representatives or through a referendum'.[9] Hanan reinforced the point that the parties had got together on this Bill 'to make a major change that will help to preserve the constitutional rights of the individual to exercise his vote and preserve his sacred right of the secrecy of the ballot'.[10]

Parliament had unanimously endorsed the entrenchment clause in the Electoral Act 1956. But where did the idea of entrenchment come from? The problem had been to find a way to reduce adversarial policy change over the electoral rules in a polity that was unicameral and had no written constitution. Furthermore, and this cannot be emphasised enough, the predominant constitutional paradigm of the times was that

Parliament was a sovereign body. No Parliament could fetter its successors, it was believed, and the substance of legislation was not subject to judicial scrutiny (unlike the implementation of the law).

So why did the decision-makers entrench parts of the law, when they believed that parliamentary supremacy excluded the feasibility of using protecting provisions? And then, despite their qualms, having decided on using the entrenchment device, why did they not also entrench the entrenching clause? Why, too, were the devices of referendum or super-majority chosen as the designated alternative pathways to amend the protected provisions? And why were not each of these two devices married with particular provisions? These are not easy questions to answer six decades after the Act was passed, since none of those involved can now tell us about it. Not all these questions can be answered definitively. Nevertheless, from combining public statements, newspaper commentary and private papers, some pieces of these puzzles fall into place.

The most important task is to understand how political ideas about the interrelationship between parliamentary powers and the constitution were constructed at the time of the development of the Electoral Act 1956. Political interpretation and imagination are constrained by dominant ideologies but frequently new ideas emerge, either deliberately or accidentally, from pervasive political paradigms.

Holland's ruthless move to make New Zealand's Parliament unicameral had put constitutional change on the government agenda. This had stimulated a wider debate both within the National Party and in the newspaper commentary. The result was Section 189, tucked in amongst the Miscellaneous Provisions in the last Part of the Electoral Act 1956, almost as if it were an afterthought.

What the politicians with their advisers achieved at the

very last stage of drafting the Bill was to bring together familiar formulae – the idea of entrenchment of constitutional provisions; and the accompanying notions that either voter referendums or legislative super-majorities might be required to repeal or amend such provisions. The legislators brought these ideas together into a somewhat eccentric package. Before this package was formalised in Section 189, however, discussions had been ongoing about the protection of some aspects of the electoral law. The idea of entrenchment was already part of the currency of exchanges about constitutional law, as I next explain.

The Idea of Entrenchment

Legislative provisions constraining the House of Representatives from easily implementing particular constitutional amendments had existed in New Zealand in the Constitution Act 1852. This had required certain changes to be approved by the Houses of Parliament at Westminster, although most of the protected features had disappeared through time. Then, after the Statute of Westminster had been ratified by New Zealand in 1946 and the Legislative Council abolished in 1950, the New Zealand House of Representatives was free to enact any constitutional legislation it wished. All that was required was a simple parliamentary majority, easily achieved by tight party discipline. And the narrowest of majorities would suffice to make the most radical of changes. Parliament could, and did (and still does), even pass significant bills through using urgency, abbreviating the usual legislative passage of bills including stand-down periods and time for legislative scrutiny, media attention and public submissions.

The doctrine of parliamentary supremacy appeared to support this state of affairs. In effect, it reinforced the constitutional powers of strong, even dictatorial, government. As explained earlier, some politicians and lawyers were aware of the inadequacy of appropriate constitutional safeguards. And New Zealand's electoral law history had thrown up highly contested issues vulnerable to adversarial, radical policy change. This turbulence had produced systemic instability that worked against both parties and all politicians.

When it comes to the rules of the game, one has to bind oneself in order to bind one's opponents. But how to achieve this situation? In 1952 the Constitutional Reform Committee had proposed that a Senate replace the former Legislative Council. This had been rejected by Sid Holland and by National Party members at an annual conference, although subsequently, as noted earlier, they asked that the recommendation be reconsidered. Nevertheless, although bicameralism was no longer on the agenda by 1956, the *Report of the Constitutional Reform Committee* would be seminal in the country's constitutional history because it discussed constitutional change processes in similar sorts of jurisdictions to New Zealand.[11] In its appendices the Constitutional Reform Committee addresses the issues of protection through entrenchment and discusses how entrenched clauses could be reconciled with the doctrine of parliamentary sovereignty.

Appendix A of the *Report of the Constitutional Reform Committee* focuses on how a constitution can be created. First, it can be imposed by 'a sovereign and superior legislature'. Second, it can originate in the 'assent or consent of those who are bound by it'. And third:

> A Constitution could be created by a 'unitary' legislature like our own and imposed upon itself by a kind of self-denying act of self-discipline; it could bind itself in a statute and hope that its successors would feel equally constrained to respect that

> enactment. But it could not easily bind them to observe it by any process that could be described as legally effective. Any Parliament can bind itself by its legislation, but in no way can a Parliament like ours by its own act bind its successors.[12]

Appendix B turns to the question of a written constitution. It endorses parliamentary sovereignty and it discusses the use and effectiveness of reserved provisions, providing examples of 20th-century efforts to change the constitutions of the Australian state of New South Wales and South Africa, jurisdictions with entrenched sections in their constitutions. The main authorities cited in Appendix B are two New Zealand legal academics, E. K. Braybrooke and J. F. Northey.[13] I report their views from the original sources.

Braybrooke comments on A. V. Dicey's view of parliamentary sovereignty. Dicey was an influential 19th-century constitutional lawyer who stressed the preeminence of parliamentary sovereignty in the British constitution. Braybrooke points out that Dicey himself suggests 'a sovereign may transfer sovereign authority to another person or body of persons'. This indicates that parliamentary sovereignty might not be as absolute as is often thought.[14]

Braybrooke goes on to discuss the case of the New South Wales Parliament attempting to amend its constitution in 1929. The new provision stated that:

> no bill for the abolition of the Legislative Council or for the alteration of its constitution or powers should be presented to the Governor for the Royal Assent until it had been approved by a majority of the electors in a referendum: the provisions of the section were to extend to any Bill for the repeal or amendment of the section itself.[15]

A year later, in 1930, an Act was passed to provide for a referendum on a bill aimed at changing the constitution of the Legislative Council of New South Wales.[16] But that Parliament came to an end the same year, before the legislation was given effect. The new Parliament, however, passed a bill through both Houses to repeal the two amending Acts and it also put through a bill to abolish the Legislative Council.[17] A lawsuit on the issue was instituted, and the case ended up in the Privy Council. It upheld the majority judgement of the Australian High Court that the approval of the electors was indeed required before constitutional amendments were made and also the upper house could be abolished.[18]

In his comparison between the two jurisdictions, Braybrooke argues that, unlike in Australia, the extent of the New Zealand Parliament's powers were not circumscribed. In Australia, Section 5 of the Colonial Laws Validity Act 1865 required that legislation must be passed in such 'manner and form' as required by any Act of Parliament.[19] Referring to the now fully sovereign New Zealand Parliament, Braybrooke writes, 'Thoughtful inquiry may pose the question whether there is not the possibility of *formal* restriction on parliamentary sovereignty, in the sense that it must proceed in a particular "manner and form".'[20] And he goes on to cite Coke's suggestion that sovereign legislatures can restrict themselves as to 'manner and form'.[21] He points out that the Bill to abolish the Legislative Council, which was before the New Zealand Parliament at the time of Braybrooke's writing, must pass the Council before it becomes law; and it would seem to follow that 'a subsequent statute which purports to amend the amending statute must also conform in "manner and form" to the statute which it will in due course amend'.[22] Braybrooke then takes up the example of South Africa, explained below. He concludes that New Zealand may be able to have a written constitution that could not be amended or repealed except by referendum. He continues:

> The foundation of this power might be either the possibility of restraining a fully-sovereign parliament as to the 'manner and form' in which future constituent legislation might be passed or that of regarding the invocation of the electoral vote as an abdication of portion of the parliamentary sovereignty in favour of the people.[23]

Jack Northey, writing during the same period, was also interested in the effect of 'manner and form' requirements in parliamentary systems such as New Zealand's, citing the South African and New South Wales examples.[24] In the South African case there was a constitutional battle over the South African legislature's removal of 'coloured persons' from the ordinary voter register. Clauses in the South Africa Act 1909 set out particular procedures for passing certain bills, namely a joint sitting of both houses and, also, achieving a two-thirds majority in the third reading. In 1951 the South African government argued that the change could be made through simple majority change of the entrenching clause. However, the relevant clause was doubly entrenched, meaning that any bill to alter the procedure itself needed the super-majority required by the constitution.[25] The government argued that because the Statute of Westminster had been enacted in South Africa in 1934, parliament was now sovereign. The Speaker, on the other hand, ruled that parliament must comply with the terms of the Act,[26] and the South African courts declared that those clauses did indeed have 'constitutional significance'.[27] (Subsequently, however, the South African parliament legislated to nullify the pronouncements of the court.)

Northey discusses the New South Wales example and

picks up an argument in *Attorney-General for New South Wales v. Trethowan* (1931):

> Dixon, J. has suggested that, even in the UK, a distinction is to be drawn between the power to make any law and the manner of exercise of that power. Although a Parliament cannot bind its successors in the sense that it can deny them certain legislative powers, it is competent to determine the manner in which legislative power can validly be exercised. If it is assumed that the Parliament of the Union enjoys the same legislative competence as does the Imperial Parliament, in the reasoning of Dixon J., the Union Parliament remains obliged to legislate in the 'manner and form' prescribed by a prior Act until that prior Act is repealed according to the procedure therein provided.[28]

Thus, Northey reports, Dixon believed that sovereign parliaments could set out the conditions to be followed when making valid laws, and 'subsequent Parliaments may, of course, amend this law, but, if the law is itself subject to amendment in a special manner, then it is submitted that the procedure prescribed must be followed, and an Act which failed to comply with these conditions would be invalid'.[29] Northey believed that some fundamental rights could be accordingly protected but a bill that set out such provisions should be endorsed by a referendum. Also, double entrenchment would be required. That is, the section of the Act that set out the entrenching requirements would have to be similarly protected.[30]

New Zealand's Constitutional Reform Committee agreed with Braybrooke's opinion: New Zealand differed from New South Wales in that the Statute of Westminster, ratified in 1947, gave New Zealand powers equivalent to those of the UK Parliament.[31] The *Report* stated:

> Our Parliament could, if it chose to do so, set up a second Chamber in this country; by the same Act it could declare that the constitution or existence of that Chamber would never thereafter be altered by legislation unless or until the approval of the electors was first secured through a referendum. But even if these elaborate precautions were taken it would seem that they would have no consequences that could be safeguarded by our Courts of Law.[32]

But, the *Report* continues, although 'legal protection' of a new upper house cannot be created, 'there might still be some practical value in inserting a similar clause in any legislation that may be proposed for setting up a Second Chamber in this country'.[33] A clause that stipulates that a referendum must be used if the constitution of a second chamber is amended would be 'a provision that will be declaratory of the moral, if not the legal, rights of our citizens. We will tell the legislators of the future – for what it is worth – that proposed alterations in the constitution of the second Chamber should first have the assent of the people.'[34] The South African case showed that entrenched clauses have 'constitutional significance'.[35]

Influenced by the advice the Committee received on these overseas examples, and believing that the effectiveness of any entrenchment would be limited by parliamentary supremacy, the Committee recommended that the constitution of its proposed second chamber 'shall not be amended or abrogated unless and until the approval of the electors has been expressed in a referendum, or unless and until both Houses sitting together have agreed to the proposal by a majority of any size that may be prescribed'.[36] The Committee stated it was not competent to answer what the effect of this might be, and noted what had happened in South Africa when legislation was passed nullifying the court decision.[37] Despite this, the Committee advocated entrenched clauses on constitutional matters.[38] The Committee did not report on the question of whether those clauses should themselves be protected by a similar entrenching clause.

During the 1952 parliamentary debate on the *Report*, various National Party MPs addressed the constitutional issues raised in its Appendices. (Clarence Skinner, speaking for Labour, had announced that his Party would not take part.[39]) Ron Algie, discussing the *Report*'s mixed reception, bemoaned the fact that New Zealand's unfettered Parliament could pass any law it chose and, 'there being no Constitution, there can be nothing that is unconstitutional'. Parliament could even change the electoral system, he argued.[40] Algie said that he had voted for abolition in the belief that bicameralism would be restored.[41] Duncan Rae retold the South Africa story, showing how powerful the government was when it was up against the courts. He pointed out that the proposal before the New Zealand House stipulated a referendum be held before the new upper house's constitution could be changed.[42] There was general agreement among the National speakers that, with the Statute of Westminster ratified, and believing that no Parliament could bind its successor, only moral restraints, such as requiring a referendum before constitutional amendment, were feasible.

Interestingly, Ralph Hanan, referring to the appendices of the *Report*, mentioned the 'unique and very important suggestion made by the Chairman of the Committee to introduce what are called entrenched provisions in any Act which would create a second Chamber', and he went on to explain what was meant by entrenchment. An Opposition speaker interjected that it could not be done, and Hanan agreed that such a clause could be rescinded but argued there would be a public reaction against such a move.[43] He described such measures as 'ingenious entrenched clauses'.[44]

Outside Parliament, other voices expressed their views on the various possibilities of creating constitutional protections. H. J. Benda and R. H. Brookes, for example, commented on the *Report of the Constitutional Reform Committee*. Where there was no second chamber other solutions might be possible:

> If constitutional checks were keenly desired, it should not prove impossible for the main parties to agree on a list of statutes (e.g. those affecting the duration of Parliament, the process for determining electoral boundaries, the independence of the judiciary) alterations to which should require approval by a referendum. If minority rights were to be protected, a Bill of Rights could be similarly entrenched.[45]

The authors observed that, although Braybrooke had been doubtful whether entrenched clauses were legally binding, he still supported such a clause on the grounds that it would provide a moral check on the government.[46] And they recommended that, if there were to be entrenched clauses, these should be submitted for approval to the voters in a referendum before such clauses became effective, not simply include the intention to implement reserved provisions in party manifesto commitments before general elections. Benda and Brookes wrote, 'Marriage is easy, but divorce difficult: let us not bind ourselves, "for better, or for worse", except by a deliberate act of choice.'[47]

As can be seen, the direct consequence of the abolition of the upper house was to raise some fundamental questions about the manner of its execution, its protection from subsequent repeal (were an upper house to be resurrected), and the absence of constitutional constraints on the unicameral Parliament. On the agenda was the whole problem of the feasibility of constraining the actions of future Parliaments, even if only by providing moral guidelines for constitutional behaviour.

So the idea of entrenchment, even in a parliament that was believed to be a sovereign body, was part of contemporary constitutional discourse in New Zealand during the 1950s, albeit amongst a minority of the political and academic elites. More fundamentally, even, questions were raised about the nature of constitutionality.

The possibility of implanting entrenchment clauses into bills as constraints on constitutional change had thus been raised and discussed before the 1956 Bill went through the House, though they were hedged by doubts around how entrenchment could and would work in a system that saw itself as bound by the doctrine of parliamentary sovereignty. And even though it was generally believed that the courts would not want to become involved if entrenched clauses were not respected by a future House of Representatives, such clauses would have 'moral' authority over all parliamentarians. In short, the sanctions were political, not legal.

Thus the idea of entrenchment existed in the contemporary parliamentary lexicon, but there were doubts about its legal powers.

Single Entrenchment

Soon after the events of 1956, Professor Ken Scott gave a lecture in the United Kingdom on New Zealand's political traditions.[48] Responding to a request to discuss New Zealand's 'recent attempt to safeguard democracy by entrenching the electoral law',[49] Scott explained the circumstances of the Electoral Act 1956 and described the entrenching conditions. He continued thus:

> It might be asked why the entrenching clause was not entrenched. What would have happened if the clause had been entrenched and a later Parliament had purported to

> legislate by a bare majority in defiance of it? Constitutional litigation would probably have resulted, and the judge would have been called upon to give what might have looked like a political decision, and the law on the subject might have been uncertain until the case had been carried on appeal to the Privy Council. I believe that the reason why the entrenching clause was not entrenched—the reason why the legal possibility of defying the spirit of the entrenching clause was left open—was from a very proper desire that the judges should not only be out of politics, but also should be seen to be out of politics, and from a very proper desire that constitutional law on this important subject should be not in a state of flux for a period perhaps of many months while a Privy Council decision was awaited.[50]

Of course the Judicial Committee of the Privy Council was New Zealand's final court of appeal until the Supreme Court Act 2003.

At the time of Scott's lecture, Sir Clifton Webb, the former National Government Attorney-General and Minister of Justice, was New Zealand's High Commissioner in London, and he chaired the seminar. Webb asked Scott to explain how, in a unicameral system such as that in New Zealand, entrenchment can happen.[51] Scott said he agreed with the view of the National Party – stated by Webb himself when he was Attorney-General, restated in the *Report of the Constitutional Reform Committee* and again in the debate on the Electoral Bill – 'that it cannot be done'. Scott said that the New South Wales and South African precedents are not comparable to New Zealand. Also, in the British Coal Corporation case the Privy Council stated that the Canadian Parliament had full power to legislate, despite Section 4 of the Statute of Westminster providing that the UK Parliament 'may not enact a Statute extending to a Dominion as part of the law of that Dominion unless it is recited in the Statute that the Statute is passed with the advice and consent of the Dominion concerned'. And Scott concludes, 'I think the same would be true in New Zealand if Parliament passed what purported to be a statute by ordinary procedure in defiance of an entrenching clause.' The Chairman agreed.[52]

Scott was very close to political and constitutional developments in New Zealand and indeed interviewed members of the select committee that considered the Electoral Bill in 1956. It seems certain that double entrenchment was avoided for precisely the reason he gives above – to avoid the judiciary becoming involved in adjudicating on the situation were a doubly entrenching clause to be overturned by a parliament.

Almost thirty years later, in the White Paper on a Bill of Rights for New Zealand where entrenchment of the Bill was proposed (although not implemented), the authors commented thus on Section 189 of the Electoral Act 1956 and the single rather than double entrenchment:

> This was not an oversight. When s. 189 of the Electoral Act was enacted, most constitutional lawyers were of the view that if Parliament passed an Act which purported to make it more difficult for future Parliaments to legislate on a certain matter, then that Act was ineffective. It was said that Parliament could not bind its successors. The theory is that a sovereign Parliament, that is a Parliament which has power to enact any legislation it wishes, cannot bind itself as to the content or the form of its future legislation. In other words, a sovereign Parliament cannot limit its sovereignty. Any Act of Parliament can be amended or repealed by another Act passed by a simple majority, despite what the earlier Act says. To avoid the appearance of promising more than could be achieved, there

> was no attempt in 1956 to entrench s. 189 itself, so that s. 189 is not, even on the face of it, fully entrenched.[53]

The White Paper then goes on to explain how constitutional opinion has changed (and see Chapter 8, p. 190). This interpretation sits alongside Scott's – there were two intersecting reasons for not doubly entrenching: the belief that manner and form clauses are overridden by the doctrine of parliamentary sovereignty; and the desire not to involve the judiciary in constitutional matters that were felt to be the proper province of the legislature.

As to who suggested that Parliament put aside the first of these doubts and go ahead with single entrenchment, we cannot be certain. Was it John Marshall, who during the debate (and subsequently) stressed the moral authority of Section 189? The constitutional lawyer Professor Brookfield refers to Marshall as the 'designer' of this crucial section.[54] Or was it one of the other lawyers in the Government? Or a group invention? Note that Ralph Hanan and Marshall were on the select committee that considered the Electoral Bill; Ron Algie had chaired the committee that had proposed instituting a Senate four years earlier, and Hanan and Marshall also sat on that committee.[55] It was Holland, Keith Holyoake (as deputy prime minister) and Marshall who met with Labour MPs on 23 October. Or was the single entrenchment an official's suggestion, perhaps? It is less likely that it was a member of the Labour Opposition who was involved in negotiations during the Bill's passage through the House. There is no hint in the public expressions of Labour MPs that they believed parliamentary supremacy could be constrained in any way.[56]

Another way of thinking about the single entrenchment is to consider which other political ideas were prevalent during the time that might have been influential but that were not directly linked to the entrenchment device. Here I am thinking in particular about the predominant and enduring New Zealand belief in the virtues of the flexible constitution, one that could be adapted to suit changing circumstances. There are many examples of this view being expressed during the 1950s. One quotation from a National Party MP will suffice:

> The strength of our democratic system of government and our democratic way of life lies in their ability to change, to grow and to alter with circumstances from time to time, to adapt themselves to the course of events and the course of history.[57]

Note also that the belief in flexibility rather than rigidity, and parliamentary sovereignty rather than political power being given to judges, were understood as essential ingredients of the Westminster political tradition. They were mutually reinforcing constitutional mantra.

The next puzzle is why the Bill's drafters decided that either a referendum of electors or three-quarters of all MPs must approve the repeal or amendment of the entrenched clauses.

Referendums and Super-Majorities

It is unsurprising that a referendum was chosen as a possible process to be followed if a protected provision is amended or repealed. As already explained, some MPs were uneasy that the upper house had been abolished without consulting voters via referendum, even though this move had been heralded before the 1946 general election as a National Party manifesto commitment. This sentiment derived from New Zealand's history of plebiscites, although there had never been one on a constitutional matter. According to Keith Jackson, both Clifton Webb and Ronald Algie advocated having a referendum on the abolition of the Legislative

Council.[58] A contemporary observer wrote, 'Mr Holland is himself quite referendum-minded: in 1948 he favoured using it on the second chamber question and, . . . later in 1956 he expressed approval of a "constitutional referendum".'[59] Holland never actually called a non-licensing referendum during his eight years as prime minister, although there were licensing referendums at each general election.

Hence the notion of the referendum as a legitimate decision-making process in a representative democracy, although unfamiliar at Westminster itself, was certainly not a new idea in New Zealand politics. There had been periodic discussion in the House about the use of referendums as checks on the legislature.[60] And there had been plenty of practice in holding plebiscites. Licensing polls – hardly a constitutional matter but certainly an issue on which both parties harboured strong views – had been held since the early 1880s. The first nationwide referendum was in 1911, on the sale of liquor.[61] In more recent history, there had been three referendums on contested issues in 1949. These were on offshore betting, the sale of liquor and military conscription. Thus, for MPs and voters alike, referendum voting was a familiar decision-making device, albeit used for controversial issues on which it was difficult for political parties to take cohesive stances. Furthermore, the idea of the popular initiative had been discussed (a proposal that, in much different form, was finally enacted in 1993 with the Citizens' Initiated Referenda Act).[62]

Thus the idea of the referendum as a legitimate constitutional device was an ingredient of contemporary discourse in 1956. It was not only promulgated by Holland but also discussed in the press. Also, as shown above, examples had been cited of its use in overseas jurisdictions. But why did the New Zealand Parliament decide upon having an alternative mechanism for repealing or amending particular provisions of the electoral law? Certainly, it allows Parliament to make minor and technical changes with cross-party support, without the expense of a nationwide referendum.[63] Fascinatingly, however, I can find no evidence of parliamentary super-majorities being used as requirements for amendment or repeal of constitutional provisions in the newspapers of the period, while there are plentiful examples of discussion of referendums. And why was the super-majority of three-quarters of all MPs chosen rather than any other fraction of the House? Again, unfortunately, there is no written record that provides a guide to the decision-makers' reasoning in 1956.

Although the UK Parliament and constitution provided scant help when it came to finding plausible models of constitutional bulwarks, the South African and Australian examples offered in the appendices to the *Report of the Constitutional Reform Committee* had provided some clues to the problem when it came to considering how the House of Representatives, in the future, could legitimately reform the protected provisions of the electoral law. The New South Wales Constitution Act 1902, as noted, required any bill that abolished, dissolved or altered the powers of the Legislative Council to be first approved by a 'majority of the electors voting' (Section 7A(5)) and then be passed through both houses. The Union of South Africa Act 1909, under Section 152, provided that certain constitutional bills be passed by both houses in a joint sitting with its third reading agreed to by no less than two-thirds of the total number of the members of both houses. Here, therefore, was an example of a super-majority requirement, albeit in a bicameral parliament in a country with a written constitution.

But the unicameral New Zealand legislature would find its own formula for a super-majority: the three-quarters of all MPs barrier. It is interesting that the two-thirds majority was not adopted in the New Zealand House of Representatives. Of course, to gain a two-thirds majority across two houses is a formidable threshold but might not have seemed high enough to those who designed the Electoral Act, given the absence of an upper house. One can only speculate that the New Zealand designers opted for the three-quarters of all MPs barrier to ensure that, in the two-party system of that period, cross-party agreement would be required to change any of the reserved provisions. It might be feasible for a single party to win two-thirds of the seats in a landslide victory, especially as the electoral system tended to over-reward the winning party, but three-quarters would be much more difficult.

Nevertheless, at least one newspaper editor at the time doubted the effectiveness of the three-quarters majority. After opining that the 'new electoral laws have no real binding force' and were merely a 'moral barrier', the editorial stated, 'The possibility that, in the event of some future political landslide, such a majority might be obtained among the Government of the day does not appear to have been envisaged.' The provisions of the Act 'should be accepted as no more than a stop-gap' and New Zealand still needed an effective second chamber.[64]

Over a decade later, during the debate in the House on the Bill providing for a referendum on the parliamentary term, Arnold Nordmeyer recited New Zealand's history on the length of the term and recalled that,

> In 1956, when the Electoral Act was being consolidated, the then National Government approached the Opposition and indicated that it felt the time had arrived when certain matters affecting elections should be entrenched in legislation, and it was agreed unanimously at that time that certain clauses, including the clause dealing with the three-year term of Parliament, should be entrenched.

He went on to say that it was agreed a 75% majority could alter the parliamentary term, which meant that 'there had to be substantial unanimity between the two main political parties'. And if there was any 'uncertainty' about a 75% majority in favour of extending the term, then 'the matter should be submitted to a referendum'.[65]

This casts a somewhat different light on the entrenchment clause. Rather than regarding the choice of alternate decision-making devices as entirely up to Government and Parliament, perhaps choosing according to the type of issue at stake, the referendum was seen as a way of taking the decision to the people when the parties were internally divided or when one party favoured change and the other did not, and hence a three-quarters majority vote of the House was unlikely or impossible. In Chapter 7 I investigate this issue further by looking at New Zealand's record of referendums and super-majorities in an effort to understand more deeply precisely why and how they were employed.

New Zealand's Entrenchment and Institutional Change

Policy decisions in stable democratic states, even those with adversarial party systems, tend to be path-dependent. That is, they follow the patterns of past policies rather than striking out in dramatically new directions. This is partly because the costs of exiting from previous decisions are greater than continuing in the same general direction as before.[66] It might be that Westminster states with strong party systems are particularly prone to this pattern of policy development, despite their absence of formal constraints on their policy actions. As explained in Chapter 3, by the 1950s, party discipline in New Zealand was strong but went alongside the habit of caucus consultation by government ministers (see p. 35 and pp. 49–50). And before mass-opinion polling and the use of focus groups, backbench MPs were important conveyors of public opinion. It can be argued that this means that policy change is built on consensus. When consensus must be negotiated, then it is easier to develop and justify policy on the basis of its connections with the familiar and the trialled rather than to propose radical reform. This is probably even more the case when constitutional decisions must be negotiated with the Opposition.

When the National Party leaders decided to make it more difficult to change certain electoral laws than others, they made two crucial choices. The first was that they introduced a self-denying rule that constrained the future actions of parties on both sides of the House. National's fear of what might happen if it were to lose the next general election added a strong measure of urgency to their actions. The second crucial decision was to find a way of doing this by proposing a new type of constraint, a 'manner and form' clause that had moral and, we should note, political authority. This was a new idea for New Zealand. The politicians took the idea of entrenchment from elsewhere and planted it in the Electoral Act 1956. By not doubly entrenching the entrenching clause, the politicians believed at the time that they had managed to avoid judicial interference with their future decisions. This has to be understood within the perceived belief in the Westminster tradition of parliamentary sovereignty. The common law prevailed. Note that rights-based movements (human, Indigenous and so forth) were yet to develop in New Zealand. And no bills of rights existed in the UK, Australian or Canada, let alone in New Zealand. These were yet to come.

The two alternative means of amending or repealing the reserved provisions, by referendum or super-majority, like the device of single entrenchment, also reflected familiarity yet demonstrated novelty. Although non-constitutional referendums were part of New Zealand history, super-majorities were the product of policy transfer from abroad. And from where else would the New Zealand architects of Section 189 draw their ideas? The proportionally elected European parliaments would not be seriously studied until MMP came on to the political agenda; and the US constitution was regarded as a different order of species altogether.[67] It was the UK and its former settler polities that provided examples and precedents.

As shown earlier, there were very few submissions to the select committee on the 1956 Bill. There was neither the time nor the inclination, it seems, to look for ideas and proposals beyond the narrow world of MPs and ministers, with their officials, legal advisers and a few academic lawyers. Despite Holland having earlier expressed his intention to take any entrenched provisions to a referendum, in the end Parliament provided the key political actors for this policy decision, almost uninfluenced by outside organised interests. This was a marked departure from the consultative policy processes that so characterised New Zealand at that time, as we saw in earlier chapters.

The decision-makers of 1956 knew they were doing something different – this is obvious from the parliamentary debates. But what they did not, and perhaps could not, realise is just how influential Section 189 would be on the development of future electoral law and general New Zealand constitutional development.

7

The Reserved Provisions: Justifications and Evolution

With the entrenchment formula agreed on, the political parties could protect the contested electoral issues and, perhaps, other issues of constitutional significance. The reserved provisions of the Electoral Act 1956 are the focus of this chapter. Without a full written record of the discussions we cannot tell exactly what went on between the two parties when they negotiated the details of the reserved provisions. But we can certainly assume that the cross-party discussions were not easy since, as shown in Chapter 5 (p. 113), the entrenchment clause and reserved provisions were inserted very late in the Bill's passage. Furthermore, we also know that the National caucus met frequently during the last stage of the passage of the Bill. It might be that the National backbenchers had to be brought on board with the proposed amendments to the Bill.

In the House, apart from discussing the entrenching provision, John Marshall outlined the principles underlying the Bill: 'that no qualified person should be deprived of the opportunity to register or to vote'; 'no vote should be invalid because of some mistake on the part of an official'; and 'voters should be free from all influence and propaganda by parties or candidates' (whereupon Walter Nash interposed, commenting that they can fetch voters 'in a motorcar and influence them while they are in it!'). Double-voting and similar abuses were made as difficult as possible; and 'where an election is contested the court should look to the substance and not to the technicality in deciding whether or not votes should be allowed or whether incorrect practices have occurred'.[1] The definition of election expenses was clarified and the party propaganda law tightened, a clause that was 'the subject of considerable scrutiny by the select committee'.[2] Marshall also elaborated on the changes that stressed examining the intentions of voters when interpreting ballot papers and the court processes to be followed when disputes occurred, with electoral petitions now going to the Supreme Court to be heard by three judges rather than to a separate election court.[3] In other words, the core value underlying these stated principles related to fairness of voting procedures and vote counting. None of these measures was entrenched.

Marshall noted that the Select Committee had 'reached almost complete unanimity on the Bill and on the amendments made in the committee'. There were one or two 'slight differences', which he did not identify.[4] Fascinatingly, Marshall at no stage during the parliamentary debates on the Electoral Bill justified the choice of provisions to be entrenched, let alone mentioned possible omissions. This chapter discusses the possible reasons for the inclusion of each of the reserved provisions and traces their subsequent amendments.

The Representation Commission and the Electorate Boundaries

In his memoirs, Marshall wrote that he wished to 'ensure that governments could not, in future, influence the shape of electorates to their own advantage'.[5] This goal was achieved through bargaining and compromise. According to K. J.

Scott, who interviewed members of the select committee that considered the Electoral Bill during the negotiations between the National Government and the Labour Opposition, there were mutual concessions over the rules around boundary-drawing and the composition of the Representation Commission:

> Four provisions in the Bill were in dispute between the parties, and two of these provisions were settled in accord with the views of one party and two in accord with the views of the other. The provisions settled in favour of the National Party were that the boundaries of the European electoral districts were to be drawn on the basis of total European population, not adult population or numbers of European electors, and that the Representation Commission's terms of reference were to remain in the existing form. The provisions settled in favour of the Labour Party were that the Representation Commission was to be reconstituted in such a way as to minimise the risk of gerrymandering, and that the tolerance (the degree by which the population of an electoral district might vary from the electoral quota) was to be reduced from 7½ percent. to 5 per cent.[6]

It is always helpful to consider what those involved in constitutional bargaining have in common as well as what they differed on. Both Labour and National had an interest in electoral stability and systemic legitimacy. The agreement on the composition of the Representation Commission gave each party, whether in government or opposition, its nominated representation on the Commission. In Parliament, noting that 'the fixing of the boundaries has been a controversial question', Walter Nash, Leader of the Opposition, praised the provision that the Government and the Opposition would each have the right to nominate a person on the Representation Commission 'almost as scrutineers'.[7] The reduction of the electoral tolerance fitted with Labour's preference, and was agreed to during the select committee phase, but was not a huge sacrifice for National, especially as, perhaps in return, electorates would continue to be based on total rather than adult population. There was no public discussion of National proposing a return to the country quota.

The entrenched provisions included a surprising number of instructions on the boundaries and the Representation Commission, even including details relating to the membership of the Representation Commission and the drawing of boundaries that might have been better placed outside the reserved provisions.[8] Section 15 defined the composition of the Representation Commission:

> 15. *Representation Commission*—(1) In order to provide for the periodical readjustment of the representation of the people in New Zealand in the House of Representatives there shall be a Commission to be known as the Representation Commission.
>
> (2) The Commission shall consist of seven members, of whom—
>
> (a) The Surveyor-General, the Government Statistician, the Chief Electoral Officer, and the Director-General of the Post and Telegraph Department shall be the official members:
>
> (b) Two persons (not being public servants or members of the General Assembly) shall be appointed by the Governor-General by Order in Council on the nomination of the House of Representatives as the unofficial members of the Commission, one of those members being nominated to represent the Government and one to represent the Opposition:
>
> (c) One person (not being a public servant of a member of the General Assembly) shall be appointed by the Governor-General by Order in Council on the nomination of the official and unofficial members of the Commission, or a majority of them, to be the Chairman of the Commission.'

[Subsections 3, 4 and 5 of Section 15 then set out further details of membership, resignation of members and provision of salaries and allowances.]

This section survived almost intact during the next decades, even after the implementation of MMP in the Electoral Act 1993 (Section 28).[9] The Royal Commission on the Electoral System had recommended that each parliamentary party should have its own representative, not just one for the Government and one for the Opposition. The Commission also recommended that the party representatives no longer be able to vote.[10] As Andrew Geddis has argued, it would be far better if there were no party representatives at all on the Representation Commission. After all, parties may make submissions.[11] That body's composition was a legacy from the Electoral Act 1956 that should have been amended when MMP was implemented, whether following the Commission's recommendation or that proposed by Geddis.

Section 16 set out the rules for drawing up the European electorate boundaries. Unlike the Māori seats, these were placed under the jurisdiction of the Representation Commission:

> 16. *Division of New Zealand into European electorates after each census*—(1) After each periodical census it shall be the duty of the Commission to divide New Zealand into European electorate districts according to the following basis, that is to say:
>
> (a) New Zealand shall be divided into seventy-six European electoral districts, so that the number of districts in the North Island bears, as nearly as may be, the same proportion to the number of districts in the South Island as the European population of the North Island bears to the European population of the South Island:
>
> (b) The European population of each Island shall be divided by the number of districts in that Island, and in each case the

> quotient thus obtained shall be the quota for that Island:
>
> (c) The extent of the districts in each Island shall respectively be such that at the time of making the division the European population thereof shall, subject to the provisions as to the allowance hereinafter contained, be equal to the quota for that Island;
>
> (d) In forming the several districts due consideration shall be given to the existing boundaries of electoral districts, to community of interest, to facilities of communications, and to topographical features.

[Subsections 2, 3 and 4 then set out further requirements concerning reporting census results, and preparing maps showing proposed boundaries of European electorates.]

Note that 'European' population was used as the basis for calculating electorate boundaries. European population was defined in Section 2, the interpretation part of the Act. 'European' meant 'not Māori' and 'European population' meant 'total population', excluding Māori, people on ships and other persons in temporary sorts of accommodation. In other words, Labour, who of course had wanted adult electors rather than total population to be counted, had lost this part of the argument. In fact, Labour had lost the argument for the foreseeable future. There was no return to its 1950s preference in the Electoral Act 1993. Indeed, the Royal Commission on the Electoral System reported that, in their submission, the Labour Party as well as the National Party supported retaining the total population base.[12] The Commission recommended continued use of total population. Its main justification was that 'the general argument for the population quota for a constituency being set in terms of the total population is that everyone is affected by the decisions of Government and therefore everyone should be equally represented in the body that makes those decisions'.[13]

One of the interesting features of the 1956 legislation was that the total number of seats was not explicitly included as an entrenched provision in the 1956 Act, an omission that was noted at the time by contemporary commentators.[14] After referring back to the Constitution Act 1852, Section 11 of the 1956 statute specifies that there are 80 members of the House, of whom:

> Seventy-six shall be elected respectively for the European electoral districts constituted under Part of the Act:
>
> Four shall be elected respectively for the Maori electorate districts constituted under this Part of this Act.

However, Section 16, as shown above, stipulates that the country be divided into 76 European constituencies, and sets out the quota formulae. Thus the total number of European MPs was protected, albeit in a rather back-door manner. Of course, if the whole of Section 11 had been entrenched, the Māori electorate districts would have also been given the same status, a discussion continued later in this chapter. Suffice to say here that contemporary MPs, including Eruera Tirikatene and Ralph Hanan, noted the disparity of treatment of the Māori seats compared with their European counterparts.

Although the total size of Parliament was not a contested issue during the 1950s, the South Island electorates were viewed as a growing problem, with the population of the North Island rising in proportion to that of the South Island, as shown in the 1956 census. It was generally agreed that, 'with the North Island population still increasing faster than that of the South Island, the South Island must as the law stands at present lose at least one seat'.[15] Evidently, Holland had expressed the view that there should be a limit to the number of seats lost to the South Island and its representation should be stabilised.[16] Nevertheless, *The Dominion* reported on 15 October 1956, the issue of the South Island seats would not be dealt with. The prime minister had told the recent National Party Conference that no bill that altered the size of Parliament would be introduced until there had been a referendum on the subject.[17]

During the term of the next National Government (1960–1972) led by Keith Holyoake, the Electoral Amendment Act 1965 fixed the number of South Island electorates at 25. Both parties agreed that stabilisation was necessary, but National's 1963 election manifesto had promised a 25-seat minimum (the existing number) while Labour wanted 26 (the number at the time of the 1956 legislation).[18] National won this argument and the quota for the South Island became the total non-Māori population of that island divided by 25. The agreement between Government and Opposition was achieved as follows:

> The 75 per cent of the vote required to change an entrenched section of the Electoral Act was obtained by the Government giving a promise that, in the words of K. J. (later Sir Keith) Holyoake, in the event of the Opposition coming into power and wishing to increase the number of South Island seats to 26, 'such a Government would have cooperation equal to that given to the National Government by the present Opposition'.[19]

Labour not only had wanted more seats given to the South Island but also more seats in total.[20]

The 1965 amendment to the Electoral Act was the occasion of an antagonistic debate between the two parties on the question of the fixed number of Māori seats. That articulate advocate for justice for Māori representation, Labour MP Eruera Tirikatene, argued that that those seats should be increased to reflect the Māori populations in those seats.

He was supported by his party. The National Government disagreed and no changes were made.[21] As we shall see, this issue would be taken up by Labour during its next spell in government between 1972 and 1975 and, much later, the Electoral Act 1993 would change the situation still further.

From 1965 onwards, because the South Island population was used to calculate the number of seats in the North Island where the population was rapidly growing, the total size of the House of Representatives rose, reaching 99 MPs in 1993, the last FPP general election. For the Labour Party, however, the total number of MPs was inadequate for the tasks they had to perform, including fulfilling their roles in select committees. The package of proposals the party tried to implement during their one-term government between 1972 and 1975 included one to increase the size of the House to 121 MPs. Because the National Party refused to support this measure which, of course, was entrenched for the reasons explained above, the Labour Government dropped it from its change agenda.[22] The 1975 initiatives, as they affected the Māori seats, are discussed below.

The last of the issues concerning boundaries and the Representation Commission was the permitted difference allowed among the populations of different electorates.

> 17. *Allowance for adjustment of Quota*—Where in the opinion of the Commission districts cannot be formed consistently with the considerations hereinbefore provided for so as to contain exactly the quota, the Commission may for any district make an allowance by way of addition or subtraction of European population not exceeding five per cent.

As with the question of using total or adult population as the basis for deciding electorate boundaries, the 5% discrepancy permitted between the constituencies – a very tight difference indeed – remained in place thereafter. It survived the radical reduction in total number of electorates after MMP was established: the Royal Commission on the Electoral System had recommended 5%.[23] Again, however, Māori electorates were not treated equally in this regard in 1956, as there was no tolerance at all defined for those constituencies until 1982, when the Representation Commission finally took over determining their boundaries.

The Triennial Parliamentary Term

As already established, the ease with which the parliamentary term could be extended had caused anxiety. When discussing the effectiveness of the entrenching provision, Scott writes, 'One of the reasons why the Coalition Government was so heavily defeated in 1935 was that many electors believed that the extension of the life of a peace-time Parliament, though legally valid, had been unconstitutional.'[24]

The wording of the Electoral Act 1927 had been as follows:

> 3.(1) It shall be lawful for the Governor-General from time to time as occasion requires, by Proclamation in His Majesty's name, to summon and call together a House of Representatives in and for New Zealand, consisting of seventy-six members, in addition to four Maori members as provided in Part IV hereof.
>
> 3.(2) Every such House of Representatives shall, unless the General Assembly is sooner dissolved, continue for a period of three years, computed from the day fixed for the return of the writs issued for choosing such House, and no longer.[25]

In 1956, Clause 12, which limited the length of the parliamentary term to three years, was in the draft Bill from early on. It stated:

> *Duration of House of Representatives*—The House of Representatives, as existing on the date of the commencement of this Act, and every House of Representatives elected after that date, shall, unless Parliament is sooner dissolved, continue for a period of three years, computed from the day fixed for the return of the writs issued for the general election of members of that House of Representatives, and no longer.

So whereas the 1927 Act included the number of members in the House and the length of the term in the same section, in 1956 they were separated, with the number of MPs defined in Section 11, *Constitution of the House of Representatives*. Because of the unhappy 20th-century experience of general election postponements, once the politicians in 1956 had decided to attempt to protect some aspects of the electoral rules, the length of the parliamentary term was an obvious and non-controversial candidate for inclusion. The Electoral Bill 1956 provided the opportunity to freeze the parliamentary term at three years, protecting the triennial term from being lengthened by reigning governments.

There had been some debate in the newspapers during 1956 over whether or not there should be a four- rather than three-year term of parliament, with speculation that the Government might hold a referendum on the question. It was suggested that this referendum would be held at the same time as one on the issue of capital punishment. (The latter had been scheduled for 1957 but was never held.[26]) It was reported that the Royal Commission on Monetary Affairs and the Chambers of Commerce had advocated the longer term.[27] From the evidence of the parliamentary debates, however, there was no appetite among MPs for such a change. This was hardly surprising given that there was no referendum held on the provisions of the Bill itself. Any Parliament that extended the parliamentary term without public approval, not even an electoral mandate, would have been trenchantly criticised.

Including the duration of the House of Representatives as one of the reserved provisions was almost certainly the most uncontroversial decision made by those who designed, and bargained over, Section 189. But there has been debate ever since over the length of the parliamentary term. Which of the two change mechanisms under Section 189 should those who wish to change the length of the parliamentary term select? Plainly, were MPs to make such a radical reform through using a super-majority, such an action would be rightly seen as self-serving. As Ralph Hanan said, 'We in this House were chosen by the people for a term of three years, and I think we would all feel it would be very wrong in any way to extend our own life.'[28] Such a decision must come from the people, and since 1956 they have been given the opportunity to make such a change on two occasions, in 1967 and 1990.

In 1967 the National Government, led by Keith Holyoake, held a referendum on extending the term of parliament to four years. This was the first attempt to change one of the reserved provisions of the Electoral Act 1956 by using a nationwide non-binding referendum.[29] Unfortunately, another poll was held at the same time. This was on the totally different – and more hotly contested – issue of hotel closing hours. In the House, Norman Kirk, Leader of the Opposition, pointed out that a referendum on the parliamentary term had been promised in Labour's 1966 election policy.[30] Keith Holyoake responded that, although it had not been National Party policy, the issue had been discussed over the years, 'and it seemed, as a liquor licensing referendum is to be held at a considerable cost of about £150,000, that it was a good opportunity to get the opinion of electors on this other issue.'[31] Such is the price of democracy. The bill was scrutinised by the House's Statutes Revision Committee, which heard submissions and recommended that the referendum be held. A leaflet on the parliamentary term was distributed to voters ('a pretty superficial document', according to a senior Labour MP) which set out the main arguments for and against change.[32]

In a turnout of 69.7% of enrolled voters, 68.1% chose 'I vote for a maximum of three years as present', while 31.9 % opted for 'I vote for a maximum of four years'.[33] The referendums were not held at the same time as a general election, lowering the numbers participating. (As for extending the opening hours of hotel bars, the reverse happened with the majority selecting change and the minority wanting a continuation of the '6 o'clock swill'.)[34] In discussing the Bill providing for the referendum, Martyn Finlay said, 'We have adopted what I might call the short-cut tactic in dealing with certain other entrenched provisions of the constitution . . . We felt justified in doing it that way, but when it comes to the life of Parliament itself I think it would be improper for us to take the short cut. The electorate itself should decide.'[35]

The issue of the length of the parliamentary term surfaced again after the Royal Commission on the Electoral System considered the matter and recommended that a 'referendum should be held no later than December 1993 to determine whether the term of Parliament should be increased to 4 years' and that this referendum 'should include a proposal to limit the power to seek a dissolution'.[36] After hearing over 600 submissions on electoral issues, including the parliamentary term, the Electoral Law Committee inquiry into the *Report of the Royal Commission on the Electoral System* made a number of recommendations.[37] One of these was that the Government hold a referendum on a four-year parliamentary term 'with appropriate limitations on the power to seek a dissolution'.[38] At the October 1990 general election voters had their second opportunity to consider extending the term of the House of Representatives. In between this referendum and the earlier one, the clause defining the parliamentary term had been shifted to the Constitution Act 1986, where it was similarly entrenched.

The collective choice of the people in 1990 echoed the earlier referendum decision: it seemed that voters had not changed their minds during the intervening years. Of the 85.2% turnout of enrolled voters, 69% chose 'I vote for 3 years as the term of Parliament as at present'. Just 30.7% opted for a four-year term.[39] As Stephen Levine and Nigel Roberts point out, voter attitudes to this matter shift according to their perceptions of the capacities of the government in office. This was demonstrated in their opinion polling of the Miramar (Wellington) electorate, where more respondents favoured an extension of the term in their 1987 survey – when the Labour Government was still popular—than in 1990, when Labour lost the general election to National. Nevertheless, a majority in both surveys favoured the status quo.[40]

Because both of the parliamentary term referendums were non-binding, Parliament would have had to have passed legislation subsequently in order to give effect to the verdict of the voters. That legislation would have had to be passed by a 75% majority in the House of Representatives.[41]

If the boundary definition rules and the triennial parliamentary term were electoral issues that needed to be stable and predictable to avoid gaming by future governments, what else was of such importance in 1956 that it was of the same status as the unsettled and contested issues? Two other matters were deemed as such: the definition of voter eligibility and the 'method of voting'. These were not issues that had recently been the focus of intense adversarial politics, although there had always been minor differences between Labour and National on the details of residency and voter enrolment rules.

Voter Eligibility

This is a particularly messy part of the 1956 Act. Section 189(e) restricts amendment or repeal for:

> Subsection one of section thirty-nine, and the definition of the term 'adult' in subsection one of section two, and paragraph (e) of section ninety-nine, as far as these provisions prescribe twenty-one years as the minimum age for persons qualified to be registered as electors or to vote:

In full, these sections and sub-sections are (in the order of Section 189(e) quoted above):

> 39. *Qualification of electors*—(1) Subject to the provisions of this Act every adult person shall be qualified to be registered as an elector of an electoral district if—
>
> (a) He is a British subject; and
>
> (b) He is ordinarily resident in New Zealand; and
>
> (c) He has at some period resided continuously in New Zealand for not less than one year; and either
>
> (d) He has resided in that electoral district for not less than three months immediately preceding the date of his application for registration; or
>
> (e) He has resided continuously in that electoral district for not less than three months and has not subsequently resided continuously for three months or upwards in any one electoral district; or
>
> (f) He resides in that electoral district, or has resided in that district and has not subsequently resided in any other electoral district, and, because of his occupation or employment or that of his spouse, whether as a seaman, an actor, or a commercial traveller, or otherwise, he has not resided continuously for three months or upwards in any one electoral district.

> 2. *Interpretation*—(1) In this Act, unless the context otherwise requires,—
>
> 'Adult' means of or over the age of twenty-one years:
>
> 99. *Who may vote*—Subject to the provisions of this Act, the following persons, and no others, shall be qualified to vote at any election in any district, namely:
>
> [and subsections (a) to (d) set out the non-reserved provisions relating to voter registration]
>
> (e) Any serviceman who is outside New Zealand, if he is or will be of over the age of twenty-one years before polling day, and his place of residence immediately before he last left New Zealand is within the district.

In his parliamentary speech during the passage of the 1956 Bill, Marshall said that the first substantial amendment to the Bill had changed the residency requirements, permitting those ordinarily resident in New Zealand to vote even if they had lived outside the country for a year (with a limit of three years).[42] Nash questioned the phrase that the voter 'shall be a British subject', pointing out that 'a foreign immigrant has the right after a period of years of residence in this country – I think five years at present – to become naturalised, which automatically gives him the right to vote. A British immigrant has the right to vote after 12 months' residence, and must reside for three months in a given district.'[43]

But these sections did not seem to be intensely divisive. It was taken for granted that being a British subject was an appropriate status for voting: it would not be until 1975 that this was redefined, when permanent residency rather than formal citizenship status would then interestingly replace being a British Subject as the key requirement for voting eligibility. During the 1950s there had been differences between Labour and National over length of residency in electorates and the position of people such as seamen, but these were mostly resolved. Neill Atkinson observes that the Raglan case (see Chapter 5, p. 96) had demonstrated the need to revise the rules on residency and the rights of those people who had been temporarily living overseas but normally lived in New Zealand.[44] The only issue that divided the parties in a mild sort of way (and we do not know whether there was also intra-party disagreement over this) was the voting age. Fixing the age-eligibility at 21 years old in 1956 had not been without its critics, particularly from the Labour Party. Nash queried the 21-year-old age eligibility.[45]

Despite the fact that voter eligibility in general was not an unsettled electoral issue in the sense that it had stimulated intense partisan differences during the 1950s, it was certainly viewed as an aspect of the New Zealand voting system that needed to be clarified. Indeed, it was one of the original reasons for revising and consolidating the Electoral Act 1927. As such, it was of high salience to MPs. Perhaps also the rules on voter eligibility might have been perceived as having the potential to be manipulated by future governments according to their own voting strengths. Labour, for example, depended more than National did on voters with occupations that involved shifting around for jobs and, also, poorer voters who might have been less likely than richer ones to enrol to vote late. Ease of registration and voting has always mattered more for left-wing than right-wing political parties, especially in systems where voting is voluntary rather than compulsory.

During the 1960s the age of voting returned to the electoral agenda and, interestingly, it was a National government who initiated the first lowering of the age of eligibility. However, the Government was at least in part responding to a petition to Parliament requesting that the age for qualification be reduced to 18 years. About 11,000 people had signed the petition, which was presented by Hugh Watt, Deputy Leader of the Opposition. This petition undoubtedly reflected changing public feelings on the appropriate age of voting, stimulated by, as Neill Atkinson argues, the increasing number of young people remaining at secondary school and entering higher education, and the Vietnam war – one did not have to be 21 years of age to fight for one's country.[46] The bill to reduce the voting age to 20 was introduced in 1969, an election year, when the petition was still being examined by a select committee. Norman Kirk, Labour leader, said National had opposed reduction during the 1966 election campaign while Labour had advocated a voting age of 18. That was Labour Party policy.[47] During the second reading debate, Watt pointed out that because the voting age was entrenched, 'The Bill could not go through the Chamber without the support of the Opposition'.[48] There was a bitter debate about the timing of the Bill, just three months before the general election with the main rolls already closed, meaning it would be a struggle for the newly enfranchised voters to get on the roll. But Labour supported the Bill to enfranchise those who were 20 years old, and so its passage complied with the provisions of Section 189.

In 1974, the voting age was lowered again, this time to 18. Again the super-majority device was used to amend the Electoral Act. Led by Norman Kirk, Labour had won the 1972 general election and had promised to lower the voting age. The Government was in a hurry to get the legislation through the House because the Sydenham by-election was scheduled for 2 November 1974 and it was already September. Although Robert Muldoon, by now leader of the National Party, proposed that implementation of the Bill be postponed until before the general election of the next year, after cross-party discussion and clarification of the enrolment details the bill was hurried through the House and had its third reading on 19 September. Although there have been proposals to lower the voting age further since 1974, by the end of 2017 the voting age remains unchanged.

The eligibility sections of the Electoral Act were, however, the occasion of an unsuccessful attempt at amendment. Alan McRobie reports that in 1966 National, who wanted to permit 'servicemen on active duty in designated special areas to be able to vote once they reached 20 years of age', failed to persuade the Labour Opposition to support this change.[49] There was no change to the Act: the entrenched section had been respected by the governing political party.

The Method of Voting

This is an intriguing part of the Electoral Act 1956. The relevant reserved provision is as follows:

> 106. *Method of Voting*—(1) The voter, having received a ballot paper, shall immediately retire into one of the inner compartments provided for the purpose, and shall there alone and secretly exercise his vote by marking his ballot paper by striking out the name of every candidate except the one for whom he wishes to vote.
>
> (2) Every voter shall, before leaving the inner compartment, fold his ballot paper so that the contents cannot be seen, and shall then deposit it so folded in the ballot box.

One of the Act's designers, Marshall, describes it as 'the method of voting, with one person having one, and only one, vote for one, and only one, candidate, in one, and only one, electorate, thus excluding proportional, preferential, or any other new system of voting, none of which, at that time, had any public support'.[50] As Alan Robinson pointed out many years ago, Sections 86 and 116 – those parts of the Electoral Act 1956 that related to the FPP electoral system – were not protected by single entrenchment.[51] Section 86 states that 'if more than one candidate is nominated, and a sufficient number do not withdraw their nominations so as to leave only one candidate, a poll for deciding between the candidates shall be taken by secret ballot at the several polling places of the district on polling day'. Section 116 deals with the declaration of the result of the poll and what would happen if candidates won equal numbers of votes (magisterial recount, and, if they were still equal, determination of the winner by lot). The secret ballot is certainly protected in Section 106 but it is extremely doubtful that on its own it protected FPP itself.

Perhaps the 'Method of Voting' was swept into the group of reserved provisions simply because, by the 1950s, FPP was deemed an essential part of the New Zealand constitution. That it was included in Section 189 was no surprise to the newspaper editor who expressed the view in August of that year, after the National Party Conference, that 'Mr Holland's idea is that the constitution of Parliament and the method of its election should be fixed by law' and only a referendum could alter or revoke that law.[52] The 'method of voting' had not been vulnerable to tit-for-tat electoral legislation in the same way as the boundary issues had been since 1935. It is probable that the unsettled issues provided reason for searching for the means of agreeing upon and stabilising the rules, while the more consensual issues – the method of voting and voter eligibility – were then slotted into Section 189 because they were deemed simply too important to remain unprotected. They were the add-ons.

When it came to considering the adoption of MMP it was assumed that any change to a non-FPP electoral system would involve complying with the entrenchment provisions. The story of how New Zealand came to switch electoral systems has been told fully elsewhere;[53] it is sufficient to note here that there were two referendums. The 1992 referendum, when

New Zealanders voted on whether they wanted to change the electoral system and selected among a range of alternative electoral systems, was an 'indicative' poll, that is, it was not legally binding. The 1993 referendum, which offered the choice between FPP and MMP, held at the same time as the general election of that year, was the only occasion (between 1956 and 2017) on which a proposal for amending a reserved provision was put to the public via a binding referendum. It was held under legislation that set out the details of the changes, repealing all the reserved provisions except the triennial term provision and amending others. The Act provided that it would go into force only if approved by a majority of voters in a referendum held for that purpose. McGee notes, 'had the legislation that became the Electoral Act 1993 not been made subject to a binding electoral referendum, those provisions would clearly have been required to be passed by a 75 per cent majority of members.'[54]

Section 168 of the Electoral Act 1993 is protected in the entrenching clause of Section 268. Like its predecessor, it is entitled 'The Method of Voting'. This time, however, as well as protecting the secret ballot it more explicitly protects the MMP electoral system than the Electoral Act 1956 protected FPP.

The Omissions and their Consequences

In Parliament in 1956, the senior Labour MP Rex Mason praised the Electoral Bill but, after querying the inclusion of the minimum voting age of 21, asked, 'Why are not other provisions put beyond the power of ready alteration?'[55] Mason did not specify what these might have been. As the Royal Commission on the Electoral System wrote in 1986, 'defining the matters which are to be protected is difficult', and the *Report* goes on to point out the detail that might have been omitted from the 1956 Act's reserved provisions.[56]

Geoffrey Palmer also observes that while 'relatively technical matters', for example the composition of the Representation Commission, are included in the reserved section of the Electoral Act, there are other matters that are not, such as the requirement that ministers must be MPs, the security of tenure of judges, 'or even the existence of the New Zealand Parliament'.[57] I do not discuss the security of tenure of judges since this is not an electoral issue, and although the political actors of the time regarded the Electoral Act 1956 as of constitutional significance, it was not regarded as 'the constitution', which remained the Constitution Act 1852.

Eligibility to Stand as a Candidate

An obvious absence from the reserved provisions in 1956 was a provision establishing the eligibility requirements for taking a seat in the House of Representatives. Section 25 states that 'registered electors may be members, unless disqualified'. Disqualification could come under any of the provisions of the Act, being an undischarged bankrupt, or being a contractor, as defined in Section 2. 'Citizenship', the principal qualification for becoming an elected member in most legislatures, was not required in the Electoral Act 1956. Perhaps the combination of lacking an historic notion of citizenship beyond being a 'British subject', along with the experience of being a society of immigrants and settlers in a country without border problems, helps explain this gap.[58]

In 1956, the candidature qualifications were complicated by the non-entrenched exclusionary clauses that related to standing for election in Māori and European electorates. Section 25 stated that:

> (2) A Maori (other than a half-caste) shall not be qualified to be elected a member for any European electoral district.

> (3) A European shall not be qualified to be elected a member for any Maori electoral district.

These stipulations of course echoed the voter eligibility rule discussed earlier. For a country with high rates of marriage between Māori and Pākehā, they were based on extraordinarily dated notions of 'race' and were difficult to administer. In 1967, the Holyoake-led National Government changed Section 25, permitting all Māori (not only those who were 'half-caste' or more) to stand in the non-Māori seats and Europeans to stand in Māori seats. This reform did not also apply to enrolment qualifications. As the Labour leader, Norman Kirk, said (not opposing the Bill), 'It seems to me that it might have been a much wiser step to have moved towards integration by leaving the Maori an area of choice to enrol either as a European or as a Maori elector, thus giving him the right to contest a seat either as a European or as a Maori'.[59] Labour would change this situation subsequently, as explained below. Whatever National's hopes in making the 1967 change, it took until 1975 for the party to elect candidates who identified as Māori.[60] Labour stood three Māori candidates for European seats in the 1969 general election,[61] although no Māori won a general seat for Labour until 1993.[62] At the time of writing, no non-Māori had been elected to represent a Māori seat – which would have been an odd situation had that happened, given that one of the arguments in favour of their retention has been to represent the Māori culture in Parliament.

The Electoral Act 1993 changed the candidature rule, again requiring that candidates must satisfy the qualifications for voting, but this time adding the extra stipulation that they must also be New Zealand citizens (Section 127).[63] This provision is not included in the entrenching section of the Act (Section 268), leaving it open to future Parliaments to alter it without the consent of either the opposition parties or voters. However, the right to stand for Parliament is now included in the Bill of Rights Act 1990. Section 12 states that:

> Every New Zealand citizen who is of or over the age of 18 years—
>
> (a) has the right to vote in genuine periodic elections of members of the House of Representatives, which elections shall be by equal suffrage and by secret ballot; and
>
> (b) is qualified for membership of the House of Representatives.

The Bill of Rights is not itself entrenched, an issue I touch on in the next chapter.

The Requirement for Ministers to be MPs

Another obvious omission from the Electoral Act 1956 was the requirement that ministers must be MPs. Exactly three decades after the passing of the 1956 Act, this requirement was included in the Constitution Act 1986. During the tenure of the 1949–57 National Government, codification of ministerial eligibility had occurred in Section 6(1) of the Civil List Act 1950, which had provided for ministerial salaries. Before that, this important aspect of the New Zealand constitution had been one of the many conventions that glued the disparate sources into some sort of coherence.

The Māori Seats

With the number of European seats entrenched, the fact that the four Māori seats were not so treated was a glaring gap. Alan Robinson points out, however, that under the 1956

Act 'it is probable that abolition of Maori districts altogether would involve an alteration in the reserved provisions defining European population and specifying the procedure for dividing New Zealand into European electorates'.[64] As explained in Chapter 4 (p. 91), the different attitudes of National and Labour towards Māori representation help explain why the Māori seats were not included in the reserved provisions.

The treatment of the four Māori seats in the Electoral Bill was the focus of debate during its passage. Walter Nash thought that the Māori electorates might have been included as one of the entrenched provisions, with boundaries fixed in the same ways as European electorates.[65] Interestingly, speaking from the government benches, Ralph Hanan agreed on the disparity of treatment between the Māori and non-Maori seats. There would be the 'curious situation' whereby the number of European seats was fixed at 76 and was an entrenched clause but Māori representation 'could be varied at the will of the future Government by a simple majority vote in the House of Representatives. I think that the House will give consideration to that anomaly in the Committee stage. I would think that the Maori representation should be similarly entrenched.'[66] Because debates in the Committee of the Whole House were not fully written down at that time, we have no record of whether or not the inclusion of the Māori electorates or, indeed, any other issues that did not result in amendments, were debated. Picking up this issue – but from a different perspective, perhaps revealing divisions within National on the Māori seats – Marshall expressed his view that he looked forward to having just one electoral roll.[67] Arnold Nordmeyer (Labour) then commented that the move to one electoral roll would have to come from Māori themselves, and Hanan agreed. [68]

Nash's colleague, Eruera Tirikatene, MP for Southern

Maori, who had led the way in attempting to democratise the seats when Labour was in office, made a substantial contribution on this topic. Although he supported the bill, he observed that the Māori electoral districts would continue to be defined by proclamation by the Governor-General. Māori favoured separate representation in the House, Tirikatene argued, but why was the process of defining the boundaries of the four seats not transferred to the Representation Commission? He also pointed out that Māori voters faced many difficulties with compulsory registration and also with voting. 'If we are compelled to register, why should we not be compelled to vote?'[69] Perhaps this was a veiled comment on the relative paucity of Māori electorate voting booths compared with non-Māori ones. If voting was compulsory then adequate provision would have to be made.

Just as in the 21st century, there was no consensus on the continued existence of the Māori seats. Nevertheless, as was expressed in the parliamentary debates of those times, it was plainly unfair that, whether or not the existence of the seats themselves should have been entrenched, the boundaries of the Māori seats would continue to be drawn by declaration of the Governor-General (that is, the government in power) rather than by the neutral Representation Commission which employed clear criteria for boundary-drawing. As Ranginui Walker observes, 'Maori Representation in the New Zealand Parliament exists only at the pleasure of the Pakeha majority'.[70]

Putting the Māori seats under the jurisdiction of the Commission had been part of Labour's Electoral Amendment Act 1975, but all returned to the status quo under the incoming National Government elected in 1975. Indeed, the 1975–76 period saw an intense wrangle between Labour and National over the Māori seats.[71] In brief, the Labour Government elected in 1972 initiated an electoral review.

As Neill Atkinson relates, the select committee included National's 'big three' – Robert Muldoon, John Marshall and Keith Holyoake – as well as Labour's Jonathan Hunt (Chair), Prime Minister Norman Kirk and the Minister of Justice, Martyn Finlay.[72] Labour desired four main reforms: the reduction of the voting age, which succeeded, as explained earlier; the redefinition of voting eligibility, shifting away from entitlement by virtue of being a 'British subject';[73] an increase in the number of parliamentary seats, as also already explained; and the further democratisation of the Māori seats.

The Electoral Amendment Act 1975 changed the definition of Māori to 'any person of the Maori race of New Zealand; and includes any descendant of such a person who elects to be considered as a Maori for the purposes of this Act'. Electors were required to state at the time of the five-yearly general census whether they were Māori and, if so, whether they wished to enrol on the Māori or general roll ('the Maori Option'). The total number of Māori seats in future would depend on the number of Māori who opted for the Māori roll. The 'total' Māori population used in boundary calculations would include those choosing to enrol in the Māori seats and their children. The problem was that the National Opposition regarded any increase in Māori seats as a way of Labour increasing its electoral gains. And National's leader argued that 'the policy of the party which I lead is that these four seats will remain until such time as the Maori people indicate their desire to be on a common roll with no special Maori seats'.[74] However, because these provisions, unlike the increase in seats, were not entrenched, Labour could and did implement them without National support. After the National Party won the 1975 general election, it repealed the sections relating to the Representation Commission as well as the link between Māori enrolment in the Māori seats and their total number, although the 'Maori Option' remained in place. Adversarial politics over electoral matters had been played out as vehemently as had occurred in the years before the passage of the Electoral Act 1956 over the country quota and the composition of the Representation Commission.

At last, in the Electoral Amendment Act 1981, the Representation Commission took over the task of drawing the boundaries of the Māori seats. The only difference between the criteria used for defining the general seats was that Māori iwi were included as a community of interest. (Also, political parties not represented on the Commission [minor parliamentary parties] were given the right to make submissions to it.[75])

In 1993, the other part of the Third Labour Government's attempt to reform the Māori seats was implemented. The Royal Commission on the Electoral System had recommended the seats be abolished, arguing that with a common electoral roll all political parties would have the incentive to seek Māori votes; that Māori would be represented by Māori standing in the party lists because parties would seek to present 'balanced' lists; and that the proposed nationwide threshold of 4% could be waived for parties representing Māori interests.[76] After representations from iwi, the Māori seats remained under MMP and, as with the 1975 legislation, would be linked with the number of Māori registering on the Māori roll. This took the total number of Māori seats to five in the first Parliament elected under the MMP rules (subsequently rising to seven). All parties would have to win 5% of the nationwide party vote to qualify for list seats. Alternatively, if a party won at least one constituency seat it would be entitled to its share of the party list vote even it did not reach the threshold, a rule that ironically would help the Māori Party until it lost its seats in the 2017 general election.

Hence the transition to MMP also encompassed the further democratisation of the Māori seats. Māori could not only choose whether to enrol in a Māori or a general seat, but also their decisions would constitute a five-yearly poll on Māori views of those constituencies. That treating the Māori seat voters fairly had taken so long can at least partly be traced to the unequal treatment of Māori representation in 1956.

Entrenchment and Tradition

Apart from the unresolved matter of the Māori seats, the other parts of the electoral constitution that might have been included in Section 189 were simply not on the political agenda at the time. Mostly, they were pieces of the constitutional edifice that were taken for granted. Note, too, that apart from the Representation Commission and boundary-drawing requirements, the details of the Electoral Bill had been under development for well over a year by officials, with input from the parties outside Parliament and from the National ministers themselves. The inclusions into Section 189 were inserted in the hurried last stages of the Bill's passage. Perhaps there was simply too little time to give thought to what ideally were the essential elements of an electoral bill.

As can be seen from this analysis of the entrenched provisions of the Electoral Act 1956, the electoral issues that had divided the parties, but which they could also compromise upon, were included in Section 189. Thus, at least on these issues, the politicians of the 1950s decided to compromise and negotiate in an attempt to provide future electoral rule stability and, in so doing, protect their own interests. The other issues that found themselves under the entrenchment umbrella were those on which there was cross-party agreement, such as the parliamentary term, an unsettled issue since the 1930s, and the generally accepted measures of the 21-year-old age-eligibility provision and the secret ballot.

Because there was no public input into the content of the

Bill, there was no knowing what inclusions or exclusions to Section 189 the wider public and constitutional experts might have proposed. There was no time for public submissions to be considered by the select committee, no tradition for this to happen, and there were no standing orders that stated that public participation was part of the normal process. There was no warning that this was a Bill that would develop constitutional significance. This was a 'constitutional moment', but it was a fleeting one, dominated by a tiny group of decision-makers. As I argue later, negotiation and compromise are essential ingredients of all constitution-building. But it is decidedly more democratic if the forum in which these sorts of vital democratic policies are decided upon is substantially wider than party caucus and select committee rooms, the offices of the prime minister and other relevant ministers, and officials.

8

The Electoral Act 1956 and Constitutional Evolution in Aotearoa New Zealand

Although it retains its basic design, by the 21st century the New Zealand constitution had been built into a very different edifice from that of the 1950s. New Zealand remains a centralised, parliamentary democracy with a unicameral legislature, Sidney Holland's legacy. It is still a constitutional monarchy. Except for the one entrenched section of the Constitution Act 1986 and the reserved provisions of the Electoral Act 1993, constitutional statutes continue to be unprotected from simple-majority amendment in the House of Representatives. Over sixty years after the passage of the Electoral Act 1956, no single document sets out the essential elements of New Zealand government, although much now is included in statutes and other documents.

Despite noticing the basic similarity in New Zealand's constitutional design, were they to walk into the House of Representatives in 2018 the makers of the Electoral Act 1956 would scarcely recognise it as the institution with which they were familiar. The MMP-elected, multi-party parliaments with their coalition and minority governments would certainly be regarded by the politicians of the 1950s as alien importations into a Westminster system. The select committees would be seen as possessing surprisingly substantial formal powers; and their public hearings and many public submissions would, or should, impress MPs accustomed to a much more closed and executive-dominated legislative process. The social composition of parliament, with its increased numbers of women (although still not 50%), Māori, Pasifika and Asian peoples might surprise and perhaps even shock MPs accustomed to their male, Pākehā-dominated political environment. The 1950s MPs would surely be startled to learn that governments, although powerful when sure of their parliamentary majorities, must frequently negotiate with members of other parliamentary parties as well as with their own caucuses in order to pass legislation through the House.

Governments today, the 1950s MPs would observe, must cope with the challenges of biculturalism, the demand for the political equality of women, and the needs of a rapidly changing multi-ethnic society. International globalisation and the prevalence of neoliberal economic ideas would challenge the policy preconceptions of those MPs.[1] The work and influence of the Waitangi Tribunal would surprise them, as would the institutions and statutes focused on fostering citizen rights, such as the Office of the Ombudsman (which some of them lived to see implemented), the Human Rights Commission, the Official Information Act 1982 and the Bill of Rights Act 1990. The MPs of the earlier era would also discover that, in the 21st century, the mass media has been transformed, political parties have many fewer members than in the earlier period, a lower proportion of the population turns out to vote at general elections, and the doctrine of the electoral mandate holds much less sway over the actions of governments. The 1950s MPs would realise that today's political culture is very different from that when they were sitting in the House of Representatives.

Above all else, those who were involved in the making

of the Electoral Act 1956 might be astonished to find that Section 189 retained its 'moral' force thereafter. Not only that, but the idea of entrenching constitutional clauses enjoyed greater authority and status. In 1993, completely uncontroversially, the new Electoral Act that implemented MMP took the earlier statute as its model and entrenched the term of parliament, the Representation Commission, the definition of the term *general population*, the allowance for the adjustment of the quota, the definition of 'adult' (with the age of voting) and the method of voting. However, despite the changing ideas about the extent to which the New Zealand Parliament was a sovereign body, there was no double entrenchment. This would not have surprised those earlier elected representatives. As Philip Joseph comments, perhaps in 1993 Parliament did not want to 'surrender any more of its legislative freedom than under the existing singly entrenched procedure'.[2] An alternative interpretation might also be that Parliament felt secure in the strength of the single entrenchment. Parliaments are notoriously 'sticky' institutions and, as such, are particularly prone to following familiar pathways when they reform themselves. By the 1990s, Section 189 had become the accepted model for making constitutional changes involving electoral law. Furthermore, however, it had become a blueprint for those who wanted a fully codified and protected constitution.[3]

Despite considerable constitutional development since 1956, much remains 'unsettled', including whether or not New Zealand should adopt a fully codified and judiciable constitution and how this might be achieved. Associated with this is the problematic constitutional status of the Treaty of Waitangi, a major and contested issue whether or not New Zealand adopts a codified constitution. This chapter is not the place to discuss these issues. However, before turning to discussing the lessons and legacy of the Electoral Act 1956,

I focus on the still unsettled aspects of the constitution that would be familiar to its makers. I do not include in this category the MMP electoral rules. Although certain aspects of the electoral system are contested, in 2011 New Zealanders voted in a referendum to retain their version of proportional representation.[4]

The Unsettled Electoral Issues in the 21st Century

As noted above, the 1956 Electoral Act's entrenchment section's direct transfer to its 1993 successor legislation is one of the most outstanding indications of its political acceptability. Yet policy-borrowing from the past brought with it some problems. For example, the new Electoral Commission, a vital institution for a functioning democratic state, was not included as one of the new entrenched provisions in the 1993 Act. The Royal Commission on the Electoral System had both recommended establishing this body and entrenching the term of the Electoral Commissioner.[5] Nevertheless, the Representation Commission remains a protected provision, despite the fact that constituencies do not matter as much for the end result of the distribution of seats under MMP as they did under FPP (although the fairness of boundary-drawing is an important value in itself).

Earlier I showed how the manner in which the Legislative Council was abolished, and the consequential arguments about the comparative virtues of bicameralism and unicameralism, influenced the making of the Electoral Act 1956. The ideal of bicameralism did not die away during the first decades after the Legislative Council disappeared. Agitation for the reinvention of an upper house continued through the 1950s and 1960s, led by the Constitutional Society, who also wanted a written constitution. In 1961 a Public Petitions Committee considered and rejected the Society's recommendations that a second chamber be created.[6] Much later, under the National Party prime minister Jim Bolger, the idea of becoming bicameral again reentered the public agenda and a proposal for a Senate (as an alternative to MMP) was drafted and dismissed by a select committee.[7] The possible construction of a new upper house remains a hardy perennial of political life, although it is difficult to imagine one reappearing in New Zealand given the arguments that would eventuate about any such body's powers and membership, especially regarding the representation of Māori. Its cost would also be a disincentive: New Zealanders are attracted to the idea of having fewer, not more, members of the political class.

The resurrection of an upper house is not a constant unsettled issue. Instead, every now and then it bounces back onto the public agenda. Sidney Holland's abolition of the Legislative Council has had an enduring effect but did not abolish altogether its possible resurrection. Rather than reviving bicameralism New Zealand should continue to improve its unicameral Parliament.

In comparison, the very existence of the Māori electorate seats is a contested part of the political system. Furthermore, if they are to continue, what should be their constitutional status? Apart from representing the Māori culture and Māori interests, an additional justification for the seats has been added since 1956. They are regarded by many as coming under the umbrella of the Treaty of Waitangi. Should the seats be protected from future abolition through entrenchment? As we saw, the democratisation of the Māori seats from 1867 onwards was a long, slow and sad process. They were not entrenched in the 1956 Act, even though there were voices that advocated their inclusion in Section 189. The attitudes between the National and Labour parties were too divided for there to be any compromise on this issue, and the parliamentary Māori voice was too weak to demand that they be protected in the same way as the non-Māori seats. That they were not entrenched in 1956, and again were not given this status in 1993, is symptomatic of their uncertain legitimacy in the Aotearoa New Zealand constitution. Note that the Royal Commission on the Electoral System recommended their abolition, arguing that proportional representation would bring Māori into the House of Representatives.[8]

The Labour Party and more recently the Green Party have consistently argued that the seats must remain so long as Māori want them, while the National Party has from time to time called for their abolition, as have Act and New Zealand First. The governing relationship between National and the Māori Party, however, preserved the seats between 2008 and 2017; and the coalition agreement signed between Labour and New Zealand First in 2017 put a stop to the latter's policy of holding a referendum on the future of the Māori seats. Debate over the Māori seats is not confined to political parties. Constitutional lawyers differ in opinion over whether they should continue to exist and their proper constitutional status.[9]

Clearly, it is only fair for the future of the Māori seats to be left in the hands of Māori voters who anyway pronounce on their effectiveness or ineffectiveness with their regular choice of whether to enrol on the general or Māori roll. This is one unresolved issue that cannot be decided legitimately by either of the processes set out in 1956. It would discriminate against minority opinion were three-quarters of the House to decide that the seats should go; and it would be undemocratic were a majority of voters at a referendum to decide on their future. The constitutional position of the Māori seats remains a major unsettled issue of the 21st century, and is one of the legacies of the 1956 negotiations.

Another particularly contested aspect of the electoral law that remains unresolved because of different parties' views is the issue of the voting rights of prisoners. In 2010 Parliament amended the Electoral Act 1993 to disqualify all prisoners from voting, whereas previously this only applied to those imprisoned for three years or more. This matter was taken through the courts. However, the Court of Appeal found against the appellant on the grounds that the disqualification did not infringe his rights under the Bill of Rights Act 1990.[10] This matter remains an unresolved part of the electoral law and of the rights of New Zealand citizens.

One piece of unfinished business is the triennial parliamentary term, an issue I touched on in the last chapter. Do three years in office allow sufficient time for governments to implement their promises and conduct stable and foresighted public policy? This argument has been balanced against the democratic accountability case: voters need to be able to hold governments and MPs to account, and those occasions need to be relatively frequent in a unicameral, highly centralised, executive-controlled political system. As the Royal Commission on the Electoral System pithily stated, 'there is a balance to be struck between voter sovereignty and effective government'.[11] New Zealand is one of the few outliers with its triennial term: not many other countries have such a short period between elections (although Australia's three-year term at the federal level seems to normalise it more in this part of the world than elsewhere). So it is not surprising that governments and others involved in the public policy process have from time to time called for an extension of the parliamentary term.

The length of the parliamentary term was revived during the Constitutional Advisory Panel's consideration of constitutional issues. This Panel was established under the relationship and confidence and supply agreement between the National Party and the Māori Party after the November 2008 general election, putting in place (along with the Act and United Future parties) a National-led government. One of the terms of reference for the Panel was to consider 'the length of the term of Parliament and whether or not the term should be fixed'.[12] The Panel noted that there was a reasonable level of support for a longer term and recommended more public consultation 'to explore what additional checks and balances might be desirable if a longer term is implemented'. Any change should be accomplished through a referendum rather than three-quarters of the House voting in approval of that change.[13] The length of the parliamentary term thus remains an unsettled aspect of the contemporary constitution.

Finally, there is the unresolved issue of how Aotearoa New Zealand continues to reform its constitution. Although, laudably, the Electoral Act 1956 gave New Zealand an enduring blueprint for constitutional amendment and repeal, it applied to a relatively narrow group of electoral issues. Most of New Zealand's constitutional rules, including the important and influential Bill of Rights 1990, are not protected against the actions of governments armed with simple-majority support in the New Zealand House of Representatives. Although the makers of the Electoral Act gave New Zealand a change formula to follow, and although their successors have faithfully followed that formula, its instructions are – in law, anyway – confined to the protected sections of electoral law. Furthermore, the referendum device for amending or repealing the reserved provisions has at times been criticised because there is no requirement for a minimum turnout of voters for a majority decision to be valid. The arguments on this point can go both ways. Clearly, if a referendum is to be binding (or even strongly recommendatory) then a higher rather than lower turnout is desirable. This is why constitutional referendums should be held with general elections.

Given that the New Zealand constitution will continue to change and, indeed, should change, what lessons can be learned from this story of the making of the Electoral Act 1956?

The Making of the Electoral Act 1956 and Constitutional Change

However much various political players and lobbyists might desire to reform existing rules, constitutional change in stable democratic systems seldom happens except under particular circumstances.[14] These conditions may not all be essential, but at least some of them are necessary for significant change to develop.

First, and most obviously, there must be underlying problems of sufficient importance that they appear on the public agenda. During the 1950s, there were serious faults with the voting and vote-counting processes which led to the revision of the Electoral Act 1927. That there was a democratic deficit was obvious. Not only was there a perceived conflict between accepted political values on the one hand and the processes and structures on the other, it was in the interests of a majority of MPs to resolve this conflict. Furthermore, there was a bitter battle between the two main political parties, National and Labour, over constituency boundary-drawing, as I have shown. When elections are won and lost according to the results of the marginal seats, as they are under FPP electoral rules, the positioning of electorate boundaries matters a great deal. And as the story of the unresolved electoral issues in Chapter 4 shows, the creation of the country quota and its abolition, arguments over whether electorates should be drawn up on the basis of total or adult populations, and disagreements over the population variance permitted between electorates were all salient and contested issues. The National and Labour parties had played adversarial politics over these aspects of the electoral law. There was also the unresolved problem of governments being free to extend the parliamentary term all too easily.

Another reason for change was an anxiety among many people, especially within the National Party, over the future of Parliament without the Legislative Council. This might be labelled a precipitating event, one that pushes political actors into actually doing something about the underlying problems. New Zealand's upper house had been weak – it had few defenders – but critics argued that it either should be reformed or abolished and other more effective constraints created. The problem was how to fetter the actions of a legislature governed by the doctrine of parliamentary sovereignty. That the Electoral Act 1927 had become outdated and inadequate provided an opportunity to attempt to revise and settle certain outstanding electoral problems, thereby helping to constrain a few of the problems of unicameralism and the unfettered power of elected governments.

Thus the conditions were ripe for political resolution: there were serious underlying and unresolved electoral and power-balance problems, and the opportunity to do something about them. But, however principled the goals of the politicians, they also needed to find a way to protect their own interests. Constitutional change is much more likely to occur when it is in the interests of those able to do so, as in 1956. The exception, of course, is the radical reform of an electoral system which happened in New Zealand in the 1990s, not only because there were perceived problems with FPP and because the 1986 Royal Commission on the Electoral System had recommended a change, but also because various decisions made by party leaders led to a range of choices in the public referendum of 1992, which was followed by a final binding referendum in 1993.

Furthermore, insofar as constitutional politics is concerned, one change tends to beget another. This is partly because those involved subsequently must deal with the almost inevitable unintended consequences of major reform, as occurred after the abolition of the Legislative Council. Also, however, a context of heightened expectations about the possibilities of reform can develop. And when what might be labelled a 'change context' evolves, networks of interested political actors become involved in debate and discussion. This occurred in the New Zealand National Party during the 1950s and, also, among academic lawyers with an interest in the constitution, as shown especially in the debate on entrenchment that developed around the possibility of instituting a new upper house. Constitutional epidemics can of course easily develop in countries without written constitutions, for example as the United Kingdom under Tony Blair's prime ministership showed, when power was devolved to Scotland and Wales, the House of Lords was reformed and the Human Rights Act 1998 was passed (to name some of the important reforms).

Frequently, also, legislatures and governments that have been newly elected instigate constitutional and institutional reform. In the early 1950s in New Zealand there was of course a new government in power, and it was also the first time the National Party had been elected to office. The abolition of the Legislative Council was followed by a series of more minor but significant constitutional changes, as outlined earlier, and then by the passing of the Electoral Act 1956.

As the story of this book also suggests, significant constitutional change needs its entrepreneurs. These may be public servants or elected representatives. For example, during the Fourth Labour Government, Sir Geoffrey Palmer (deputy prime minister and then prime minister) took the initiative to make a wide range of changes, including the Constitution

Act 1986, the Bill of Rights Act 1990, reform of the select committee system, and the appointment of the Royal Commission on the Electoral System. During the late 1940s and 1950s New Zealand had that unlikely constitutional leader, Sidney Holland, promoting the abolition of the Legislative Council, followed by, of course, by the lawyer and Minister of Justice, John Marshall, and other interested MPs. Prime Minister Sidney Holland, however, continued to provide the necessary political management for negotiating political solutions to constitutional problems.

Thus, from the evidence of this story, a number of circumstances help explain the small, quiet constitutional revolution carried out in 1956: there were underlying problems with the operation of the electoral system, including some outstanding and unsettled electoral issues; it was in the political actors' interests to try to solve those problems; there was the opportunity to remedy the contested issues when the Electoral Act 1927 was revised; a general context of constitutional change existed that was important in fostering further reforms; there was a brand new governing team in power, thirsty to make its mark on history; and there was a network of reformers led by constitutional entrepreneurs.

Constitutional decisions are inevitably the products of bargaining and compromise because, as shown here, different political actors have different interests. Electoral systems are particularly vulnerable to alteration by political parties, simply because they represent different sections of the community and/or benefit from different electoral mechanisms. Hence it is unsurprising that, wherever possible, legislatures attempt to hold tight their power to change electoral rules. Without a fully codified constitution to stabilise and protect existing rules, the decisions made on the shape and details of the New Zealand electoral system have almost always been made in the House of Representatives. The exceptions were the triennial term referendums in 1967 and 1990, when the electors decided not to change the status quo. The major exception, however, was the adoption of MMP, made by referendum.

From 1956 onwards New Zealand's parliament has turned itself temporarily into a 'constituent' assembly through employing its select committee system. There, decisions are debated, traded, discarded, or implemented through a series of compromises. This process developed over the years into a much more democratic process than during the 1950s. Since 1979, a committee has reviewed electoral law and practice after every general election. It calls for public submissions and holds public hearings.[15]

Although most of the changes included in the Electoral Act 1956 were the fruit of consultation by officials with political parties outside Parliament, the making of Section 189, as explained here, was hurried and secretive. It was an elite process, not a democratically defensible one. In that way, it was certainly not an ideal model of how to change a constitution. Citizens did not even have the opportunity to make submissions to the select committee that formally approved the inclusion of Section 189. It would not be until 1979 that bills (except for money bills) would automatically go to select committees, and not until after the standing orders review that resulted in the committee reforms of 1985 that committees would invariably advertise for submissions, thus democratically involving voters.[16] Public involvement in constitutional decision-making is essential because the public have a legitimate voice in expressing their views on future changes, and legitimacy is enhanced when reform is widely debated and all voices heard and heeded. Parliamentary committees can achieve that participation. However, there is a very strong case to be made for creating independent constituent conventions when making radical constitutional change. Such conventions remove decisions from those with political interests to pursue.[17]

The voters should have been consulted in 1956. Haste – getting the legislation in place for the next general election, just one year away – and, perhaps, policy complexity meant that there was no referendum on the issue, as indeed had been suggested by various MPs, including the prime minister. The select committee appointed to scrutinise the Electoral Bill 1956 should have been allowed more time to consider it. That committee should have called for and heard a wide range of submissions on its proposals. The use of urgency, an unsavoury legislative process unless under certain narrow and justifiable circumstances,[18] meant that Section 189 was implemented in a highly undemocratic fashion. A tiny political elite played around with the New Zealand constitution behind closed doors.

The undemocratic making of Section 189 meant that, apart from the admirably dutiful attention paid by the newspapers to the Electoral Act 1956, this constitutional fiddling was never a 'noisy' constitutional issue. Its lack of publicity at the time may help to explain its absence from almost all of New Zealand's political histories.

The Legacy of Section 189

The most remarkable legacy of the single entrenchment in Section 189 of the 1956 Electoral Act is that parliamentarians have complied with it. As has been demonstrated, none of the reserved provisions was amended or repealed without either being approved by a majority of voters at a general election or the support of at least three-quarters of the House.

Indeed, on only one occasion between 1956 and 2017 was a reserved provision amended that was contested and did not have the full consent of the House. This happened when, after the binding referendum on the Electoral Act 1993, the major political parties decided to change the layout of the new ballot paper so that there would be a single ballot paper rather than one for the electorate vote and a separate ballot paper for the party vote. The minor parties disagreed with the proposal. As David McGee writes, 'This involved a repeal and replacement of the provision relating to the method of voting. The proposal was carried by a vote of 79 to 13, four more than the 75 percent majority of votes required.'[19]

Not only was the single entrenchment clause respected but, also, each time a protected provision of the Act was amended, the process followed was appropriate for the measure being considered. The parliamentarians followed the analysis of the Royal Commission on the Electoral System:

> A referendum should be required, it could be argued, when a major constitutional change is being introduced. More specifically the people should be asked to consent if the change means that parliamentarians are either enhancing their power or reducing the rights of the electorate. Sometimes those 2 circumstances will overlap as with an increase in the term of Parliament. An example of the first alone (at least so far as the major parties are concerned) would be the replacement of a proportional representation system by a plurality one. An example of the second alone would be a reduction of the rights of suffrage, for example by increasing the voting age.[20]

Thus, deciding to reduce the voting age through the decisions of the House was appropriate, as happened in 1969 and 1974. An increase in the length of the parliamentary term, however, should be the people's choice (although a national emergency might justifiably see that decision in the hands of the MPs, but only as a temporary measure).[21] Changing the ratio between the South Island and North Island seats did not appreciably affect voters' rights and powers, and thus was properly agreed to in Parliament. This is an example of a policy change that is inappropriate for decision by referendum because its complexity makes public education a difficult task. Public submissions on complicated constitutional matters, however, should be invoked. Despite the ambiguity of the provision in Section 189 protecting 'the method of voting', radical electoral system change, as happened with the transition from FPP to MMP, could only legitimately be made by the electors.

As can be seen, behavioural norms developed in the House of Representatives concerning the appropriateness of each change mechanism. These norms were not only based on what was deemed constitutionally appropriate but also on the anticipated reactions of voters were those norms to be infringed. Political interests and democratic values are intertwined in democratic politics. The secret is to find rules and practices where the interests have the incentive to fulfil the values.

The legacy of Section 189 was even more far-reaching than compliance with its provisions and the development of norms about the appropriateness of each change mechanism. As is apparent from the story told in this book, the notion that parliamentary compliance with single entrenchment might actually be, or become, a constitutional convention was simply not part of the vocabulary of the 1950s. This changed over time after 1956. Writing decades later, David McGee observes, 'An attempt to exploit single entrenchment to circumvent the protection of the reserved provisions would be constitutionally improper and arguably a breach of constitutional convention.'[22] Perhaps Section 189 is an example of how constitutional conventions emerge. A convenient and plausible norm develops, usually justified in terms of behavioural principles, and that norm then acquires 'convention' status, a more formal rule that helps to regulate the allocation, distribution and use of political power.

In New Zealand's case, the 'moral' obligation to respect single entrenchment was significantly fortified not only through tradition and practice but also by several other factors: a significant change to the standing orders of the House of Representatives; the institutionalisation of the committee system of the House, especially the development of consensual norms when considering electoral issues; and changing ideas about the nature and extent of parliamentary sovereignty.

In 1988, recognising that there should be limits on what one parliament could impose on its successors when it came to writing 'manner and form' legislative clauses, the Electoral Law Committee of the New Zealand House of Representatives recommended:

> That certain stated provisions of the Electoral Act should be subject to repeal or amendment only if the legislation recites that it is repealing or amending a reserved provision and is supported by three-quarters of all members of the House or comes into force if subsequently endorsed by the electorate in a referendum. The protecting legislation should itself be protected in the same way.[23]

No change was made, however, until 1995, when the Standing Orders Committee conducted a major review of the House's rules in preparation for the multi-party Parliament expected to be elected after the first MMP general election in 1996. After observing that the rule at that time allowed proposals for entrenched provisions to be carried by a 'bare majority' and observing that this was 'inequitable', it recommended that when proposing a provision is entrenched, that proposal 'can only be carried if it can itself secure the special majority it proposed for any future amendment of it. Thus, if a proposal requires a 65 percent majority for amendment, that proposal itself must be agreed to by a 65 percent majority.'[24] This was accepted. The relevant standing order is as follows:

> A proposal for entrenchment must itself be carried in a committee of the whole House by the majority that it would require for the amendment or repeal of the provision to be entrenched.
>
> A proposal for entrenchment is any provision in a bill or amendment to a bill that would require that that provision or amendment or any other provision can be amended or repealed only by a majority of more than 50 percent plus one of all the members of the House.[25]

The single entrenchment clause was strengthened by this change in standing orders because, while it made it more difficult to propose changes that did not have sufficient support behind them, it also recognised the importance of requiring super-majorities to repeal or amend particular aspects of the constitution. Note, however, that the standing order applies only to the use of super-majorities, not to the use of the referendum when changing what is now Section 268 of the Electoral Act 1993, as pointed out by Philip Joseph.[26]

The conventions under which decisions were made in parliamentary committees that examined and reviewed the electoral rules, also underwent change after the passage of the Electoral Act 1956. From then on, proposed electoral changes were discussed and settled in post-election electoral committees that employed consensual means of agreeing on such matters, including issues that were not covered by the entrenching clause, according to research by James Christmas.[27] The bipartisan negotiations that characterised the making of that Act, and their pursuit of compromise and consensus, became the accepted pattern of behaviour for settling electoral issues.

Section 189 also had a contagion effect that reached beyond the scope of the electoral matters covered in the 1956 legislation. Under Section 131 of the Electoral Act 1993, if an electorate seat in the House of Representatives is vacated and that happens within six months of the date of the expiration of the parliament, a by-election can be waived if approved by a 75% majority of all MPs.

A further significant legacy of the Electoral Act 1956 was that it helped stimulate more nuanced interpretations of parliamentary sovereignty than presented in the political debates of the 1950s. However, as shown in the course of this book, even at that time some constitutional lawyers were arguing that parliamentary sovereignty was not so absolute a constitutional doctrine as often believed: 'manner and form' statutes, insofar as constitutional provisions are concerned (not substantive public policy measures), could indeed bind successor parliaments. The subsequent development in legal thinking about the effectiveness of entrenchment measures was in part due to constitutional scholars having to consider the legal as well as political efficacy of the single entrenchment clause contained in Section 189.

Note that the Bill of Rights 1990 in its draft form was doubly entrenched. The parliamentary committee that considered the draft agreed with the White Paper that accompanied the draft legislation, which stated:

> The courts [then] are likely to hold, if the matter is raised with them, that a provision in the Bill of Rights protecting its guarantees from abrogation and encroachment except following the support of a referendum or a three-quarters majority in the House would be effective. Future Parliaments would have to comply with it.[28]

In order for such a bill to be accepted by the courts, however, it would have to have been passed either by a referendum or by the near-unanimous support of the House.[29] In the end, dominant opinion, including that of most lawyers, was against entrenchment of the Bill of Rights Act.

Despite the paradigmatic nature of parliamentary sovereignty at the time of the drafting of Section 189, that provision placed parliamentary sovereignty on the constitutional agenda and made it just that much more vulnerable to challenge. This is not to downplay the influence of other social and legal forces on ideas about parliamentary sovereignty, especially in light of considering Māori rights under the Treaty of Waitangi 1840 and human rights generally. 'Parliamentary sovereignty', as a convention of the constitution, depends for its effectiveness on its general acceptance by the public and by members of the political elite in particular, including the judiciary. At the heart of the convention of parliamentary sovereignty is the normative notion of where responsibility sits in a political system. Like all conventions, however, the interpretation of parliamentary sovereignty can differ, often quite subtly, through time, and it stimulates much debate and discussion.[30] This has been described by Chief Justice Sian Elias as a 'merry-go-round'.[31]

The primary normative usefulness of the convention of parliamentary sovereignty is its assumption that democratic power is best situated in the hands of those who are elected by, and responsible to, voters. This is the argument that, in New Zealand, has always underpinned its strength. Concomitantly, it can be reasoned, decision-making powers should be in the hands of those who can be unseated by voters, not held by unelected judges. Integral to this democratic formulation is the often-neglected convention that there is a legitimate parliamentary opposition: the parliamentary minority (or collection of minorities) with the constitutional right and duty to criticise, propose alternative ideas, and delay and even obstruct the parliamentary majority in its pursuit of policy implementation. Hence the doctrine of parliamentary sovereignty is closely linked with the Westminster concept of responsible, representative government and a loyal opposition. The acceptance in 1956 that the Opposition has a legitimate role to play in deciding upon certain constitutional and electoral matters contributed an important democratic practice to the functioning of Parliament and government.

The development of the New Zealand constitution, at least until the early part of the 21st century, demonstrated a continuing belief in the supremacy of parliament alongside more nuanced interpretations of the actual limitations of its sovereignty, including obligations to follow its own formal rules such as single entrenchment clauses. It is interesting that, by 2017, no attempt had been made by MPs to doubly entrench any procedural rule. In that way, parliamentarians continue to have an escape clause – if desired they could go against established convention and repeal the entrenching clause. Nevertheless, as indicated above, contemporary legal thinking is that such a move could well be challenged in the courts. Writing about the United Kingdom, one commentator notes:

> Though it is hardly ever remarked upon in discussions of the role of convention, any listing of conventional rules in the United Kingdom would have to include the most basic – the rule that the legally unlimited power of the legislature is not used to its limits, but is exercised in accordance with broad principles described in such terms as constitutionalism, the rule of law and toleration of minority rights. It is a good example of a convention that is both general in its formulation and founded on principle rather than precedent.[32]

In New Zealand, to comply with the single entrenchment clause in Section 189 is to act constitutionally.

We can be quite sure that the makers of the Electoral Act 1956 would have been amazed and pleased at the impact of their negotiated and bargained attempt to constrain the actions of future political actors when it came to electoral rule change. The Act's architects would also have been interested, but not perhaps quite as pleased, to learn that legal thinking concerning the role of the courts in protecting 'manner and form' legislative processes had developed considerably during the last five decades. The insertion of Section 189 into the Electoral Act 1956 might have been a quiet and seemingly unimportant innovation but, like all constitutional reforms, it has had unanticipated consequences.

The Electoral Act 1956: Constitutional Principles and Ideas

It is easy to depict the making of the Electoral Act 1956 as a consequence of MPs intent on protecting and pursuing their own party interests within the framework of accepted ideas such as parliamentary sovereignty and powerful single-party governments. This interpretation is too simple.

Whereas Britain had developed an indigenous political structure, New Zealand continued to borrow ideas and practices from the former imperial power. By 1984, as Colin James writes, 'The legislative and legal systems were closely modelled on the British in structure and procedure and followed British precedent almost slavishly.'[33] Yet, in the course of its political development, Aotearoa New Zealand developed its own character as it adapted its politics to its distinctive environment. New Zealand formed its own political identity through the politics of distance, isolation and an almost careless adaptation of the original British model given to it in the early 19th century. The local adaptations included the creation of the Māori seats (1867), the early enfranchisement of women (1893) and, of course, the move to become a unicameral Parliament in 1950. With the advantage of hindsight, we can now see that this last action signalled a marked shift away from the inherited model of Parliament and government.

Leaving aside the innovation of entrenching parts of the electoral law, note that the Office of Ombudsman (1962) was picked up from the Scandinavian states, and the 1982 legislation that made government information more accessible to the public was certainly not a feature of the British constitution until relatively recently. The Bill of Rights Act 1990 owed more to the Canadian Charter of Rights and Freedoms and the US Constitution than that of the UK's, and later New Zealand adopted a system of proportional representation modelled on the German rules. The transfer of constitutional ideas and institutions from one polity to another commonly occurs: New Zealand, however, borrowed ideas from a range of models. As shown in this book, when the New Zealand Parliament drafted Section 189 of the Electoral Act 1956, it borrowed from its own past and from other Westminster jurisdictions. Later, it looked further afield.

Constitutional policy transfer is endemic in democratic systems, partly because there are fads and fashions in constitutional ideas but also because of the universality of certain principles, such as the separation of powers and the protection of individuals against the state.[34] But has New Zealand shown a particular propensity to borrow its constitutional ideas from abroad? This is unanswerable without extensive comparative analysis. However, overseas and local observers of New Zealand constitutional practices have noted the readiness with which decision-makers experiment with existing political arrangements. It is a willingness that has led to refreshing and rejuvenating reforms, some of them controversial and hotly contested. Reform exercises inevitably involve looking elsewhere for new ideas. Rather than seeing New Zealand's frequent practice of transferring constitutional ideas from abroad as merely copying others, it can be viewed as an openness to entertain fresh political ideas and a demonstration of an absence of intellectual insularity. These traits were apparent in the creation of Section 189 of the Electoral Act 1956.

That New Zealand MPs in 1956 were willing to limit their future freedom to change aspects of the electoral rules was without doubt partly a desire to protect their own party interests. In a sense this was a pragmatic adjustment to the realities of the two-party political system of the times and its alternating fortunes of political power. However, the historical episode explored in this book also illustrates the decision-makers' awareness of the importance of complying with particular constitutional doctrines and democratic principles. Most obviously, the MPs were operating within a worldview dominated by the constitutional idea of parliaments that could not bind the actions of their successors, the cultural notion that governments must respect electoral mandates, and the institutional ideal of the two-party system with alternating governments. Parliamentary parties either won political power and held it completely or else went into opposition to criticise and play the role of government-in-waiting. The important modification of these ideas was that it incorporated the views of the Opposition – the parliamentary minority – into decision-making on a select group of electoral rules. Alternatively, the powers of decision-making were transferred to the voters. Either way, the mechanisms employed were consensual in style and the desired outcome was to secure a measure of consensus across parliament or society, and hence argue a strong legitimacy for change.

However, as well as fulfilling the principle of achieving a consensus of political views, other democratic values were also influential. First, the principle of fairness, which should be pursued when electorate boundaries are drawn. Second, the principle of due process was a significant normative influence to those involved in the making of the Electoral Act. This had been put into practice when the Representation Commission was established decades previously, with its independent and final decisions on electorate boundaries. But the existence and subsequent brusque abolition of the country quota and the partisan appointments to the Representation Commission had led to accusations of partisan bias when it came to the rules of the electoral system. Respect for due process, as well as fairness, led to the 1956 agreement that each major party should have just one voice on the Commission. Third, the principle of equality influenced the negotiations over the content of Section 189. While fairness and due process are natural democratic twins, reinforce each other and can relatively easily be put into practice, equality is a much more difficult goal to achieve. This is because it refers to policy outcomes rather than policy processes. It is far easier to settle on how to resolve matters in ways that respect all political interests than it is to design guidelines to make interests count equally. When it came to counting voters and determining electorate boundaries Labour and National had different views, as explained earlier. On this issue, compromises had to be negotiated and, as happens with many bargains, each side had to give way on something that mattered to them.

Hence, democratic principles as well as constitutional and cultural characteristics played their part in influencing political behaviour during the development of Section 189, both in terms of limiting each party's future constitutional flexibility and, also, in terms of the content of the provisions themselves. That there was bargaining between the National and Labour parties was to be expected: different political interests place different values on certain formulae. It was to the credit of those involved that, for once, partisanship was set aside in the search of cross-party consensus in order to resolve unsettled electoral issues. In the process, the National and Labour MPs, guided by their advisers, put in place a formula that borrowed ideas from the past and from elsewhere. They also invented something new. The single entrenchment, that 'moral' constraint, was a creative solution to the problems that they faced, were the electoral rules to continue to be the subject of partisan politics.

Constitutional Change and the Electoral Act 1956

The crafting of Section 189 of the Electoral Act 1956 was a considerable achievement that set the New Zealand Parliament in a new direction. John Marshall and his colleagues introduced a measure of balance to the constitution by putting in place procedural constraints that have had a long and valuable impact on how New Zealanders repeal and amend certain parts of the electoral law. They did this by constraining their own future actions. 'Moral' constraint became a parliamentary convention and then, when 'manner and form' legislative instructions became more acceptable, evolved into a form of constitutional law.

Section 189 laid down principled pathways to constitutional change that have affected how New Zealanders continue to redesign and rebuild their constitution ever since the 1950s. Thus the story of the Electoral Act 1956 shows how the creation of institutional norms and the prevalence of democratic principles can act as significant limitations on self-interested political behaviour.

The makers of the Electoral Act 1956, with their inclusion of Section 189, solved some problems, and those solutions proved to be lasting ones. Their agenda was confined to electoral matters; their own attitudes and interests influenced their framing of the Bill; their timeline was the immediate future; and, as always, there were unanticipated consequences of their decisions and non-decisions. Nevertheless, the decision-makers of the 1950s also found a solution that fulfilled democratic principles such as fairness and equal treatment within the electoral law. They did this by hoping that their parliamentary successors would, as they did, respect the moral sanction of single entrenchment. In so doing they made a remarkable contribution to their country's future.

The constitution of Aotearoa New Zealand has been rather like the development of this country's 19th- and early 20th-century wooden villas. Rooms have been removed and added on over the years, walls knocked down and then reinstated, and second stories have been placed over the original roofs. Nevertheless, the house remains identifiably an old villa with its original character. Wooden houses are resilient in earthquakes, as New Zealand's flexible constitution has proved to be. But sometimes houses need new foundations. Section 189 of the Electoral Act was a stouter support than expected at the time, but it became a pillar of the constitution. The question is whether the old wooden structure needs further strengthening.

Notes

Preface

1 Bernard Grofman, ed., *Political Science as Puzzle Solving* (The University of Michigan Press, Ann Arbor, 2001). The chapters fall within the 'soft' rational choice tradition of political analysis.
2 Grofman, 4.
3 Claudia Geiringer, Polly Higbee and Elizabeth McLeay, *What's the Hurry? Urgency in the New Zealand Legislative Process, 1987–2010* (Victoria University Press, Wellington, 2011).

1: The 'Remarkable' Electoral Act 1956

1 Sidney Holland, *NZPD*, Vol. 310 (1956), 2902.
2 The Act can be seen at: http://www.nzlii.org/nz/legis/hist_act/ea19561956n107130/. Accessed 6 April 2017.
3 Sir Kenneth Keith, 'On the Constitution of New Zealand: An Introduction to the Foundations of the Current Form of Government', in *Cabinet Manual* (Cabinet Office, Department of Prime Minister, Wellington, 2017), 6. At: https://cabinetmanual.cabinetoffice.govt.nz/files/cabinet-manual-2017.pdf. Accessed 21 August 2017; See Standing Order 266, *Standing Orders of the New Zealand House of Representatives* (Wellington, 2017). At: https://www.parliament.nz/en/pb/parliamentary-rules/standing-orders-2017/. Accessed 27 October 2017; See also Mary Harris and John Wilson, eds., *McGee: Parliamentary Practice in New Zealand*, 4th edn, (Oratia Books, Auckland, 2017), 246, 445–6.
4 There was a promising but unsuccessful attempt in 1914 to reform the Legislative Council by making it an elected upper house. See Keith Jackson, *The New Zealand Legislative Council: A Study of the Establishment, Failure and Abolition of an Upper House* (University of Otago Press, Dunedin, 1972), Chapter 14.
5 Keith Jackson, 'The Abolition of the New Zealand Upper House of Parliament', in Lawrence D. Langley and David M. Olson, eds., *Two into One. The Politics and Processes of National Legislative Cameral Change* (Westview Press, Boulder, 1991), 45.

6 The classic work on veto points is: George Tsebelis, *Veto Players. How Political Institutions Work* (Princeton University Press, Princeton, 2002).

7 Jan-Erik Lane, *Constitutions and Political Theory* (Manchester University Press, Manchester and London, 1966), 9. See also Matthew S. R. Palmer, 'What is New Zealand's Constitution and who interprets it? Constitutional realism and the importance of public office-holders', *Public Law Review*, Vol. 17 (2006), especially 134–41. Palmer makes the valuable point that one of the problems in New Zealand is that we –as a political culture – are not always 'sure what is constitutional', and he sets out the consequences of this, 141.

8 One review was by a parliamentary select committee: Constitutional Arrangements Committee, 'Inquiry to Review New Zealand's Existing Constitution: Report of the Constitutional Arrangements Committee' (August 2005). At: http://www.converge.org.nz/pma/cacrep05.pdf. Accessed 26 February 2017. The other review was by a government-appointed panel: Constitutional Advisory Panel, 'A Report on a Conversation. He Kōtunga Kōrero mō Te Kaupapa Ture O Aotearoa' (November 2013). At: http://www.ourconstitution.org.nz/store/doc/FR. Accessed 26 February 2017.

9 The conferences resulted in books: Alan Simpson, ed., *The Constitutional Implications of MMP* (Occasional Publication No. 9, School of Political Science and International Relations, Victoria University of Wellington, 1998); Colin James, ed., *Building the Constitution* (Institute of Policy Studies, Victoria University of Wellington, 2000); and Caroline Morris, Jonathan Boston and Petra Butler, eds., *Reconstituting the Constitution* (Springer, Heidelburg Dordrecht London New York, 2011).

10 Andrew Butler and Geoffrey Palmer, *A Constitution for Aotearoa New Zealand* (Victoria University Press, Wellington, 2016), Section 116, 75; 231–34. See: http://constitutionaotearoa.org.nz. Accessed 26 February 2017.

11 See especially the following chapters, all from James, ed., *Building the Constitution*: Moana Jackson, 'Where Does Sovereignty Lie?', 196–200; Justice Edward Durie, 'The Treaty in the Constitution', 201–4; Whata Winiata, 'How Can or Should the Treaty be Reflected in Institutional Design?', 205–6; and Denese Henare, 'Can or Should the Treaty be Replaced', 207–13.

12 Mark Hickford, 'Considering the Historical-Political Constitution and the Imperial Inheritance in Mid-Nineteenth Century New Zealand: Balance, Diversity and Alternative Constitutions', *New Zealand Journal of Public and International Law*, Vol. 12 (2014), 146.

13 For a similar observation see Peter Franks and Jim McAloon, *The New Zealand Labour Party 1916–2016* (Victoria University Press, Wellington, 2016), 18.

14 Philippa Mein Smith, *A Concise History of New Zealand*, 2nd edn., (Cambridge University Press, Melbourne, 2005), 183. I gratefully

borrow the notion of 'unsettling' and apply it to aspects of the New Zealand constitution.

15 Michael King, *The Penguin History of New Zealand* (Penguin, Auckland, 2003), pp. 411–32.

16 Robert Chapman, 'From Labour to National', in W. H. Oliver, ed., with B. R. Williams, *The Oxford History of New Zealand* (The Clarendon Press, Oxford; and Oxford University Press, Wellington, 1981), 333–68. On National's origins, development and policies see 334–37 and 356–63. Two recent interesting histories discuss the 1950s but, again, do not discuss the Electoral Act 1956. See: Jenny Carlyon and Diana Morrow, *Changing Times: New Zealand Since 1945* (Auckland University Press, Auckland, 2013); and Paul Moon, *New Zealand in the Twentieth Century: The Nation, The People* (Harper Collins, Auckland, 2011).

17 John Marshall, *Memoirs. Volume One: 1912 to 1960* (Collins, Auckland, 1983), 246–8.

18 See Keith Eunson, 'Sidney Holland', in *Mirrors on the Hill. Reflections on New Zealand's Political Leaders* (Dunmore Press, Palmerston North, 2001), 29–46.

19 Ross Doughty, *The Holyoake Years* (Ross A. Doughty, Feilding, 1977); Barry Gustafson, *Kiwi Keith. A Biography of Keith Holyoake* (Auckland University Press, Auckland, 2007); and Margaret Clark, ed., *Keith Holyoake: Towards a Political Biography* (The Dunmore Press, Palmerston North, 1997).

20 Sheila M. Belshaw, *Man of Integrity. A Biography of Sir Clifton Webb* (Dunmore Press, Palmerston North, 1979).

21 John L. Robson, *Sacred Cows and Rogue Elephants: Policy Development in the New Zealand Justice Department* (Government Printing Office, Wellington, 1987). The Secretary of Justice at that time was S. T. Barnett.

22 King, *The Penguin History of New Zealand*, 447–465. King entitles his chapter on that period 'A Revolution Begun'.

23 See: Andrew Geddis, *Electoral Law in New Zealand: Practice and Policy* (Wellington, LexisNexis, 2007); and Philip Joseph, *Constitutional and Administrative Law in New Zealand*, 4th edn. (Brookers, Wellington, 2014)

24 Constitutional Arrangements Committee, 'Inquiry to Review New Zealand's Existing Constitutional Arrangements'.

25 The Royal Commission on the Electoral System [RCES], *Report of the Royal Commission on the Electoral Commission: Towards a Better Democracy* (The Government Printer, Wellington, 1986), 287–92.

26 Department of Justice, 'The Electoral Law of New Zealand: A Brief History', in RCES, *Report of the Royal Commission on the Electoral Commission*, Appendix A, 68–81. According to The Hon. Mr Justice Wallace in his 'Foreword' to the electoral history, B. Ritchie wrote much

of the electoral history and after he died the work was completed by H. G Hoffman.

27 Neill Atkinson, *Adventures in Democracy. A History of the Vote in New Zealand* (University of Otago Press, Dunedin, in association with the Electoral Commission, 2003), 166–67.

28 James Christmas, 'Consensus Gained, Consensus Maintained? Changing New Zealand's Electoral Law 1927–2007', MA Thesis (Victoria University of Wellington, 2010), especially 35–40. At http://researcharchive.vuw.ac.nz/xmlui/handle/10063/1214. Accessed 15 October 2017.

29 K. J. Scott, *The New Zealand Constitution* (Oxford University Press, London, 1962), 6–16.

30 As Richard Boast observes, New Zealand historians have tended to neglect constitutional and legal history. See 'New Zealand Legal History and New Zealand Historians: A Non-Meeting of Minds', *Journal of New Zealand Studies*, No. 9 (2010), 1–36.

2: New Zealand's Constitution in the 1950s

1 John Marshall, *Memoirs. Volume One: 1912 to 1960* (William Collins, Auckland, 1983), 248.

2 Alan Ward, *An Unsettled History. Treaty Claims in New Zealand Today* (Bridget Williams Books, Wellington, 1999), 20.

3 Ibid., 20.

4 Jan-Erik Lane, *Constitutions and Political Theory* (Manchester University Press, Manchester and London, 1966), 198.

5 Leslie Lipson, *The Politics of Equality: New Zealand Adventures in Democracy* (University of Chicago Press, Chicago, 1948), 10.

6 See G. A. Wood, 'The Former "Dominion" of New Zealand', *Political Science*, Vol. 26 (1974), 2–10.

7 Elizabeth McLeay, *The Cabinet and Political Power in New Zealand* (Oxford University Press, Auckland, 1995); and Geoffrey Palmer, 'The Cabinet, the Prime Minister and the Constitution: The Constitutional Background to Cabinet', *New Zealand Journal of Public and International Law*, Vol. 4 (2006), 1–36.

8 Keith Jackson, 'Government Succession in New Zealand', *Journal of Commonwealth and Comparative Politics*, Vol. 15 (1977), 151.

9 Ibid., 151.

10 See Elizabeth McLeay, 'Buckle, Board, Team or Network? Understanding Cabinet', *New Zealand Journal of Public and International Law*, Vol. 4 (June 2006), 37–54.

11 On leadership selection and tenure see: William P. Cross and André Blais, *Politics at the Centre. The Selection and Removal of Party Leaders in the Anglo Parliamentary Democracies* (Oxford, Oxford University Press, 2012).

12 David Lange, 'Foreword', 9 October 1984, in *Cabinet Office Manual (*Cabinet Office, Prime Minister's Department, Wellington, 1979).
13 P. G. Millen, 'Introduction and Historical Note', 1983, in ibid.
14 John Martin, 'The Changing Governance: The State Services in the Holyoake Years', in Margaret Clark, ed., *Sir Keith Holyoake: Towards a Political Biography* (The Dunmore Press, Palmerston North, 1997), 61.
15 Ibid., 62.
16 See especially, Robert Chapman, 'The Response to Labour and the Question of Parallelism of Opinion, 1928–1960', in Robert Chapman and Keith Sinclair, eds., *Studies of a Small Democracy* (University of Auckland, Auckland, 1963), 221–54, reprinted in Elizabeth McLeay, ed., *New Zealand Politics and Social Patterns: Selected Works by Robert Chapman* (Victoria University Press, Wellington, 1999), 132–62.
17 See W. K. Jackson and G. A. Wood, 'The New Zealand Parliament and Māori Representation', *Historical Studies,* Vol. 11 (1963–65), 383–96; E. M. McLeay, 'Political Argument about Representation: The Case of the Māori Seats', *Political Studies,* Vol. 28 (1980), 43–62; New Zealand Parliamentary Library, 'The Origins of the Māori Seats' (2003). At: https://www.parliament.nz/resource/en-NZ/00PLLawRP03141/e27e432e971eb1f60ea75b00c987a39e4b2e62ce. Accessed 24 May 2017; M.P. Sorrenson, 'A History of Māori Representation in Parliament', in RCES, *Report of the Royal Commission on the Electoral System: Towards a Better Democracy* (Government Printer, Wellington, 1986), B, 13–21.
18 Ibid., Sorrenson, B, 18.
19 Ibid., B, 15.
20 Neill Atkinson, *Adventures in Democracy. A History of the Vote in New Zealand* (Dunedin University of Otago Press, 2003), 50.
21 Paul Pierson, 'The Limits of Design: Explaining Institutional Origins and Change', *Governance,* Vol. 13 (2000), 479.
22 On the 1950s committees see John Halligan, 'Continuity and Change in the New Zealand Parliament', PhD Thesis (Victoria University of Wellington, 1980), especially 203–5.
23 Ibid., 217–8.
24 Claudia Geiringer, Polly Higbee and Elizabeth McLeay, *What's the Hurry? Urgency in the New Zealand Legislative Process 1987–2010* (Victoria University Press, Wellington, 2011). See 21–44 for a brief history of the urgency provision and an explanation of how it has worked.
25 See Elizabeth McLeay, 'The Opposition in New Zealand: Evolution; Institutionalisation; Opportunity', Paper prepared for 'Her Majesty's Oppositions', Roundtable, Public Policy Institute, Australian Catholic University, Canberra, 21–23 February 2011.
26 Arend Lijphart, 'Democratic Political Systems: Types, Cases, Causes, and Consequences', *Journal of Theoretical Politics,* Vol. 1 (1989), 34.
27 Arend Lijphart, *Patterns of Democracy. Government Forms and*

Performances in Thirty-Six Countries (Yale University Press, New Haven and London, 1999), 2–30.

28 Ibid., 25.

29 R. A. W. Rhodes, John Wanna and Patrick Weller, *Comparing Westminster* (Oxford University Press, Oxford, 2009), 7, Table 1.1.

30 See George Tsebelis, *Veto Players. How Political Institutions Work* (Princeton University Press, Princeton, New Jersey, 2002).

31 Jack Vowles, Peter Aimer, Helena Catt, Jim Lamare and Raymond Miller, *Towards Consensus? The 1993 Election in New Zealand and the Transition to Proportional Representation* (Auckland, Auckland University Press, 1995), 4. The authors then go on to discuss the loss of consensus, 5–8.

32 Richard Mulgan, 'Political Culture', in G. R. Hawke, ed., *Changing Politics? The Electoral Referendum 1993* (Institute of Policy Studies, Victoria University of Wellington, 1993), 45.

33 Ibid., 44–9.

34 Shaun Goldfinch and Brian Roper, 'Treasury's role in State Policy Formulation During the Post-war Era', in Brian Roper and Chris Rudd, eds., *State and Economy in New Zealand* (Auckland, Oxford University Press, 1993), 54.

35 Mulgan, 'Political Culture', 47. For an excellent description of the constituency work of MPs during the period see Robert K. Kelson, *The Private Member of Parliament and the Formation of Public Policy. A New Zealand Case Study* (University of Toronto Press, Toronto, 1964), 119–26.

36 J. Theodore Anagnoson, 'Home Style in New Zealand'. *Legislative Studies Quarterly*, Vol. 8 (May 1983), 172. The author interviewed a sample of 30 MPs.

37 See the discussion in K. J. Scott, *The New Zealand Constitution* (Oxford, Oxford University Press, 1962), 52–55. Scott construes 'mandate' more narrowly than the usage of politicians suggests. Scott confines the term mainly to constitutional matters.

38 Ibid., 52.

39 Richard Mulgan, *Democracy in New Zealand. A Study of New Zealand Politics*, 2nd edn. (Auckland, Oxford University Press, 1984). See the discussion of election policy and mandate, 63–8. See also R. G. Mulgan, 'The Concept of Mandate in New Zealand Politics', *Political Science*, Vol. 30 (1978), 88–96.

40 'Press Statement Issued to Morning Papers, 19.6.1950 for publication 29/6/50, 'The Legislative Council. Its Future Decided. Government Majority Essential. Abolition at End of Session', Sir Alister McIntosh Papers, MS Papers 6759-051, ATL. This file also contains a letter from the Prime Minister's Office to a number of National Party loyalists asking them to consider appointment to the Council in order to abolish it. Some signed acceptances and letters are included.

41 'Papers re implementation of 1949 Policy', 23 /11/53, Sir Sidney Holland

Political Papers, MS-1624-117/4, ATL.

42 New Zealand Labour Party, 'Constitution and Platform' (as amended at the Third Annual Conference, July 3, 4, 5, 1919), reprinted in Paul Harris and Stephen Levine, eds., with Margaret Clark, John Martin and Elizabeth McLeay, *The New Zealand Politics Source Book* (Dunmore Press, Palmerston North, 1992), 120.

43 Bruce Brown, *The Rise of New Zealand Labour: A History of the New Zealand Labour Party* (Wellington, Price Milburn, 1962), 172.

44 Ibid., 172.

45 Janet McLean, 'The Political, the Historical and the Universal in New Zealand's Unwritten Constitution', *New Zealand Journal of Public and International Law*, Vol. 12 (2014), especially 325; Bruce Ackerman, *We the People: Foundations* (Harvard University Press, Cambridge, Mass., 1993), Vol. 1.

46 McLeay, 'Political Argument about Representation' especially 51-8.

47 I could find no evidence in any of the personal papers of those involved in constitutional issues, or in departmental files, that anything more than piecemeal reform – and that strictly limited – was required to improve New Zealand's democracy.

48 Robert Chapman, 'From Labour to National', in W. H. Oliver, ed., with B. R. Williams, *The Oxford History of New Zealand* (The Clarendon Press, Oxford; and Oxford University Press, Wellington, 1981), 359.

49 David McGee argues that the requirement that ministers must be MPs might better have remained as a constitutional convention. If it had, then the constitutional crisis of 1984 (concerning devaluation) might have been more easily dealt with. Muldoon and the National ministers could have resigned and then the incoming Labour ministers could be appointed by the Governor-General. See 'Constitutional Conventions', in Mark Francis and Jim Tully, eds., *In the Public Interest: Essays in Honour of Professor Keith Jackson* (Canterbury University Press, Christchurch, 2009), especially 78–80.

50 The Commission took written evidence, employed statistical data, compared salaries with other Commonwealth parliamentarians and looked at the cost of living. The reports were tabled in the House and an Order in Council (thus determined by ministers with the Governor-General) then implemented the recommendations. This meant that a political element remained in the process. This was not changed until 1974 when the Independent Higher Salaries Commission was formed.

51 Ministers' Private Interests Committee, 'Report', *AJHR* (1956), Vol. 4, I.17. See the discussion in McLeay, *Cabinet and Political Power in New Zealand*, 192–3.

52 Ibid., 'Report'.

53 John Marshall, 'Draft of Speech Delivered April 23 1957 to the 10th Dominion Legal Conference', Sir John Marshall Collection, MS Papers 98-116-07/05, ATL.

3: Politics and Government in the 1950s

1 Michael King, *The Penguin History of New Zealand* (Penguin, Auckland, 2003), 406.
2 See Peter Aimer, 'Labour Party – Origins of the Labour Party' *Te Ara – the Encyclopedia of New Zealand.* At http://www.teara.govt.nz/en/labour-party/page-1. Accessed 16 March 2017.
3 See Barry Gustafson, *The First 50 Years: A History of the New Zealand National Party* (Reed Methuen, Auckland, 1986), 2–36.
4 For a succinct summary see Barry Gustafson, 'Holyoake and the National Party', in Margaret Clark, ed., *Sir Keith Holyoake: Towards a Political Biography* (The Dunmore Press, Palmerston North, 1997), 132.
5 Ibid., 135.
6 E.M. McLeay, 'Parliamentary Careers in a Two-Party System: Cabinet Selection in New Zealand', PhD thesis (University of Auckland, 1978), 176.
7 Ibid., 178.
8 Elizabeth McLeay, Interview with former National minister, February 1972, for 'Parliamentary Careers in a Two-Party System'.
9 Gustafson, 'Holyoake and the National Party', 136; and see also Keith Eunson, 'Sidney Holland', in *Mirrors on the Hill. Reflections on New Zealand's Political Leaders,* (Dunmore Press, Palmerston North, 2001), 32.
10 Austin Mitchell, 'Caucus: The New Zealand Parliamentary Parties', *Journal of Commonwealth Studies,* Vol. 6 (1968) 8.
11 Robert K. Kelson, *The Private Member of Parliament and the Formation of Public Policy. A New Zealand Case Study* (University of Toronto Press, Toronto, 1964), 50. Kelson provides other examples also, both of consultation and non-consultation, 49–52.
12 McLeay, 'Parliamentary Careers in a Two-Party System', Table 8.6, 343.
13 McLeay, Interview with former National Minister, February 1972.
14 Information about MPs and ministers from G. A. Wood, *Ministers and Members in the New Zealand Parliament,* 2nd edn. (University of Otago Press, Dunedin, 1996).
15 Gustafson, *The First 50 Years.* 20.
16 See Hugh Templeton, 'Algie, Ronald Macmillan', first published in the Dictionary of New Zealand Biography, Vol. 4 (1998) *Te Ara – The Encyclopedia of New Zealand.* At https://teara.govt.nz/en/biographies/4a8/algie-ronald-macmillan. Accessed 31 August 2017.
17 John Marshall, *Memoirs: Volume One: 1912 to 1960* (William Collins, Auckland, 1983), 213.
18 Eunson, *Mirrors on the Hill*, 36.
19 Jim Lundy, 'Oram, Matthew Henry', *Te Ara—The Encyclopedia of New Zealand.* At: http://www.teara.govt.nz/en/biographies/5o5/oram-matthew-henry. Accessed 4 April 2017. Oram continued his interest

in matters constitutional after leaving Parliament in 1957, with his involvement in the Constitutional Society.

20 Erik Schwimmer, 'The Man and His Work: The Hon. Ernest Bower Corbett' *Te Ao Hou*, No. 21 (December 1957), 7. There is no author provided so the writer was almost certainly the Editor of the time, Schwimmer. At: teaohou.natlib.govt.nz/journals/teaohou/issue/Moa21TeA/c9.html. Accessed 20 August 2017.

21 Keith Sinclair, *Walter Nash (*John McIndoe, Dunedin, 1976), 281.

22 Gustafson, *The First 50 Years*, 40.

23 Austin Mitchell, *Politics and People in New Zealand* (Christchurch, Whitcombe and Tombs Ltd., 1969), 106.

24 Marshall, *Memoirs: Volume One*, 140. Marshall notes on the same page that Holland did not read books. He was also a 'practised magician'(141).

25 Ibid., 254.

26 Ibid., 255.

27 Eunson, *Mirrors on the Hill*, 46.

28 McLeay, Interview with former National MP, October 1971.

29 Marshall, *Memoirs*, 254–5. In October 1956, during the Suez Crisis, Holland had either a stroke or a heart attack. See Barry Gustafson, 'Holland, Sidney George', *Te Ara* – th*e Encyclopedia of New Zealand*. At: http://www.TeAra.govt.nz/en/biographies/5h30/holland-sidney-george. Accessed 9 March 2017.

30 Sinclair, *Walter Nash*, especially 274–89.

31 Ibid., 292. Sinclair shows how Nash roundly defeated his opponents, 292–4.

32 Holland at the National Party Conference, July 1948, quoted by W. B. Sutch, *The Quest for Security in New Zealand 1840–1966* (Oxford University Press, Wellington, 1966), 364.

33 Robert Chapman, 'From Labour to National', in W. H. Oliver, ed., with B. R. Williams, *The Oxford History of New Zealand* (The Clarendon Press, Oxford; and Oxford University Press, Wellington, 1981), 358.

34 Letter from Sidney Holland to Keith Holyoake (copy), 22 October 1954, Sir Keith Holyoake Political Papers, 1814-044/3, ATL.

35 Chapman, 'From Labour to National', 360.

36 See, for example, Marshall's description of the National Housing Conference 1953 which influenced government policy: *Memoirs*, 150–3.

37 John Martin, *A Profession of Statecraft? Three Essays on Some Current Issues in the New Zealand Public Service* (Institute of Policy Studies, Victoria University of Wellington, 1987), 5. Martin identifies the shared beliefs of the era, 5–6.

38 Mitchell, *Politics and People in New Zealand*, 106–7.

39 Jack Vowles, Peter Aimer, Helena Catt, Jim Lamare and Raymond Miller, *Towards Consensus? The 1993 Election in New Zealand and the Transition to Proportional Representation* (Auckland, Auckland University Press, 1995), 4.

40 The New Zealand National Party, 'Russianising New Zealand' (Hawera Star Publishing Co., Lts. Undated) The pamphlet attacks the 1947 Supply Regulations Bill.
41 Under Labour between 1957 and 1960 no one was executed. In 1961 a free parliamentary vote abolished the death penalty except for treason, which was also abolished in 1989.
42 Mitchell, *Politics and People in New Zealand*, 103–39.
43 See the discussion by Jack Vowles: 'Aspects of Electoral Studies, Present and Past: New Zealand Voters and "the System", 1949–1996', *Political Science*, Vol. 50 (1998), 90–110.
44 For figures on Māori voting see M. K. Sorrenson, 'History of Maori Representation in Parliament', in Royal Commission on the Electoral System [RCES], *Report of the Royal Commission on the Electoral System: Towards a Better Democracy* (Wellington, 1986), B 82, Appendix 7. The turnout of valid votes is expressed as a percentage of total eligible population.
45 Neill Atkinson, *Adventures in Democracy. A History of the Vote in New Zealand* (University of Otago Press in Association with the Electoral Commission, Dunedin, 2003), 187.
46 See the profiles in Janet McCallum, *Women in the House: Members of Parliament in New Zealand* (Cape Catley, Auckland, 1993), 36–79
47 McLeay, 'Parliamentary Careers in a Two-Party System', 28.
48 On the origins of National and the development of both parties, see especially Mitchell's excellent brief analysis in *Politics and People in New Zealand*, 103–41.
49 R. S. Milne, *Political Parties in New Zealand* (Clarendon Press, Oxford, 1966), 211, citing Louise Overacker, 'The New Zealand Labor Party', *American Political Science Review*, Vol. 49 (1955), 718.
50 Milne, *Political Parties in New Zealand*, 211.
51 See Gustafson, *The First 50 Years*, 22–6.
52 R. N. Kelson, 'The New Zealand National Party', *Political Science*, Vol. 6 (1954), 5.
53 Milne, *Political Parties in New Zealand*, 164.
54 Department of Statistics, 'The New Zealand Official Year-Book, 1951–1952. At: https://www3.stats.govt.nz/New_Zealand_Official_Yearbooks/1951-52/NZOYB_1951-52.html#idsect1_1_980. Accessed 1 March 2017. The figure on 31 March was 1,984,730.
55 Milne, *Political Parties in New Zealand*, 204. Milne's source is the *President's Address* to the Nineteenth Annual Conference, 1956 (footnote 5, 204).
56 Ibid., 205; and Kelson, 'The New Zealand National Party', 5.
57 See Raymond Miller, *Party Politics in New Zealand* (Oxford University Press, Melbourne, 2005), 69–70 and 73–4.
58 Milne, *Political Parties in New Zealand*, 206.
59 Ibid., 174.

60 See Kelson, 'The New Zealand National Party', 22–4.
61 Ibid., 'The New Zealand National Party', 23.
62 Milne, *Political Parties in New Zealand*, 177–8. See 179–80 for a description of the party administrative staff.
63 Ibid., 172.
64 Ibid., 211.
65 Ibid., 106–7. Milne lists some issues discussed, 107.
66 Robert Bremer with an historical introduction by Tom Brooking, 'Federated Farmers and the State', in Brian Roper and Chris Rudd, eds., *State and Economy in New Zealand*' (Auckland, Oxford University Press, 1991), 116.
67 Milne, *Political Parties in New Zealand*, 99. Emphasis in the original.

4: The Unsettled Electoral Issues

1 See Leslie Lipson, who also sketches out the variety of arguments about just representation put forward at this period: *The Politics of Equality* (University of Chicago Press, 1948), 28–31.
2 Neill Atkinson, *Adventures in Democracy: A History of the Vote in New Zealand* (University of Otago Press in association with the Electoral Commission, Dunedin, 2003), 72.
3 Atkinson, *Adventures in Democracy*, 72–3. As with its predecessor, the 1881 Act increased the number of European seats to 91.
4 Alan McRobie, *New Zealand Electoral Atlas* (GB Books, Wellington, 1989), 11.
5 The Royal Commission on the Electoral System [RCES], *Report of the Royal Commission on the Electoral System: Towards a Better Democracy* (Government Printing Office, Wellington, 1986), 134.
6 Lipson, *The Politics of Equality*, 32.
7 Ibid., 180 and see 174–82 for a general discussion.
8 Ibid., 182.
9 Ibid., 183.
10 Ibid., 73.
11 Atkinson, *Adventures in Democracy*, 150.
12 See R. M. Chapman on the situation during the 1920s as it affected the political parties: 'Appendix: The Effect of the Country Quota', *The Political Scene 1919–1931*' (Heinemann Educational Books, Auckland, 1969), 66–68.
13 Department of Justice, 'The Electoral Law of New Zealand: A Brief History', in RCES, *Report of the Royal Commission on the Electoral System*, A, 64–6.
14 'Farmers Stand Firm', *The Evening Post* (8 November 1945). *The Evening Post* Vertical File Collection, WPL.
15 'Flouting the People's Rights', *The Evening Post* (19 October 1945). *The Evening Post* Vertical File Collection, WPL.

16 John E. Martin, *The House. New Zealand's House of Representatives 1854–2004* (Dunmore Press, Palmerston North, 2004), 215.
17 Atkinson, *Adventures in Democracy*, 156.
18 Ibid., 157.
19 Ibid., 158.
20 Department of Justice, 'The Electoral Law of New Zealand', A, 64–5.
21 Ibid., A, 65.
22 Ibid., A, 64.
23 James Christmas, 'Consensus Gained, Maintenance Maintained? Changing New Zealand's Electoral Law 1927-2007', MA Thesis (Victoria University of Wellington, 2010), 73.
24 Christmas, 'Consensus Gained, Maintenance Maintained?', 71–4; Department of Justice, 'The Electoral Law of New Zealand', A, 68–9.
25 New Zealand National Party, 'Policy General Election 1946; and New Zealand National Party, 'Policy. General Election 1949'. The manifestos are in the Victoria University of Wellington Library, J. C. Beaglehole Room, Les Cleveland Research Papers (Alan Robinson), Roba 1987. 010. Location 49/C/1.
26 McRobie, *New Zealand Electoral Atlas*, 25, fn. 16.
27 New Zealand Labour Party, 'Constitution and Platform' (as amended at the Third Annual Conference, July 3, 4, 5, 1919), reprinted in Paul Harris and Stephen Levine, eds., with Margaret Clark, John Martin and Elizabeth McLeay, *The New Zealand Politics Source Book* (Dunmore Press, Palmerston North, 1992), 120.
28 Keith Jackson, 'The Abolition of the New Zealand Upper House of Parliament', in L. D. Longley and D. M. Olson, eds., *Two into One: The Politics and Processes of National Legislative Cameral Change* (Westview Press, Boulder, 1991), 55.
29 For a discussion of the relationship between the UK and New Zealand parliaments including arguments about parliamentary sovereignty see Peter C. Oliver, *The Constitution of Independence: The Development of Constitutional Theory in Australia, Canada and New Zealand* (Oxford, Oxford University Press, 2005), 185–201.
30 See Peter Oliver, 'Cutting the Imperial Link – Canada and New Zealand', in Philip A. Joseph, ed., *Essays on the Constitution* (Brookers, Wellington, 1995), 383. Oliver summarises the arguments around the capacities of the New Zealand Parliament before and after 1947, and the subsequent acts designed to clarify any continuing confusion around New Zealand's sovereignty.
31 Harshan Kumarasingham, *Onward with Executive Power: Lessons from New Zealand 1947–57* (Institute of Policy Studies, Wellington, 2010), 27. The author stresses New Zealand's reluctance to embrace constitutional change or to threaten the country's close relationship with the UK.
32 Ibid., 101–35.

33 Jackson, 'The Abolition of the New Zealand Upper House of Parliament', 55.
34 New Zealand House of Representatives, *New Zealand Sovereignty: 1857. 1907, 1947, or 1987?* Parliamentary Research Paper, August 2007, 8–9. At: https://www.parliament.nz/en/pb/research-papers/document/00PLLawRP07041/new-zealand-sovereignty-1857-1907-1947-or-1987. Accessed 13 September 2016.
35 Supporting documents, the submissions, and parts of a university thesis are in 'New Zealand Joint Constitutional Reform Committee 1948, *Statements etc. Prepared for the New Zealand Joint Constitutional Reform Committee 1948* (Wellington Legislative Department, 1948). A copy is in the Law Library, Victoria University of Wellington.
36 Atkinson, *Adventures in Democracy*, 163.
37 Sidney Holland, *NZPD*, Vol. 283 (22 September 1948), 2612.
38 New Zealand National Party, 'Policy. General Election 1949.'
39 Keith Jackson, *The New Zealand Legislative Council: A Study of the Establishment, Failure and Abolition of an Upper House* (Dunedin, University of Otago Press, 1972), 191.
40 Jackson, *The New Zealand Legislative Council*, 192.
41 Clifton Webb, *NZPD*, Vol. 289 (25 July 1950), 621.
42 Robert N. Kelson, *The Private Member of Parliament and the Formation of Public Policy* (Toronto, University of Toronto Press, 1964), 116.
43 Jackson, *The New Zealand Legislative Council*, 186.
44 D. Whyte, Letter to the Hon. T. C. Webb marked 'Personal', 1 August 1950, Sir John Marshall Political Papers, 'Constitution Bill', MS-Papers 1403-069/5, ATL. These papers seem to have come from Clifton Webb, Marshall's predecessor as Minister of Justice and Attorney-General.
45 Clifton Webb, Letter to Mr D. O. Whyte, 4 August 1950, Sir John Marshall Political Papers, 'Constitution Bill', MS-Papers-1403-069/5, ATL. Also in the files there is a letter from Les Munro on the same topic. He refers to the South African case, agreeing with Webb's view on parliamentary sovereignty, 25 July 1950.
46 Clifton Webb, *NZPD*, Vol. 289 (25 July 1950), 621.
47 Ronald Algie, *NZPD*, Vol. 289 (25 July 1950) 633.
48 Jack Watts, *NZPD*, Vol. 289 (26 July 1950), 709.
49 Sidney Holland, *NZPD*, Vol. 289 (26 July 1950), 726.
50 Walter Nash, *NZPD*, Vol. 289 (26 July 1950), 726.
51 For example see 'Preparation of New Zealand Constitution', *The Evening Post* (22 May 1950). *The Evening Post* Vertical File Collection, WPL.
52 H. D. G. Adams, 'New Zealand Constitution Act', 27 February 1950, Sir John Marshall Political Papers, 'Constitution Bill', MS-Papers-1403-069/5, ATL. These papers seem to have come from Clifton Webb.
53 Robert McGechan, 'Written Constitution' (undated Memorandum) and Clifton Webb, 'Written Constitution', 6 July 1950, Sir John

Marshall Political Papers, 'Constitution Bill', MS-Papers-1403-069/5 ATL. These papers seem to have come from Clifton Webb.

54 'Memorandum for Rt Hon. Prime Minister, 'Substitute for Legislative Council' 13 July 1950, Sir Alister McIntosh Papers, MS Papers 6759-051, ATL. A handwritten note on the submission says that it is from Webb.

55 Constitutional Reform Committee, 'Report of the Constitutional Reform Committee', *AJHR* (1952) I–18, 8.

56 Constitutional Reform Committee, 'Report of the Constitutional Reform Committee', 8.

57 Hugh Templeton, 'Algie, Ronald Macmillan', first published in the Dictionary of New Zealand Biography, Vol. 4 (1998) *Te Ara - The Encyclopedia of New Zealand*. At: https://teara.govt.nz/en/biographies/4a8/algie-ronald-macmillan, 2. Accessed 31 August 2017.

58 Thirty-four people gave evidence to the committee, most wanting an indirectly elected second chamber.

59 H. J. Benda and R. H. Brookes, 'SPQR: A Note on the Proposed Senate', *Political Science*, Vol. 4 (September 1952), 40.

60 E. A. Olssen, 'A Second Chamber: The Report of the Constitutional Reform Committee', *Landfall*, Vol. 6 (1952), 325.

61 John Marshall, *Memoirs: Volume One: 1912 to 1960* (Collins, Auckland, 1983), 160.

62 Kelson, *The Private Member of Parliament and the Formation of Public Policy*, 104.

63 Barry Gustafson, *The First 50 Years: A History of the New Zealand National Party* (Reed Methuen, Auckland, 1986), 59.

64 For a brief discussion see: Department of Justice, 'The Electoral Law of New Zealand', A 71–2.

65 'The New Zealand National Party: Remits for Consideration by Executive Meeting 1st and 2nd December, 1953', Sir Keith Holyoake Political Papers, MS Papers 1814-38/1, ATL.

66 'Decisions on Remits', 17th Annual Dominion Conference, held in Wellington, 5–6 July 1954, Sir Keith Holyoake Political Papers, MS Papers 1814-044/3, ATL. One remit was not carried and the other was withdrawn.

67 'Lobby Letter', *Dominion* (9 April 1956), 8.

68 See the discussion in Keith Sinclair, *Walter Nash* (Auckland University Press/Oxford University Press, Auckland, 1976), 205–7.

69 Ibid., 206.

70 Ibid., 207.

71 Sidney Holland, *NZPD*, Vol. 260, 15 October 1941, 1144.

72 Sinclair, *Walter Nash*, 207.

73 Peter Fraser, *NZPD*, Vol. 260, 15 October 1941, 1152–3.

74 Sidney Holland, *NZPD*, Vol, 261, 10 July 1942, 544.

75 Olssen, 'A Second Chamber', 322.

76 Department of Justice, 'The Electoral Law of New Zealand', A, 66.
77 See M. Sorrenson, 'A History of Maori Representation in Parliament' in RCES, *Report of the Royal Commission on the Electoral System: 'Towards a Better Democracy'*, (Wellington, 1986), B, 43.
78 John Wilson, 'The Origins of the Māori Seats', in Maria Bargh, ed., *Māori and Parliament: Diverse Strategies and Compromises* (Huia Publishers, Wellington, 2010), 55.
79 Ibid., 55.
80 For further information see Sorrenson, 'A History of Maori Representation in Parliament', B, 37.
81 Ibid., B, 43.
82 Department of Justice, 'The Electoral Law of New Zealand', A, 67.
83 Ibid., A, 67.
84 Ibid., A, 67-8.
85 Sorrenson, 'A History of Maori Representation in Parliament', B, 45.
86 Ibid., B, 65–6, Appendices 1 and 2.
87 Ibid., B, 45.
88 Ibid., B, 45. Sorrenson also notes that the first Māori Under-Secretary to the Department of Maori Affairs was appointed, 46.
89 Sorrenson, 'A History of Maori Representation in Parliament', B 47.
90 For further discussion on this point see E. M. McLeay, 'Political Argument about Representation: The Case of the Maori Seats', *Political Studies*, Vol. 28 (1980), 43–62.
91 Department of Justice, 'The Electoral Law of New Zealand', A, 62.
92 Leon Gotz, *NZPD*, Vol. 308 (19 April 1956), 369.
93 Richard S. Hill, *Maori and the State: Crown-Maori Relations in New Zealand/Aotearoa, 1950–2000* (Victoria University Press, 2009), 25. Hill adds that National placed no Māori MPs on the Board of Maori Affairs (which supervised the work of the Department of Maori Affairs).
94 Sorrenson, 'A History of Maori Representation in Parliament', B, 47.
95 Ibid., 47
96 Richard H. T. Thompson, 'Maori Affairs and the New Zealand Press', *The Journal of the Polynesian Society*, Vol. 64 (1955), 22. At: http://www.jps.auckland.ac.nz/document/. Accessed 10 May 2017.
97 Thompson, 'Maori Affairs and the New Zealand Press', 22.

5: The Making of the Electoral Act 1956

1 Neill Atkinson, *Adventures in Democracy. A History of the Vote in New Zealand* (University of Otago Press, Dunedin, 2003), 159.
2 Andrew Geddis, *Electoral Law in New Zealand: Practice and Policy* (LexisNexis, Wellington, 2007), 98, citing Re Raglan Election Petition (No 4) [1948] 65, 87–88.
3 Department of Justice, 'The Electoral Law of New Zealand: A Brief History', in Royal Commission on the Electoral System [RCES],

Report of the Royal Commission on the Electoral System: Towards a Better Democracy (Wellington, 1986), A, 72.

4 Ibid., A, 72.

5 Quoted in ibid., A, 72.

6 Ibid., A, 72; and see 'Electoral Regulations 1954' (140), *Statutory Regulations 1954*, Vol. I (8 September 1954), 624–57. The regulations revoked certain schedules of the Electoral Act 1927 and covered the registration of electors, absent, postal and declaration voting, overseas postal voting, the voting of servicemen, and voting in the Chatham Islands.

7 Ibid., A, 72.

8 Ibid., A, 74.

9 Ibid., A, 74.

10 Department of Justice, 'Report of the Department of Justice for the Year 1956–57', *AJHR*, Vol. IV (1957), 4.

11 John Marshall, 'Press Statement. New Electoral Act', 28 February 1956, Sir John Marshall Collection, MS Papers 98-116-07/05, ATL.

12 'Speech from the Throne', *NZPD*, Vol. 308 (4 April 1956), 6.

13 Frank Kitts, *NZPD*, Vol. 308 (12 April 1956), 156. The information on MPs and ministers is from G. A. Wood, *Ministers and Members in the New Zealand Parliament* 2nd ed. (University of Otago Press, Dunedin, 1996).

14 Arthur Kinsella, *NZPD*, Vol. 308, (12 April 1956), 160.

15 General Secretary's Report, 'Electorate and Divisional Questionnaires (1956) in Relation to Organisation (Confidential)', Sir Sidney Holland Political Papers, National Party Correspondence and Papers, MS Papers 1624-113/5, ATL. The report is signed by the General Secretary and contains the results of the questionnaires.

16 'Second Parliamentary Chamber', Letter from Holland to Alex McKenzie, National Party president, 30 April 1956, Sir Sidney Holland Political Papers, 'Second Chamber', MS Papers-1624-093/4, ATL.

17 'Second Parliamentary Chamber', Letter from Holland to Alex McKenzie, 30 April 1956.

18 Ibid.

19 See, for example, Harry Combs, *NZPD*, Vol. 289 (25 July 1950), 637.

20 Sidney Holland, *NZPD*, Vol. 289 (26 July 1950), 724. Holland asked Peter Fraser for similar assurances. The Bill passed its third reading in the House without a division.

21 'Some Notes with Reference to the Establishment of a Second Chamber in New Zealand, and with Special Reference to the Report of the Constitutional Reform Committee', Letter from the Speaker, Matthew Oram, to Sidney Holland, 1 May 1956, Sir Sidney Holland Political Papers, 'Second Chamber', MS Papers 1624-093/4, ATL.

22 Copy of letter from Sidney Holland to 'Alex', 'Upper House', 7 May 1956, Sir Sidney Holland Political Papers, 'Second Chamber', MS

Papers 1624-093/4, ATL. 'Alex' is Alex McKenzie.

23 Ibid.

24 Ibid. The emphasis is in the original.

25 'Legislative Reform', Meeting in Prime Minister's Office, 16 May 1956, Sir Sidney Holland Political Papers, 'Second Chamber', MS Papers 1624-093/4, ATL.

26 Ibid.

27 Copy of unsigned letter received by Sidney Holland, probably from Algie, 'Upper House', 7 May 1956, Sir Sidney Holland Political Papers, 'Second Chamber', MS Papers 1624-093/4, ATL.

28 'Party Branches Want Upper House Restored', *The Evening Post* (9 August 1956). *The Evening Post* Vertical File Collection, WPL.

29 New Zealand National Party, 'A Record of Progress: Policy. General Election 1954', Les Cleveland Research Papers (Alan Robinson), Roba 1987. 010. Location 49/C/1, Beaglehole Room, Victoria University of Wellington Library.

30 Sidney Holland, quoted in 'Law to Safeguard Constitution. Avoiding Dangers of No Second Chamber', *The New Zealand Herald* (21 August 1956) 10.

31 Ibid., 10.

32 'PM Explains New Proposal', *The Evening Post* (22 August 1956). *The Evening Post* Vertical File Collection, WPL.

33 'Mr Holland Unquestioned Leader. Rumours of National Party Split Dispelled', *The Evening Post* (22 August 1956). *The Evening Post* Vertical File Collection, WPL.

34 'That Blessed Word "Referendum"', *New Zealand Herald* (21 August 1956) 8.

35 'Mr Nash Watching Second Chamber Question', *The New Zealand Herald* (22 August 1956) 19.

36 For example, Walter Hudson, *NZPD*, Vol. 309 (24 August 1956), 1385.

37 Walter Hudson, *NZPD*, Vol. 308, (24 August 1956), 1386.

38 John Mathison, *NZPD*, Vol. 308 (11 September 1956), 1685.

39 'Ministers' Private Interests. Report Shortly Before Parliament', *New Zealand Herald* (28 August 1956) 12.

40 Copy of Letter from R. L. Hutchins, Secretary to Cabinet, to the Minister of Justice, 8 May 1956, 'Electoral Act – General Re-Enrolment (CM(56)22', Sir John Marshall Papers, 'Cabinet Minutes (1–29), MS Papers 1403-433/1, ATL.

41 Copy of Letter from R. L. Hutchins, Secretary to Cabinet, to the Minister of Justice, 12 June 1956, 'Compulsory Enrolment of Maori Electors (CM(56)417', Sir John Marshall Papers, 'Cabinet Minutes (1–29), MS Papers 1403–433/1, ATL.

42 Letter from R. L. Hutchens, Secretary of the Cabinet, to the Minister of Justice, 'Electoral Act – Basis of Right to Vote CM(56)41', 4 September 1956, Sir John Marshall Political Papers, 'Cabinet Minutes (31–59)', MS

Papers 1403–433/2, ATL.

43 Letter from R. L. Hutchens, Secretary of the Cabinet, to the Minister of Justice, 'Proposed Electoral Bill – Ballot Papers CM(56)42, 11 September 1956, Sir John Marshall Political Papers, 'Cabinet Minutes (31–59)', MS Papers 1403–433/2, ATL.

44 Cabinet Committee on Legislation, 'Minutes', 8 October 1956, 'Legislation. Cabinet Committee on Legislation – Minutes of Meetings', AAFD, Series 811, Acc W23, [R20819762] ANZ.

45 Electoral Bill L.D.O. 59/2, 'Legislation – The Electoral Act 1956', [EL] 1268, Record No. 14/6/20, [R11288408], ANZ.

46 Cabinet Committee on Legislation, 'Minutes of the Cabinet Committee on Legislation held in the office of the Hon. J. R. Marshall, Parliament Buildings, on Tuesday 9 October 1956, from 11.30 a.m. to 1 p.m., 4 p.m. to 5.45 p.m. and 7 p.m. to 9.40 p.m', Legislation, Cabinet Committee on Legislation – Minutes of Meetings, AAFD, Series 811, Box 224, Acc W2347, [R20819762], ANZ.

47 Letter from R. L. Hutchens, Secretary of the Cabinet, to the Minister of Justice, 11 October 1956, Sir John Marshall Political Papers, 'Cabinet Minutes (31–59)', MS Papers 1403-433/2, ATL.

48 PM S. G. Holland, 'Prime Minister's Diary', 1956, PM 1011, AECO, Series 18654. Item 31, [R20834043], ANZ. This is Holland's Private Secretary's diary. The topic of the meeting is seldom included.

49 John Marshall, *NZPD*, Vol. 310 (12 October 1956), 2840.

50 'Voters Given Additional Protection in Electoral Bill', *The Dominion* (13 October 1956),14. The article summarises the content of the Bill.

51 John Marshall, *NZPD*, Vol. 310 (12 October 1956), 2450.

52 *The Dominion* (13 October 1956), 14.

53 'Electoral Reforms in Train', *The New Zealand Herald* (15 October 1956) 8.

54 John Marshall, *NZPD*, Vol. 310 (12 October 1956), 2450.

55 Sidney Holland, *NZPD*, Vol. 310 (12 October 1956), 2451.

56 John Marshall, *NZPD*, Vol. 310 (12 October 1956), 2450.

57 *NZPD*, Vol. 310, (12 October 1956), 2451.

58 Copy of letter from the Secretary of Justice, 15 October 1956, 'Electoral Act and Regulations 1927 – Proposed Amendments to Electoral Regulations 1954', J1 159, O-1957, [R16365909], ANZ. This file includes copies of the letters of thanks sent to the Registrars on 6 November 1956. The letters also include the following: 'As we explained, circumstances beyond our control prevented our giving officials an opportunity for the careful and leisurely scrutiny that would have been desirable'. There are some responses from the Registrars in the file. None suggests creating reserved provisions.

59 *NZPD*, Vol. 310 (17 October 1956), 2540.

60 Department of Justice, 'The Electoral Law of New Zealand', A, 67. The source is *The Dominion* (22 October 1956), 10.

61 'Last Rushed Week of Session. Several Major Bills to be Considered', *The New Zealand Herald* (22 October 1956), 10. Note that the Riccarton by-election took place on Saturday 27 October.
62 'Last Rushed Week of Session', *The New Zealand Herald*, 10.
63 PM S. G. Holland, 'Prime Minister's Diary' 1956.
64 Electoral Bill Committee, 'Minutes of meeting held at 5.30pm on Wednesday, 17 October, 1956'. 'Committee on the Electoral Bill-Administration-Minutes, ABGX W3706 16127, Box (74), [C354211], ANZ. This Box includes a copy of Electoral Bill No 89–1.
65 Electoral Bill Committee, 'Minutes of meeting held at 1.45pm on Thursday, 19 October, 1956'. Committee on the Electoral Bill-Administration-Minutes, ABGX W3706 16127, [C354211], ANZ.
66 The Liberal Party had renamed itself the United Party and subsequently amalgamated with Reform in 1936, producing the National Party.
67 Electoral Bill Committee, 'Minutes of meeting held at 1.45pm on Thursday, 19 October, 1956.
68 'Press Statement for Morning Papers', Sir John Marshall Papers, MS Papers 98-116-07-05, ATL.
69 A. P. O'Shea, 'Submission to the Electoral Committee', Legislation – The Electoral Act 1956, EL 1268, Record No. 14/6/20, [R11288408], ANZ. This file also contains notes for the Select Committee by officials, including members of the Justice Department. None, however, mentions the reserved provisions.
70 Electoral Bill Committee, 'Minutes of meeting held at 9am on Thursday, 25 October 1956. 'Committee on the Electoral Bill-Administration-Minutes, ABGX W3706 16127, [C354211], ANZ; and 'Electoral [As reported from the Electoral Bill Committee]', House of Representatives, 25 October 1956, 'Legislation-The Electoral Act 1956', EL 1268, Record No.15/6/20, [R11288408], ANZ.
71 'Electoral [As Reported from the Electoral Bill Committee]', House of Representatives, 25 October 1956], Legislation – The Electoral Act 1956, EL 1268, Record No. 14/6/20, [R11288408], ANZ.
72 'Electoral [As Reported from the Electoral Bill Committee]', House of Representatives, 25 October 1956].
73 *Journals of the House of Representatives of New Zealand* [*JHRNZ*], 1956, 4 April 1956, 26 October 1956 inclusive (Wellington 1957), 353.
74 John Marshall, *NZPD*, Vol. 310 (6 October 1956), 2839
75 *JHRNZ*, 1956, 4 April 1956-26 October 1956 inclusive (Wellington 1957), 356.
76 *JHRNZ*, 1956, 4 April 1956-26 October 1956 inclusive (Wellington 1957), 356–7.
77 *NZPD*, Vol. 310 (26 October 1956), 2853.
78 Geoffrey Palmer, *Unbridled Power? An Interpretation of New Zealand's Constitution and Government* (Oxford University Press, Wellington, 1979), Table 6, 81.

79 *JHRNZ*, 1956, 4 April 1956, 26 October 1956 inclusive (Wellington 1957), 413.
80 For a full description, including an analysis of the new clauses' various influences, see Department of Justice, 'The Electoral Law of New Zealand', A, 74–75.
81 Department of Justice, 'Report of the Department of Justice for the Year 1956-57', *AJHR*, Vol. IV (1957), 5.
82 Department of Justice, 'Report of the Department of Justice for the Year 1956–57', 5.

6: Entrenchment

1 John Marshall, *NZPD*, Vol. 310 (26 October 1956), 2852.
2 Ibid, 2840.
3 Walter Nash, *NZPD*, Vol. 310 (26 October 1956), 2843.
4 James Edwards, *NZPD*, Vol. 310 (26 October 1956), 2847.
5 Duncan Rae and Ron Algie, *NZPD*, Vol. 310 (26 October 1956), 2848.
6 Nash, *NZPD*, Vol. 310 (26 October 1956), 2844.
7 Phil Holloway, *NZPD*, Vol. 310 (26 October 1956), 2848.
8 Ralph Hanan, *NZPD*, Vol. 310 (26 October 1956), 2850.
9 Ibid., 2850.
10 Ibid., 2852.
11 This point is also made in the Department of Justice history: 'The Electoral Law of New Zealand: A Brief History', in Royal Commission on the Electoral System, *Report of the Royal Commission on the Electoral System: Towards a Better Democracy* (Wellington, 1986), A, 71–2.
12 Constitutional Reform Committee, Appendix A, 'How Constitutions Can be Created', *Report of the Constitutional Reform Committee*', *AJHR* (1952), I-18, 38.
13 E. K. Braybrooke, 'A Written Constitution. Is it Possible in New Zealand?' *Political Science*, Vol. 3 No. 1 (March 1951), 32–42, reprinted in L. Cleveland and A. D. Robinson, eds., *Readings in New Zealand Government* (A. H. and A. W. Reed, Wellington, 1972), 257–65; and J. F. Northey, 'Can our Liberties be Safeguarded?', *New Zealand Law Journal*, Vol. 27 No. 9 (22 May 1951), 140–43. Professor Braybrooke was born in New Zealand and taught at Victoria University of Wellington before shifting to Australia. Professor Northey taught at the University of Auckland.
14 Ibid., 259. Braybrooke cites A. V. Dicey, 6th ed., *The Law of the Constitution* (Macmillan, London, 1902). Dicey's book was first published in 1885.
15 Ibid.
16 Ibid.
17 Ibid., 260.
18 Ibid. The Privy Council case was *Attorney-General for New South Wales*

v. Trethowan (1931), CLR 394.

19 Ibid., 261.

20 Ibid., 262.

21 Ibid., 260. Edward Coke published his works in the 18th century.

22 Ibid., 262.

23 Ibid., 265.

24 Northey, 'Can our Liberties be Safeguarded?', 141–3.

25 Ibid., 140–1.

26 Ibid., 141.

27 Constitutional Reform Committee, Appendix B, 'Can We Have a Written or More or Less Rigid Constitution?' *Report of the Constitutional Reform Committee, AJHR* (1952), I-18, 43.

28 Northey, 'Can our Liberties be Safeguarded?', 141–2, citing Dixon, J. in Attorney-General for New *South Wales v. Trethowan* (1931) 44 C.L.R. 394.

29 Northey, 'Can our Liberties be Safeguarded?', 142.

30 Ibid.

31 Braybrooke, 32–42. An exchange on these and other issues continued in *Political Science* in a section entitled 'Civil Liberties and a Written Constitution', Vol. 6 (March 1954): K. J. Scott, 'Civil Liberties and a Written Constitution', 29–37; and Braybrooke, 'A Reply', 41–2.

32 Constitutional Reform Committee, Appendix B, 41.

33 Ibid., 42.

34 Ibid.

35 Ibid., 43.

36 Ibid., 44.

37 Constitutional Reform Committee, Appendix B, 44.

38 Ibid., 45.

39 Clarence Skinner, *NZPD*, Vol. 297, 5 August 1952, 728.

40 Ronald Algie, *NZPD*, Vol. 297, 5 August 1952, 726.

41 Ronald Algie, *NZPD*, Vol. 297, 5 August 1952, 727.

42 Duncan Rae, *NZPD*, Vol. 297, 5 August 1952, 730–1.

43 Ralph Hanan, *NZPD*, Vol. 297, 5 August 1952, 742.

44 Ralph Hanan, *NZPD*, Vol. 297, 5 August 1952, 743.

45 H. J. Benda and R. H. Brookes, 'SPQR. A Note on the Proposed Senate', *Political Science*, Vol. 42 (September 1952), 43.

46 Ibid., 44.

47 Ibid.

48 K. J. Scott, 'New Zealand's Political Traditions', *Journal of the Royal Society of Arts*, Vol. 106, No. 5021 (April 1958), 354–66. At: www.jstor.org/stable/41366253?seq=1#page_scan_tab_contents. Accessed 8 April 2016. At the time Scott was associate professor of Political Science at Victoria University of Wellington. He kept a close watch on constitutional developments, especially the Electoral Act 1956.

49 Ibid., 365.

50 Ibid., 365–6.
51 Ibid., 366.
52 Ibid. The case alluded to was decided by the Judicial Committee of the Privy Council in: *British Coal Corporation v. The King* (6 June 1935) and involved whether or not the Canadian Parliament was empowered by the Statute of Westminster Act 1931 to prohibit appeals to the Privy Council.
53 Department of Justice, 'A Bill of Rights for New Zealand: A White Paper', (Government Printer, Wellington, 1985), 54.
54 F. M. Brookfield, 'Referendums: Legal and Constitutional Aspects', in Alan Simpson, ed., *Referendums: Constitutional and Political Perspectives* (Occasional Publication 4, Department of Politics, Victoria University of Wellington, Wellington, 1992), 8 and 16.
55 The other members, all National, were Eric Halstead, Thomas Hayman, Duncan Rae and William (Blair) Tennent. Tennent lost his seat in 1954 and would return in 1957.
56 One might also think that if any Labour MPs had been the prime movers of Section 189, this would have been mentioned in the various biographies of the political actors of that period.
57 Jack Watts, Minister of Health, *NZPD*, Vol. 289 (26 July 1950), 707.
58 Keith Jackson, *The New Zealand Legislative Council: A Study of the Establishment, Failure and Abolition of an Upper House* (University of Otago Press, Dunedin, 1972), 191.
59 R. S. Milne, 'The Referendum Revived', *Landfall*, Vol. 11 (1957), 160.
60 Keith Jackson and Alan McRobie, *New Zealand Adopts Proportional Representation. Accident? Design? Evolution?* (Ashgate, Aldershot, 1998), 31–2.
61 See the excellent chapter on referendums in Mary Harris and David Wilson, eds., *McGee: Parliamentary Practice in New Zealand*, 4th ed., (Oratia Books, Auckland, 2017), 662–71. For lists of referendums and citizens' initiated referendums since 1949 see Electoral Commission, 'Referenda'. At: www.elections.org.nz/voting-system/referenda. Accessed 20 March 2017.
62 Jackson and McRobie, *New Zealand Adopts Proportional Representation*, 32–3.
63 Paul Harris, Personal Communication.
64 'New Electoral Laws Have no Real Binding Force', *The Dominion* (29 October 1956), 8.
65 Arnold Nordmeyer, *NZPD* Vol. 351, 19 July 1967, 2033.
66 See especially Paul Pierson, 'Increasing Returns, Path Dependence, and the Study of Politics', *American Political Science Review*, Vol. 94 (2000), 251–67.
67 However, other parliaments did provide models for the composition and election of upper houses. D. J. Riddiford, for example, took an interest in 'vocational' representation, taking Eire as an example. D. J.

Riddiford, 'An Effective Second Chamber', *New Zealand Law Journal*, Vol. 20 (1950), 329–32.

7: The Reserved Provisions: Justifications and Evolution

1 John Marshall, *NZPD*, Vol. 310 (26 October 1956), 2840.
2 Ibid., 2842.
3 Ibid., 2842–3.
4 Ibid., 2841.
5 John Marshall, *Memoirs: Volume One: 1912 to 1960* (Collins, Auckland, 1983), 247.
6 K. J. Scott, *The New Zealand Constitution* (Oxford, Clarendon Press, 1962), 8.
7 Walter Nash, *NZPD*, Vol. 310 (26 October 1956), 2844.
8 Paul Harris, 'Democracy and Referendums' in Alan Simpson, ed., *Referendums: Constitutional and Legal Perspectives* (Occasional Publication 5, Department of Politics, Victoria University of Wellington, 1992), 51; and Royal Commission on the Electoral System [RCES], *Report of the Royal Commission on the Electoral System: Towards a Better Democracy* (Wellington, Government Printer, 1986), 287–90.
9 The four Commission members are the Surveyor-General, the Government Statistician, the Chief Electoral Officer and the Chairperson of the Local Government Commission (Section 28, Electoral Act 1993).
10 RCES, *Report of the Royal Commission on the Electoral System*, 137.
11 Andrew Geddis, *Electoral Law in New Zealand: Practice and Policy* (LexisNexis, Wellington, 2007) 87.
12 RCES, *Report of the Royal Commission on the Electoral System*, 141.
13 Ibid., 142.
14 'Proposals for Amendments to Electoral Law', *The Dominion* (26 October 1956). The editor did not note that the Māori seats were not included in Section 189.
15 The Lobby Letter, *The Dominion* (16 April 1956), 8.
16 Ibid.
17 'Electoral Reforms in Train', *The New Zealand Herald* (15 October 1956), in 'Legislation: The Electoral Act 1956', EL 1268, *Record No. 14/6/20*, [R11288408], ANZ.
18 Department of Justice, 'The Electoral Law of New Zealand: A Brief History', in RCES, *Report of the Royal Commission on the Electoral Commission*, Appendix A, 81.
19 Ibid, quoting from *NZPD*, Vol. 344, 2707 (no date provided).
20 Department of Justice, A, 81–2.
21 See Department of Justice, A, 82.
22 Harris, 66, fn 6.
23 RCES, 147.
24 Scott, *The New Zealand Constitution*, 8.

25 Electoral Act 1927. At: www.nzlii.org/nz/legis/hist_act ea192718gv1927 n44175/. Accessed 29 September 2017.
26 Paul Moon explains that Keith Holyoake, who replaced Sidney Holland as prime minister in September 1957, decided not to hold the referendum, instead promising legislation on the death penalty if re-elected to government: *New Zealand in the Twentieth Century: The Nation, The People* (Auckland, Harper Collins, 2011), 329.
27 Lobby Letter, *The Dominion* (30 April 1956), 8.
28 Ralph Hanan, *NZPD*, Vol. 350 (25 May 1967), 862.
29 Neill Atkinson. *Adventures in Democracy. A History of the Vote in New Zealand* (University of Otago Press, Dunedin, 2003), 179.
30 Norman Kirk, *NZPD*, Vol. 350 (25 May 1967), 863.
31 Keith Holyoake in ibid., 863.
32 Martyn Finlay, *NZPD*, Vol. 352 (1 September 1967), 2766; and for a copy of the ministerial statement circulated to voters before the 1967 poll see: 'The Term of Parliament', in L. Cleveland and A. D. Robinson, eds., *Readings in New Zealand Government* (Wellington, A.H. and A. W. Reed Ltd, 1972), 134–5.
33 Electoral Commission, 'Elections'. At: www.elections.org.nz/voting-system/referenda. Accessed 7 August 2017.
34 Nigel Roberts, 'Referendums—Consultative Referendums before 1970', *Te Ara – The Encyclopedia of New Zealand.* At: https://teara.govt.nz/n/referendums/page-3. Accessed 7 August 2017.
35 Martyn Finlay, *NZPD*, Vol. 351 (19 July 1967), 2037.
36 RCES, 166.
37 Electoral Law Committee, 'Inquiry into the Report of the Royal Commission of the Electoral System', *AJHR*, I 17B (1988).
38 Ibid., 60.
39 Electoral Commission, 'Elections'. At: www.elections.org.nz/voting-system/referenda,. Accessed 8 August 2017.
40 Stephen Levine and Nigel Roberts, 'A Mirror for Miramar? The 1990 Election in Perspective', in E. M. McLeay, ed., *The 1990 General Election: Perspectives on Political Change in New Zealand* (Occasional Publication No. 3, Department of Politics, Victoria University of Wellington, 1991), 140–1.
41 See Mary Harris and David Wilson, eds., *McGee: Parliamentary Practice in New Zealand*, 4th ed. (Auckland, Oratia Books, 2017), 663–4.
42 John Marshall, *NZPD*, Vol. 310 (26 October 1956), 2841.
43 Walter Nash in ibid., 2843.
44 Atkinson, *Adventures in Democracy*, 166.
45 *NZPD*, Vol. 310 (26 October 1956), 2843.
46 Atkinson, *Adventures in Democracy*, 180–1.
47 Norman Kirk, *NZPD*, Vol. 362, 5 August 1969, 1723–4.
48 Hugh Watt, *NZPD*, Vol. 362, 13 August 1969, 1939.
49 Alan McRobie, 'The Electoral System', in Philip A. Joseph, ed., *Essays on*

the Constitution (Brooker's, Wellington, 1995), 319.

50 John Marshall, *Memoirs*, 247.

51 Alan Robinson, 'Parliament in New Zealand', in Sir John Marshall, ed., *The Reform of Parliament. Papers Presented in Memory of Dr Alan Robinson* (New Zealand Institute of Public Administration and Government Printing Office, Wellington, 1978), 145.

52 'That Blessed Word "Referendum"', *New Zealand Herald* (21 August 1956), 8.

53 See especially: David Denemark, 'Choosing MMP in New Zealand: Explaining the 1993 Electoral Reform', in Matthew Soberg Shugart and Martin P. Wattenburg, eds., *Mixed-Member Electoral Systems: The Best of Both Worlds?* (Oxford University Press, Oxford, 2001), 70–95; Keith Jackson and Alan McRobie, *New Zealand Adopts Proportional Representation: Accident? Design? Evolution* (Ashgate, Aldershot, 1998); Jack Vowles et al., *Towards Consensus? The 1993 Election in New Zealand and the Transition to Proportional Representation* (Auckland University Press, Auckland, 1995).

54 Harris and Wilson, ed., *McGee: Parliamentary Practice in New Zealand*, 663.

55 Rex Mason, *NZPD*, Vol. 310 (26 October 1956), 2845.

56 RCES, 289.

57 Geoffrey Palmer, 'The Hazards of Making Constitutions: Some Reflections on Comparative Constitutional Law', in David Carter and Matthew Palmer, eds., *Roles and Perspectives in the Law. Essays in Honour of Sir Ivor Richardson* (Victoria University Press, Wellington, 2002), 219.

58 On voting qualifications and, also, candidature requirements see Fiona Barker and Kate McMillan, 'Constituting the Democratic Public: New Zealand's Extension of National Voting Rights to Non-Citizens', *New Zealand Journal of Public and International Law*, Vol. 12 (September 2014), 61–80.

59 Department of Justice, 'The Electoral Law of New Zealand', A, 83, citing Norman Kirk, *NZPD*, Vol. 353, 3264.

60 Rex Austin, Awarua; and Ben Couch, Wairarapa.

61 Atkinson, *Adventures in Democracy*, 180.

62 Jill Pettis, Wanganui.

63 See Geddis, *Electoral Law in New Zealand*, 72–3.

64 Robinson, 'Parliament in New Zealand', 145.

65 Walter Nash, *NZPD*, Vol. 310 (26 October 1956), 2844.

66 Ralph Hanan, *NZPD*, Vol. 310 (26 October 1956), 2850.

67 John Marshall, *NZPD*, Vol. 310 (26 October 1956), 2851.

68 Arnold Nordmeyer and Ralph Hanan, *NZPD*, Vol. 310 (26 October 1956), 2851.

69 Eruera Tirikatene, *NZPD*, Vol. 310 (26 October 1956), 2849.

70 Ranginui Walker, 'The Maori People: Their Political Development' in Hyam Gold, ed., *New Zealand Politics in Perspective* (Auckland,

Longman Paul, 1985), 255.

71 See especially: Atkinson, *Adventures in Democracy*, 186–88 and 190; Department of Justice, 'The Electoral Law of New Zealand', A, 84–7; E. M. McLeay, 'Political Argument about Representation: The Case of the Maori Seats', *Political Studies*, Vol. 28 (1980), especially 47–9; and M. P. K. Sorrenson, 'A History of Maori Representation in Parliament', in RCES, *Report of the Royal Commission on the Electoral System: Towards a Better Democracy* (Government Printer. Wellington, 1986), B, 52–3.

72 Atkinson, *Adventures in Democracy*,186.

73 See Barker and McMillan, 'Constituting the Democratic Public' for a full analysis.

74 McLeay, 'Political Argument about Representation', 48, citing Robert Muldoon, *NZPD*, Vol. 389 (1975), 2090.

75 Department of Justice, A, 91.

76 RCES, 81–114.

8: The Electoral Act and Constitutional Evolution in Aotearoa New Zealand

1 See especially Margaret Wilson, *The Struggle for Sovereignty. New Zealand and Twenty-First Century Statehood* (Bridget Williams Books, Wellington, 2015).

2 Philip A. Joseph, *Constitutional and Administrative Law in New Zealand*, 4th ed. (Brookers, Wellington, 2014), 590.

3 See Andrew Butler and Geoffrey Palmer, *A Constitution for Aotearoa New Zealand* (Victoria University Press, Wellington, 2016), especially 231–37.

4 Subsequently the Electoral Commission conducted a review of the details of MMP, consulting widely. See: Electoral Commission, 'Report of the Electoral Commission on the Review of the MMP Voting System' (29 October 2012). At: www.elections.org.nz/sites/default/files/bulk-upload/documents/Final_Report_2012_Review_of_MMP.pdf. Accessed 28 November 2017. The then Government did not put the Commission's recommendations to Parliament.

5 Royal Commission on the Electoral System [RCES], *Report of the Royal Commission on the Electoral System: Towards A Better Democracy* (Government Printer, Wellington, 1986), 274 and 292.

6 Public Petitions M to Z Committee 1961, 'Report of the Public Petitions M to Z Committee on the Petition of J. Scott-Davidson and Others, Together with Written Submissions Made to Committee', *AJHR* (1961) I 2A.

7 See Geoffrey Palmer, 'The Constitutional Significance of the Abolition of the Legislative Council in 1950', *New Zealand Journal of Public and International Law*, Vol. 15 (2017), especially 136–39.

8 RCES, *Report of the Royal Commission on the Electoral System*, 81–113.

9 Philip A. Joseph opposes the existence of the Māori seats and therefore their entrenchment in 'The Māori Seats in Parliament', Working Paper 2 (New Zealand Business Roundtable, May 2008), mainly on the grounds that they are politically contested. Matthew S. R. Palmer favours their entrenchment in *The Treaty of Waitangi in New Zealand's Law and Constitution* (Victoria University Press, Wellington, 2008).

10 *The Attorney-General v. Taylor and Others* [2017], New Zealand Court of Appeal, 215.

11 RCES, *Report of the Royal Commission on the Electoral System*, 155.

12 Constitutional Advisory Panel Te Ranga Kaupapa Ture, *New Zealand's Constitution: A Report on a Conversation. He Kōtinga Kōrero mō Te Kaupapa Ture o Aotearoa* (New Zealand Government, Wellington, 2013), 152. The Panel was co-chaired by Professor John Burrows and Sir Tipene O'Regan.

13 Ibid., 17.

14 Elizabeth McLeay, 'The Move to Mixed Electoral Systems', paper prepared for the panel sponsored by the Committee on Viable Constitutionalism, American Political Science Association Annual Meeting, 2–5 September 1999.

15 See Andrew Geddis, *Electoral Law in New Zealand: Practice and Policy* (LexisNexis, Wellington, 2007), 239–46.

16 See Elizabeth McLeay, 'Parliamentary Committees in New Zealand: A House Continuously Reforming Itself', *Australasian Parliamentary Review*, Vol. 16 (2001), 121–39.

17 See especially Jon Elster, 'Forces and Mechanisms in the Constitution-Making Process', in Sujit Choudhry and Tom Ginsburg, eds. *Constitution Making* (Edward Elgar, Cheltenham, Glos., 2016), 5–37 (reprinted from *Duke Law Journal*, Vol. 45 (1995)); and his 'Legislatures as Constituent Assemblies', also in Choudhry and Ginsburg, eds., 181–97 (reprinted from Richard Bauman and Tsvi Kahana, eds., *The Least Examined Branch: The Role of Legislatures in the Constitutional State* (Cambridge University Press, Cambridge, 2006).

18 See Claudia Geiringer, Polly Higbee and Elizabeth McLeay, *What's the Hurry? Urgency in the New Zealand Legislative Process* (Victoria University Press, Wellington, 2011), 48–54 and 153–57.

19 Mary Harris and David Wilson, eds., *McGee: Parliamentary Practice in New Zealand*, 4th ed. (Oratia Books, Auckland, 2017), 446, referring to the Electoral Reform Bill, 1995, *NZPD*, Vol. 551, 10326–7. For a full discussion see Keith Jackson and Alan McRobie, *New Zealand Adopts Proportional Representation: Accident? Design? Evolution* (Ashgate, Aldershot, 1998), 289–92.

20 RCES, *Report of the Royal Commission on the Electoral System*, 290–1.

21 Ibid., 291.

22 Harris and Wilson, eds., *McGee: Parliamentary Practice in New Zealand*, 10. See also Joseph, *Constitutional and Administrative Law in New*

Zealand, 588–95; and David McGee, 'The Legislative Process and the Courts', in Philip A. Joseph, ed., *Essays on the Constitution* (Wellington, Brookers, 1995), 84–111.

23 Electoral Law Committee, 'Inquiry into the Report of the Royal Commission of the Electoral System', *AJHR*, I.17B (1988), 122.

24 Standing Orders Committee, 'Report of the Standing Orders Committee', *AJHR* (1995), I. 18A, 57. See Harris and Wilson, eds., *McGee: Parliamentary Practice in New Zealand*, 246.

25 New Zealand House of Representatives, *Standing Orders* (2017), No. 266. At: www.parliament.nz/media/4384/standing-orders-2017.pdf. Accessed 28 October 2017.

26 Joseph, *Constitutional and Administrative Law in New Zealand*, 592.

27 James Christmas, 'Consensus Gained, Consensus Maintained? Changing New Zealand's Electoral Law 1927–2007', Victoria University of Wellington, MA Thesis, 2010. At http://researcharchive.vuw.ac.nz/xmlui/handle/10063/1214.

28 Interim Report of the Justice and Law Reform Select Committee, 'Inquiry into the White Paper – A Bill of Rights for New Zealand', *AJHR* (1986–87), 1.8A, 72–73.

29 Ibid., 73.

30 New Zealand has had some interesting recent debates on this topic. For example, see Michael Cullen, 'Parliament: Supremacy over Fundamental Norms?' *New Zealand Journal of Public and International Law*, Vol. 3 (2005), 1–5; Jeffrey Goldsworthy, 'Is Parliament Sovereign? Recent Challenges to the Doctrine of Parliamentary Sovereignty', *New Zealand Journal of Public and International Law*, Vol. 3 (2005), 7–37; E. W. Thomas, 'Centennial Lecture. The Relationship of Parliament and the Courts: A Tentative Thought or Two for the New Millennium', *Victoria University Law Review*, Vol. 31 No. 5 (2000), 5–36

31 Sian Elias, 'Another Spin on the Merry-Go-Round', in A Series on Sovereignty in the 21st Century Organised by the Institute for Comparative and International Law at the University of Melbourne, Australia (2003). The Rt Hon. Dame Sian Elias, is citing J. Mitchell, 'Sovereignty of Parliament – Yet Again', *Law Quarterly Review*, 196 (1963), 196. See also Matthew S. R. Palmer, 'New Zealand Constitutional Culture' *New Zealand Universities Law Review*, Vol. 22 (2007), especially 582–86.

32 Geoffrey Marshall, *Constitutional Conventions: The Rules and Forms of Political Accountability* (Clarendon Press, Oxford, 1984), 201.

33 Colin James, *New Territory: The Transformation of New Zealand 1984-92* (Bridget Williams Books, Wellington, 1992), 10–11.

34 On policy transfer see especially David P. Dolowitz and David Marsh, 'Learning From Abroad: The Role of Policy Transfer in Contemporary Policy-Making', *Governance: An International Journal of Policy and Administration*, Vol. 13 (2000), 5–24.

Bibliography

Manuscripts and Archives

Alexander Turnbull Library, Wellington [ATL]

Holland, Sir Sidney, Political Papers, MS-1624.
Holyoake Sir Keith Jacka, Political Papers, MS-1814.
McIntosh, Sir Alister, Papers, MS-6759.
Marshall, Sir John Ross, Political Papers, MS-98; MS-1403.

Archives New Zealand, Wellington [ANZ]

Electoral Department [EL] 1268, Legislation-The Electoral Act 1956.
Justice [JI] 159, 0-1957, Electoral Act and Regulations 1927 – Proposed Amendments and Electoral Regulations 1954.
Office of the Clerk of the House of Representatives [ABGX], W3706, Committee on the Electoral Bill – Administration – Minutes.
Prime Minister [PM 1011], Series 18654, PM S. G. Holland.
Prime Minister's Department, AAFD Series 811, Cabinet Committee on Legislation.

The Beaglehole Room, Victoria University of Wellington Library (VUW)

Les Cleveland Research Papers (Alan Robinson), Beaglehole Room, Roba 1987. 010.

Wellington Public Library [WPL]

Vertical File Collection, *The Evening Post*

Official Publications

Appendices to the Journals of the New Zealand House of Representatives [AJHR]

Journals of the House of Representatives of New Zealand [JHRNZ]

New Zealand Parliamentary Debates [NZPD]

Constitutional Advisory Panel Te Ranga Kaupapa Ture, *New Zealand's Constitution. A Report on a Conversation. He Kōtinga Kōrero mō Te Kaupapa Ture o Aotearoa* (New Zealand Government, Wellington, 2013).

Constitutional Arrangements Committee, 'Inquiry to Review New Zealand's Existing Constitution: Report of the Constitutional Arrangements Committee' (August 2005). At: http://www.converge.org.nz/pma/cacrep05.pdf.

Constitutional Reform Committee 'Report on Petition of J. B. Donald et al. on New Zealand Bill of Rights', *AJHR* (1964), I 14.

Constitutional Reform Committee, 'Report of the Constitutional Reform Committee', *AJHR* (1952), I–18.

Constitutional Reform Committee, Appendix A, 'How Constitutions Can be Created', Report of the Constitutional Reform Committee', *AJHR* (1952), I–18.

Constitutional Reform Committee, Appendix B, 'Can We Have a Written or More or Less Rigid Constitution?' 'Report of the Constitutional Reform Committee', *AJHR* (1952), I–18.

Department of Justice, 'A Bill of Rights for New Zealand: A White Paper', *AJHR* (Government Printer, Wellington, 1985).

Department of Justice, 'The Electoral Law of New Zealand: A Brief History', in Royal Commission on the Electoral System, *Report of the Royal Commission on the Electoral Commission: Towards a Better Democracy* (The Government Printer, Wellington, 1986), Appendix A.

Department of Statistics, 'The New Zealand Official Year-Book, 1951–1952'. At: https://www3.stats.govt.nz/New_Zealand_Official_Yearbooks/1951-52/NZOYB_1951–52.html#idsect1_1_980.

Electoral Commission, 'Report of the Electoral Commission on the Review of the MMP Voting System' (29 October 2012). At: ' http://www.elections.org.nz/sites/default/files/bulk-upload/documents/Final_Report_2012_Review_of_MMP.pdf.

Electoral Law Committee, 'Inquiry into the Report of the Royal Commission on the Electoral System', *AJHR* (1988), I 17B.

Electoral Law Committee, 'Inquiry into the Report of the Royal Commission of the Electoral System', *AJHR* (1988), I 17B .

'Electoral Regulations 1954' (140), *Statutory Regulations 1954*, Vol. I (8 September 1954), 624–57.

Interim Report of the Justice and Law Reform Select Committee, 'Inquiry into the White Paper – A Bill of Rights for New Zealand', *AJHR* (1986–7), 1.8A.

Keith, Sir Kenneth, 'On the Constitution of New Zealand: An Introduction to the Foundations of the Current Form of Government', in *Cabinet Manual* (Cabinet Office, Department of Prime Minister, Wellington, 2017). At: https://cabinetmanual.cabinetoffice.govt.nz/files/cabinet-manual-2017.pdf.

Lange, David, 'Foreword', 9 October 1984, in *Cabinet Office Manual* (Cabinet Office, Prime Minister's Department, Wellington, 1979).

Millen, P. G., 'Introduction and Historical Note', 1983, in *Cabinet Office Manual* (Cabinet Office, Prime Minister's Department, Wellington, 1979).

Ministers' Private Interests Committee, 'Report', *AJHR* (1956), Vol. 4, I.17.

New Zealand Government, 'The Term of Parliament', in L. Cleveland and A. D. Robinson, eds., *Readings in New Zealand Government* (Wellington, A.H. and A. W. Reed Ltd, 1972), 134–5.

New Zealand House of Representatives, *Standing Orders of the New Zealand House of Representatives* (Wellington, 2017). At: https://www.parliament.nz/en/pb/parliamentary-rules/standing-orders-2017/.

New Zealand Joint Constitutional Reform Committee 1948, *Statements etc. Prepared for the New Zealand Joint Constitutional Reform Committee 1948* (Wellington Legislative Department, 1948).

New Zealand Parliamentary Library, 'New Zealand Sovereignty: 1857. 1907, 1947, or 1987?' (2007). At: https://www.parliament.nz/en/pb/research-papers/document/00PLLawRP07041/new-zealand-sovereignty-1857-1907-1947-or-1987.

New Zealand Parliamentary Library, 'The Origins of the Maori Seats', New Zealand House of Representatives (2003). At: https://www.parliament.nz/resource/en-NZ/00PLLawRP03141/e27e432e971eb1f60ea75b00c98/a39e4b2e62ce.

Public Petitions M to Z Committee 1961, 'Report of the Public Petitions M to Z Committee on the Petition of J. Scott-Davidson and Others, Together with Written Submissions Made to Committee', *AJHR* (1961) I 2A.

Royal Commission on the Electoral System [RCES], *Report of the Royal Commission on the Electoral Commission: Towards a Better Democracy* (The Government Printer, Wellington, 1986).

Sorrenson, M. P., 'A History of Maori Representation in Parliament', in Royal Commission on the Electoral System, *Report of the Royal Commission on the Electoral System: Towards a Better Democracy* (Government Printer, Wellington, 1986), Appendix B.

Standing Orders Committee, 'Report of the Standing Orders Committee', *AJHR* (1995), I. 18A.

Newspapers

Dominion
The Evening Post
New Zealand Herald

Books, Articles and Book Chapters

Aimer, Peter, 'Labour Party – Origins of the Labour Party' *Te Ara – the Encyclopedia of New Zealand*, http://www.teara.govt.nz/en/labour-party/page-1.

Anagnoson, J. Theodore, 'Home Style in New Zealand'. *Legislative Studies Quarterly*, Vol. 8 (May 1983), 157–75.

Atkinson, Neill, *Adventures in Democracy: A History of the Vote in New Zealand* (University of Otago Press in association with the Electoral Commission, Dunedin), 2003.

Barker, Fiona and Kate McMillan, 'Constituting the Democratic Public: New Zealand's Extension of National Voting Rights to Non-Citizens', *New Zealand Journal of Public and International Law*, Vol. 12 (September 2014), 61–80.

Belshaw, Sheila M., *Man of Integrity. A Biography of Sir Clifton Webb* (Dunmore Press, Palmerston North, 1979).

Benda, H. J., and R. H. Brookes, 'SPQR: A Note on the Proposed Senate', *Political Science*, Vol. 4 (September 1952), 40–44.

Boast, Richard, 'New Zealand Legal History and New Zealand Historians: A Non-Meeting of Minds', *Journal of New Zealand Studies*, No. 9 (2010), 1–36.

Braybrooke, E. K., 'A Reply', *Political Science*, Vol. 6 (March 1954), 41–2.

Braybrooke, E. K., 'A Written Constitution. Is it Possible in New Zealand?' *Political Science*, Vol. 3 (March 1951), 32–42, reprinted in L. Cleveland and A. D. Robinson, eds., *Readings in New Zealand Government* (A. H. and A. W. Reed, Wellington, 1972).

Bremer, Robert, with Tom Brooking, 'Federated Farmers and the State', in Brian Roper and Chris Rudd, eds., *State and Economy in New Zealand* (Auckland, Oxford University Press, 1991), 108–27.

Brookfield, F. M., 'Referendums: Legal and Constitutional Aspects', in Alan Simpson, ed., *Referendums: Constitutional and Political Perspectives* (Occasional Publication 5, Department of Politics, Victoria University of Wellington, Wellington, 1992), 7–25.

Brown, Bruce, *The Rise of New Zealand Labour: A History of the New Zealand Labour Party* (Wellington, Price Milburn, 1962).

Butler, Andrew and Geoffrey Palmer, *A Constitution for Aotearoa New Zealand* (Victoria University Press, Wellington, 2016). At: http://

constitutionaotearoa.org.nz.

Carlyon, Jenny and Diana Morrow, *Changing Times: New Zealand Since 1945* (Auckland University Press, Auckland, 2013).

Chapman, R. M., *The Political Scene 1919–1931* (Heinemann Educational Books, Auckland, 1969).

Chapman, Robert, 'From Labour to National', in W. H. Oliver, ed., with B. R. Williams, *The Oxford History of New Zealand* (The Clarendon Press, Oxford; and Oxford University Press, Wellington, 1981), 333–68.

Chapman, Robert, 'The Response to Labour and the Question of Parallelism of Opinion, 1928–1960', in Robert Chapman and Keith Sinclair, eds., *Studies of a Small Democracy* (University of Auckland, Auckland, 1963), 221–54, reprinted in Elizabeth McLeay, ed., *New Zealand Politics and Social Patterns: Selected Works by Robert Chapman* (Victoria University Press, Wellington, 1999), 32–62.

Clark, Margaret, ed., *Keith Holyoake: Towards a Political Biography* (The Dunmore Press, Palmerston North, 1997).

Cooke, Robin (Lord Cook of Thorndon), 'Unicameralism in New Zealand: Some Lessons', *Canterbury Law Review*, Vol. 1 (1999), 1–13. At: http:/www.nziii.org/nz/journals/CanterLawRw/1999/1.html.

Cross, William P. and André Blais, *Politics at the Centre. The Selection and Removal of Party Leaders in the Anglo Parliamentary Democracies* (Oxford, Oxford University Press, 2012).

Cullen, Michael, 'Parliament: Supremacy over Fundamental Norms?' *New Zealand Journal of Public and International Law*, Vol. Vol. 13 (2005), 1–5.

Denemark, David, 'Choosing MMP in New Zealand: Explaining the 1993 Electoral Reform', in Matthew Soberg Shugart and Martin P. Wattenburg, eds., *Mixed-Member Electoral Systems: The Best of Both Worlds?* (Oxford University Press, Oxford, 2001), 70–95.

Dicey, A. V., *The Law of the Constitution*, 6th edn., (Macmillan, London, 1902).

Dolowitz, David P. and David Marsh, 'Learning From Abroad: The Role of Policy Transfer in Contemporary Policy-Making', *Governance: An International Journal of Policy and Administration*, Vol. 13 (2000), 5–24.

Doughty, Ross, *The Holyoake Years* (Ross A. Doughty, Feilding, 1977).

Durie, Justice Edward 'The Treaty in the Constitution', in Colin James, ed., *Building the Constitution* (Institute of Policy Studies, Victoria University of Wellington, 2000), 201–4.

Elster, Jon, 'Forces and Mechanisms in the Constitution-Making Process', in Sujit Choudhry and Tom Ginsburg, eds., *Constitution Making* (Edward Elgar, Cheltenham, Glos., 2016), 5–37.

Elster, Jon, 'Legislatures as Constituent Assemblies', in Sujit Choudhry and Tom Ginsburg, eds., *Constitution Making* (Edward Elgar, Cheltenham, Glos., 2016), 181–97.

Eunson, Keith, *Mirrors on the Hill. Reflections on New Zealand's Political*

Leaders, (Dunmore Press, Palmerston North, 2001).

Fischer, David Hackett, *Fairness and Freedom: A History of Two Open Societies: New Zealand and the United States* (New York, Oxford University Press, 2012).

Franks, Peter and Jim McAloon, *The New Zealand Labour Party 1916–2016* (Victoria University Press, Wellington, 2016).

Geddis, Andrew, *Electoral Law in New Zealand: Practice and Policy* (LexisNexis, Wellington, 2007).

Geiringer, Claudia, Polly Higbee and Elizabeth McLeay, *What's the Hurry? Urgency in the New Zealand Legislative Process 1987–2010* (Victoria University Press, Wellington, 2011).

Goldfinch Shaun and Brian Roper, 'Treasury's Role in State Policy Formulation During the Post-war Era', in Brian Roper and Chris Rudd, eds., *State and Economy in New Zealand* (Auckland, Oxford University Press, 1993), 50–73.

Goldsworthy, Jeffrey, 'Is Parliament Sovereign? Recent Challenges to the Doctrine of Parliamentary Sovereignty', *New Zealand Journal of Public and International Law*, Vol. 3 (2005), 7–37.

Grofman, Bernard, ed., *Political Science as Puzzle Solving* (The University of Michigan Press, Ann Arbor, 2001).

Gustafson, Barry, 'Holland, Sidney George', from 'The Dictionary of New Zealand Biography', *Te Ara* – th*e Encyclopoedia of New Zealand*. At: http://www.TeAra.govt.nz/en/biographies/5h30/holland-sidney-george.

Gustafson, Barry, 'Holyoake and the National Party', in Margaret Clark, ed., *Sir Keith Holyoake: Towards a Political Biography* (The Dunmore Press, Palmerston North, 1997), 131–40.

Gustafson, Barry, *Kiwi Keith. A Biography of Keith Holyoake* (Auckland University Press, Auckland, 2007).

Gustafson, Barry, *The First 50 Years: A History of the New Zealand National Party* (Reed Methuen, Auckland, 1986).

Harris, Mary and David Wilson, eds., *McGee: Parliamentary Practice in New Zealand*, 4th edn., (Oratia Books, Auckland, 2017).

Harris, Paul, 'Democracy and Referendums' in Alan Simpson, ed., *Referendums: Constitutional and Legal Perspectives* (Occasional Publication 5, Department of Politics, Victoria University of Wellington, 1992), 47–67.

Henare, Denese, 'Can or Should the Treaty be Replaced', in Colin James, ed., *Building the Constitution* (Institute of Policy Studies, Victoria University of Wellington, 2000), 207–13.

Hickford, Mark, 'Considering the Historical-Political Constitution and the Imperial Inheritance in Mid-Nineteenth Century New Zealand: Balance, Diversity and Alternative Constitutions', *New Zealand Journal of Public and International Law*, Vol. 12 (2014), 145–86.

Hill, Richard S., *Maori and the State: Crown-Maori Relations in New Zealand/*

Aotearoa, 1950–2000 (Victoria University Press, 2009).
Jackson, Keith and Alan McRobie, *New Zealand Adopts Proportional Representation: Accident? Design? Evolution* (Ashgate, Aldershot, 1998).
Jackson, Keith, 'Government Succession in New Zealand', *Journal of Commonwealth and Comparative Politics*, Vol. 15 (1977), 151–69.
Jackson, Keith, 'The Abolition of the New Zealand Upper House of Parliament', in Lawrence D. Langley and David M. Olson, eds., *Two into One. The Politics and Processes of National Legislative Cameral Change* (Westview Press, Boulder, 1991), 43–76.
Jackson, Keith, *The New Zealand Legislative Council: A Study of the Establishment, Failure and Abolition of an Upper House* (University of Otago Press, Dunedin, 1972).
Jackson, Moana, 'Where Does Sovereignty Lie?', in Colin James, ed., *Building the Constitution* (Institute of Policy Studies, Victoria University of Wellington, 2000), 196–200.
Jackson. W. K. and G. A. Wood, 'The New Zealand Parliament and Maori Representation', *Historical Studies*, Vol. 11 (1963–65), 383–96.
James, Colin, ed., *Building the Constitution* (Institute of Policy Studies, Victoria University of Wellington, 2000).
James, Colin, *New Territory: The Transformation of New Zealand 1984–92* (Bridget Williams Books, Wellington, 1992).
Joseph, Philip A., 'The Future of Electoral Law', in Caroline Morris, Jonathan Boston and Petra Butler, eds., *Reconstituting the Constitution* (Springer_ Verlag Berline Heidelberg, 2011), 237–41.
Joseph, Philip A., *The Maori Seats in Parliament* (Working Paper 2, New Zealand Business Roundtable), 2008.
Joseph, Philip, *Constitutional And Administrative Law in New Zealand*, 4th edn. (Brookers, Wellington, 2014).
Kelson, R. N., 'The New Zealand National Party', *Political Science*, Vol. 6 (1954), 3–32.
Kelson, Robert K., *The Private Member of Parliament and the Formation of Public Policy. A New Zealand Case Study* (University of Toronto Press, Toronto, 1964).
King, Michael, *The Penguin History of New Zealand* (Penguin, Auckland, 2003).
Kumarasingham, Harshan, *Onward with Executive Power: Lessons from New Zealand 1947–57* (Wellington, Institute of Policy Studies, 2010).
Lane, Jan-Erik, *Constitutions and Political Theory* (Manchester University Press, Manchester and London, 1966).
Levine, Stephen and Nigel Roberts, 'A Mirror for Miramar? The 1990 Election in Perspective', in E. M. McLeay, ed., *The 1990 General Election: Perspectives on Political Change in New Zealand* (Occasional Publication No. 3, Department of Politics, Victoria University of Wellington, 1991), 119–50.
Lijphart, Arendt, 'Democratic Political Systems: Types, Cases, Causes, and

Consequences', *Journal of Theoretical Politics*, Vol. 1 (1989), 33–48.

Lijphart, Arendt, *Patterns of Democracy. Government Forms and Performances in Thirty-Six Countries* (Yale University Press, New Haven and London, 1999).

Lipson, Leslie, *The Politics of Equality: New Zealand Adventures in Democracy* (University of Chicago Press, Chicago, 1948).

Lundy, Jim, 'Oram, Matthew Henry', from the Dictionary of New Zealand Biography. *Te Ara—The Encycolpedia of New Zealand.* At: http://www.teara.govt.nz/en/biographies/5o5/oram-matthew-henry.

Marshall, Geoffrey, *Constitutional Conventions: The Rules and Forms of Political Accountability* (Clarendon Press, Oxford, 1984).

Marshall, John, *Memoirs: Volume One: 1912 to 1960* (William Collins Publishers Ltd, Auckland, 1983).

Martin, John E., *The House. New Zealand's House of Representatives 1854–2004* (Dunmore Press, Palmerston North, 2004).

Martin, John, 'The Changing Governance: The State Services in the Holyoake Years', in Margaret Clark, ed., *Sir Keith Holyoake: Towards a Political Biography* (The Dunmore Press, Palmerston North, 1997), 57–84.

Martin, John, *A Profession of Statecraft? Three Essays on Some Current Issues in the New Zealand Public Service* (Institute of Policy Studies, Victoria University of Wellington, 1987).

McCallum, Janet, *Women in the House: Members of Parliament in New Zealand* (Cape Catley, Auckland, 1993).

McGee, David, 'Constitutional Conventions', in Mark Francis and Jim Tully, eds., *In the Public Interest: Essays in Honour of Professor Keith Jackson* (Canterbury University Press, Christchurch, 2009), 76–92.

McGee, David, 'The Legislative Process and the Courts', in Philip A. Joseph, ed., *Essays on the Constitution* (Wellington, Brookers, 1995), 84–111.

McLean, Janet, 'The Political, the Historical and the Universal in New Zealand's Unwritten Constitution', *New Zealand Journal of Public and International Law*, Vol. 12 (2014), 321–44.

McLeay, E. M., 'Political Argument about Representation: The Case of the Maori Seats', *Political Studies*, Vol. 28 (1980), 43–62.

McLeay, Elizabeth, 'Building the Constitution: Debates; Assumptions; Developments 2000–2010', in Caroline Morris, Jonathan Boston and Petra Butler, eds., *Reconstituting the Constitution* (Springer-Verlag, Berline, Heidleburg, 2011), 3–33.

McLeay, Elizabeth, 'Buckle, Board, Team or Network? Understanding Cabinet', *New Zealand Journal of Public and International Law*, Vol. 4 (June 2006), 37–54.

McLeay, Elizabeth, 'Parliamentary Committees in New Zealand: A House Continuously Reforming Itself', *Australasian Parliamentary Review*, Vol. 16 (2001), 121–39.

McLeay, Elizabeth, *The Cabinet and Political Power in New Zealand* (Oxford

University Press, Auckland, 1995).

McRobie, Alan, 'The Electoral System', in Philip A. Joseph, ed., *Essays on the Constitution* (Brooker's, Wellington, 1995), 312–43.

McRobie, Alan, *New Zealand Electoral Atlas* (GB Books, Wellington, 1989).

Mein Smith, Philippa, *A Concise History of New Zealand*, 2nd edn., (Cambridge University Press, Melbourne, 2005).

Miller, Raymond, *Party Politics in New Zealand* (Oxford University Press, Melbourne, 2005).

Milne, R. S., 'The Referendum Revived', *Landfall*, Vol. 11 (1957), 158–64.

Milne, R. S., *Political Parties in New Zealand* (Clarendon Press, Oxford, 1966).

Mitchell, Austin, 'Caucus: The New Zealand Parliamentary Parties', *Journal of Commonwealth Studies*, Vol. 6 (1968), 3–33.

Mitchell, Austin, *Politics and People in New Zealand* (Christchurch, Whitcombe and Tombs Ltd., 1969).

Moon, Paul, *New Zealand in the Twentieth Century: The Nation, The People* (Harper Collins, Auckland, 2011).

Morris, Caroline, Jonathan Boston and Petra Butler, eds., *Reconstituting the Constitution* (Springer, Heidelburg Dordrecht London New York, 2011).

Mulgan, R. G., 'The Concept of Mandate in New Zealand Politics', *Political Science*, Vol. 30 (1978), 88–96.

Mulgan, Richard, 'Political Culture', in G. R. Hawke, ed., *Changing Politics? The Electoral Referendum 1993* (Institute of Policy Studies, Victoria University of Wellington, 1993), 43–67.

Mulgan, Richard, *Democracy in New Zealand. A Study of New Zealand Politics*, 2nd edn. (Auckland, Oxford University Press, 1984).

New Zealand Labour Party, 'Constitution and Platform (as amended at the Third Annual Conference, July 3, 4, 5, 1919), reprinted in Paul Harris and Stephen Levine, eds., with Margaret Clark, John Martin and Elizabeth McLeay, *The New Zealand Politics Source Book* (Dunmore Press, Palmerston North, 1992), 12–1.

Northey, J. F. 'Can our Liberties be Safeguarded?', *New Zealand Law Journal*, (22 May 1951), 140–3.

Northey, J. F., 'The New Zealand Constitution', in J. F. Northey, ed., *The A. G. Davis Essays in Law* (Butterworths, London, 1965), 149–79.

Oliver, Peter C., *The Constitution of Independence: The Development of Constitutional Theory in Australia, Canada and New Zealand* (Oxford, Oxford University Press, 2005).

Oliver, Peter, 'Cutting the Imperial Link—Canada and New Zealand', in Philip A. Joseph, ed., *Essays on the Constitution* (Wellington, Brooker's, 1995), 368–403.

Olssen, E. A. 'A Second Chamber: The Report of the Constitutional Reform Committee', *Landfall*, Vol. 6 (1952), 322–5.

Palmer, Geoffrey, 'The Hazards of Making Constitutions: Some Reflections on Comparative Constitutional Law', in David Carter and Matthew

Palmer, eds., *Roles and Perspectives in the Law. Essays in Honour of Sir Ivor Richardson* (Victoria University Press, Wellington, 2002), 207–38.

Palmer, Geoffrey, 'The Cabinet, the Prime Minister and the Constitution: The Constitutional Background to Cabinet', *New Zealand Journal of Public and International Law*, Vol. 4 (June 2006), 1–36.

Palmer, Geoffrey, 'The Constitutional Significance of the Abolition of the Legislative Council in 1950', *New Zealand Journal of Public and International Law*, Vol. 15 (2017), 123–47.

Palmer, Geoffrey, *Unbridled Power? An Interpretation of New Zealand's Constitution and Government* (Oxford University Press, Wellington, 1979).

Palmer, Matthew S. R., 'New Zealand Constitutional Culture', *New Zealand Universities Law Review*, Vol. 22 (2007), 565–97.

Palmer, Matthew S. R. 'What is New Zealand's Constitution and who interprets it? Constitutional realism and the importance of public office-holders', *Public Law Review*, Vol. 17 (2006), 133–62.

Palmer, Matthew S. R., *The Treaty of Waitangi in New Zealand's Law and Constitution* (Wellington, Victoria University Press, 2008).

Pierson, Paul, 'Increasing Returns, Path Dependence, and the Study of Politics', *American Political Science Review*, Vol. 94 (2000), 251–67.

Pierson, Paul, 'The Limits of Design: Explaining Institutional Origins and Change', *Governance*, Vol. 13 (2000), 475–99.

Prebble, Mark, *With Respect: Parliamentarians, Officials, and Judges Too* (Institute of Policy Studies, Victoria University of Wellington, Wellington, 2010.

Rae, Douglas W., *The Political Consequences of Electoral Laws* (Yale University Press, New Haven, 1967).

Rhodes, R.A.W., John Wanna and Patrick Weller, *Comparing Westminster* (Oxford University Press, Oxford, 2009).

Riddiford, D. J. 'An Effective Second Chamber', *New Zealand Law Journal*, Vol. 20 (7 November 1950), 313–5.

Roberts, Nigel, 'Referendums—Consultative Referendums before 1970', *Te Ara – The Encyclopedia of New Zealand*. At: https://teara.govt.nz/n/referendums/page-3.

Robinson, Alan, 'Parliament in New Zealand', in Sir John Marshall, ed., *The Reform of Parliament. Papers Presented in Memory of Dr Alan Robinson* (New Zealand Institute of Public Administration and Government Printing Office, Wellington, 1978), 129–236.

Robson, John L., *Sacred Cows and Rogue Elephants: Policy Development in the New Zealand Justice Department* (Government Printing Office, Wellington, 1987).

Schwimmer, Erik, 'The Man and His Work'. The Hon. Ernest Bower Corbett *Te Ao Hou*, (No. 21 (December 1957), 7.

Scott, K. J., 'Civil Liberties and a Written Constitution', *Political Science*, Vol. 6 (March 1954), 29–37.

Scott, K. J., 'New Zealand's Political Traditions', *Journal of the Royal Society of Arts*, Vol. 106, No. 5021 (April 1958), 354–66.

Scott, K. J., *The New Zealand Constitution* (Oxford University Press, London, 1962).

Simpson, Alan, ed., *The Constitutional Implications of MMP* (Occasional Publication No. 9, School of Political Science and International Relations, Victoria University of Wellington, 1998).

Sinclair, Keith, *Walter Nash* (Auckland University Press/Oxford University Press, Auckland), 1976.

Sutch, W. B., *The Quest for Security in New Zealand 1840–1966* (Oxford University Press, Wellington, 1966).

Templeton, Hugh, 'Algie, Ronald Macmillan', first published in the Dictionary of New Zealand Biography, Vol. 4 (1998) *Te Ara – The Encyclopedia of New Zealand*. At https://teara.govt.nz/en/biographies/4a8/algie-ronald-macmillan.

Thomas, E. W., 'Centennial Lecture. The Relationship of Parliament and the Courts: A Tentative Thought or Two for the New Millennium', *Victoria University Law Review*, 31:5 (2000), 5–36.

Thompson, Richard H. T., 'Maori Affairs and the New Zealand Press IV', *The Journal of the Polynesian Society*, Vol. 64 (1955), 22–34. At http://www.jps.auckland.ac.nz/document/.

Tsebelis, George, *Veto Players. How Political Institutions Work* (Princeton University Press, Princeton, New Jersey, 2002).

Vowles, Jack, 'Aspects of Electoral Studies, Present and Past: New Zealand Voters and "the System", 1949–1996', *Political Science*, Vol. 50 (1998), 90–110.

Vowles, Jack, Peter Aimer, Helena Catt, Jim Lamare and Raymond Miller, *Towards Consensus? The 1993 Election in New Zealand and the Transition to Proportional Representation* (Auckland University Press, Auckland, 1995).

Walker, Ranginui, 'The Maori People: Their Political Development' in Hyam Gold, ed., *New Zealand Politics in Perspective* (Auckland, Longman Paul, 1985), 251–65.

Ward, Alan, *An Unsettled History. Treaty Claims in New Zealand Today* (Bridget Williams Books, Wellington, 1999).

Wilson, John, 'The Origins of the Maori Seats', in Maria Bargh, ed., *Maori and Parliament: Diverse Strategies and Compromises* (Huia Publishers, Wellington, 2010), 55–71.

Wilson, Margaret, *The Struggle for Sovereignty: New Zealand and the Twenty-First Century Statehood* (Wellington, Bridget Williams Books, 2015).

Winiata, Whata, 'How Can or Should the Treaty be Reflected in Institutional Design?', in Colin James, ed., *Building the Constitution* (Institute of Policy Studies, Victoria University of Wellington, 2000), 205–6.

Wood, G. A. *Ministers and Members in the New Zealand Parliament*, 2nd edn, (University of Otago Press, Dunedin, 1996).

Wood, G. A., 'The Former "Dominion" of New Zealand', *Political Science*, Vol. 26 (1974), 2–10.

Theses and Conference Papers

Christmas, James, 'Consensus Gained, Consensus Maintained? Changing New Zealand's Electoral Law 1927–2007', Victoria University of Wellington, MA Thesis, 2010. At http://researcharchive.vuw.ac.nz/xmlui/handle/10063/1214.

Elias, Sian, 'Another Spin on the Merry-Go-Round', in A Series on Sovereignty in the 21st Century Organised by the Institute for Comparative and International Law at the University of Melbourne, Australia (2003).

Halligan, John, 'Continuity and Change in the New Zealand Parliament', PhD Thesis (Victoria University of Wellington, 1980).

McLeay, Elizabeth, 'The Move to Mixed Electoral Systems', Paper prepared for the panel sponsored by the Committee on Viable Constitutionalism, American Political Science Association Annual Meeting, 2–5 September 1999.

McLeay, E. M. 'Parliamentary Careers in a Two-Party System: Cabinet Selection in New Zealand' (PhD thesis, University of Auckland, 1978).

McLeay, Elizabeth, 'The Opposition in New Zealand: Evolution; Institutionalisation; Opportunity', Paper prepared for 'Her Majesty's Oppositions', Roundtable, Public Policy Institute, Australian Catholic University, Canberra, 21–23 February 2011.

Websites

Electoral Commission, 'Elections'. At: http://www.elections.org.nz/voting-system/referenda.

Electoral Commission, 'Referenda', At: http://www.elections.org.nz/voting-system/referenda.

Index